"Becoming a Healthy Disciple is a perfect co[...] earlier work, *Becoming a Healthy Churc*[...] healthy church is now added ten traits of [...] [...] [...] habits of the heart are all too frequently but needlessly missing when our Lord has provided more than enough supply for all who sense their spiritual hunger and spiritual bankruptcy and who wish to be genuine disciples of the Master. I commend this work for all thoughtful and genuine disciples of our Lord who want to mature and see the power of the living Lord working in and through them."

—Walter C. Kaiser Jr., president, Gordon-Conwell Theological Seminary

"If I wanted to answer the biblical question 'How shall we then live?' it would be difficult to find a more comprehensive and well-thought-through response than that given by Steve Macchia in this excellent book. I want to please Jesus in my life; like most of us I need to know how. At last, courtesy of Steve Macchia, I have an answer."

—Clive Calver, president, World Relief

"We will give our lives to someone or we will throw them away on nothing. For men and women who have given their lives to Jesus, *Becoming a Healthy Disciple* will give you workable leads on how to live with Jesus and for him."

—Haddon Robinson, Gordon-Conwell Theological Seminary

"This foundational and practical book on Christian discipleship will be useful both for the individual Christian and for congregations seeking renewal. Comprehensive and clearly written, with a good understanding of challenges facing Christians today, it is solidly biblical and can be read on its own or in conjunction with other resources on building healthy churches. I heartily recommend it."

—Roberta Hestenes, international minister, World Vision

"Becoming a Healthy Disciple is a must read for all who wish to grow in their personal walk. Stephen Macchia unfolds the secrets to a vital Christian life and asks the direct and challenging questions that every individual needs to answer in their daily attempt to emulate Jesus. This book is a classic. I highly recommend it for anyone who is seeking a genuine Christian walk."

—Ted Haggard, president, National Association of Evangelicals

"In *Becoming a Healthy Disciple*, Steve articulates a clear call for healthy disciple making in the context of healthy churches. One senses Steve's heart not only for the church but for the people who are the church and offers wise guidance for their growth in Christ."

—Ruth Haley Barton, cofounder, The Transforming Center

"This is a dangerous book. Reading it will be hazardous to your spiritual inertia. Macchia is out to build healthy churches by nurturing healthy disciples in down-to-earth ways. This book will transform you. You won't be the same after reading it. Macchia challenges you with gritty, realistic growth-producing strategies for healthy disciples."

—George K. Brushaber, president, Bethel College & Seminary

"With practical prescriptions and concise challenges, Steve Macchia delineates life-changing truths for day-to-day followers of Jesus Christ. *Becoming a Healthy Disciple* should come with a warning label. READERS BEWARE: THE TRUTHS IN THIS BOOK WILL CHANGE YOUR LIFE."

—Paul Borthwick, author, speaker, and leadership development consultant

"Sometimes the most profound truths are also the most basic. In *Becoming a Healthy Disciple*, Stephen Macchia takes us back to some basics that will profoundly impact our lives and the life of the church if we will embrace and practice them. Macchia reminds us that there is no seminar or toolkit for becoming a healthy church. Rather, healthy churches are the result of Christ followers who are committed to becoming healthy disciples. I pray that many people will read this book. More importantly, I pray that all who read it will begin living its message from the inside out."

—Samuel D. Rima, director, Doctor of Ministry program, Bethel Seminary

Becoming a
Healthy Disciple

Also by Stephen A. Macchia

Becoming a Healthy Church: Ten Characteristics
Becoming a Healthy Church Workbook

Becoming a Healthy Disciple

Ten Traits of a Vital Christian

Stephen A. Macchia

Baker Books

A Division of Baker Book House Co
Grand Rapids, Michigan 49516

© 2004 by Stephen A. Macchia

Published by Baker Books
a division of Baker Book House Company
P.O. Box 6287, Grand Rapids, MI 49516-6287
www.bakerbooks.com

Printed in the United States of America

Library of Congress Cataloging-in-Publication Data
Macchia, Stephen A., 1956–
    Becoming a healthy disciple: ten traits of a vital Christian / Stephen A. Macchia.
        p.   cm.
    Includes bibliographical references.
    ISBN 0-8010-9141-1 (pbk.)
    1. Christian life. 2. Spiritual life—Christianity. I. Title.
BV4501.3.M22 2004
248.4—dc22   2003021509

For Ruth, Nathan, and Rebekah
With all my love and gratitude

Contents

Foreword by George H. Gallup, Jr.   11
Introduction   13

Ten Traits of a Vital Christian
   1. Experiences God's Empowering Presence   27
   2. Engages in God-Exalting Worship   43
   3. Practices the Spiritual Disciplines   62
   4. Learns and Grows in Community   86
   5. Commits to Loving and Caring Relationships   106
   6. Exhibits Christlike Servanthood   126
   7. Shares the Love of Christ Generously   145
   8. Manages Life Wisely and Accountably   170
   9. Networks with the Body of Christ   194
  10. Stewards a Life of Abundance   217

   Conclusion   239
   Overview   246
   Afterword by Leith Anderson   250
   Notes   252

Foreword

One of the most profound yet perhaps most overlooked trends in the U.S. over the last decade, clearly identified in national surveys, is the surge of interest in spiritual matters and an intense hunger for God. This is coupled with another prominent trend—the desire on the part of the public for deeper, more meaningful relationships with other people, where nurture and support can be provided.

Eight in ten Americans place themselves in the Christian tradition, yet the stark fact is many of these people do not know what they believe, or why. Many dutifully attend church, but this act in itself has not made them a "different people," ready to take unpopular stands on issues of the day. The bottom line is that many who place themselves in the Christian tradition are wandering about in spiritual confusion and uncertainty.

Now comes a much needed and timely book, *Becoming a Healthy Disciple: Ten Traits of a Vital Christian*, which speaks powerfully to the current spiritual condition of the nation. It is written by a man who brings much to the task—a strong academic background and many years as a pastor and the head of an organization, Vision New England, which has helped lead countless numbers of people to Christ through its many creative ministries.

The purpose of this book is to "broaden and strengthen our understanding of what it means to be a fully devoted follower of Jesus Christ." In searching the Gospel of John to learn from the disciples, the author draws on the deep wellsprings of his own faith and a love of Jesus that is immediately apparent to all who meet him. A dear friend and spiritual mentor to me and members of my family, Stephen Macchia writes clearly and compellingly about each of ten traits exhibited by Christians who seek to grow as disciples.

What would happen if an ever-growing number of churches in this nation were to take a new look at their core mission of encouraging people to respond to Jesus' call to take up his cross? The results of a recent study offer some thrilling prospects.

In this study a new scale (developed by a partnership between the Gallup Institute and a team headed by Bob Buford and Randy Frazee, senior pastor of Pantego Bible Church in Dallas) was used to try to put statistical calipers on the extent to which love of God relates to love of neighbor and outreach to society as a whole.

Those who indicated on the basis of fifteen items that they have a deep love of God are *far more likely* than the total group (all those who place themselves in the Christian tradition—80 percent of the total sample) to believe that one should love all people, regardless of background; be involved in the lives of the poor and suffering; find hope in Jesus Christ; pray for Christians to accept Jesus as Lord and Savior; share one's faith with others; and believe that the community of true believers is Christ's body on earth.

Huge majorities of those who have a deep love of God hold these beliefs. The survey percentages translate into millions of Americans and point to the enormous potential impact that clergy, religious educators, and others can have if discipleship is restored to the number one priority.

Today is a historical moment of opportunity for the churches of America. It is for faith communities to "seize the day" and to make a wholesale commitment to encourage people through God's grace to come into a transforming personal relationship with the living Christ. Stephen Macchia's book is, I believe, destined to play an important role in helping to guide and invigorate this process of transformation.

George H. Gallup, Jr.
The Gallup Organization
Princeton, New Jersey

Introduction

September 11, 2001. In our lifetime, this date will stand out among the rest. We will recall with clarity where we were when terrorism invaded the United States. We will relive the emotions of the day. We will revisit the pictures etched in our minds. We will renew our ties to family and friends. We will remember afresh the words "God bless America," "United we stand," "firefighter," "police officer," "rescue worker," "World Trade Center." Those of us who lived through this experience will recall, relive, revisit, renew, and remember. Doing so helps us to face courageously all of our tomorrows while dealing with the duties of today.

The disciples must have had a similar experience as they walked away from the crucifixion of Christ. The tragedy had struck at the center of their souls, and they must have thought life without Jesus at their side would be impossible. Three days later when they discovered the tomb was empty and Jesus was alive, they regrouped around the truth of the resurrection and the cloud began to lift. As recipients of the Holy Spirit with a charge to be Christ's witnesses to the ends of the earth, their lives together were marked by prayer, worship, teaching, fellowship, community, and challenging ministry opportunities on the front lines of battle. They moved ahead with hope and joy, convicted and convinced that they were destined to fulfill the Great Commission.

What about you? If you are a follower of Jesus Christ, there is hope for all of your tomorrows as well. It may be time to regroup and return to the basics of your discipleship experience. You may find that you need to realign your priorities around those espoused by God. You may need to revisit the Gospels to discover afresh what it means to be a disciple of Jesus Christ.

Becoming a healthy disciple is a lifelong journey. We won't ever arrive at the fullest picture of what God requires of us. Discipleship is apprenticeship, and the Master doesn't expect perfection, only skill development that leads to a deeper relationship along the way. We will fall short of his glory, and we will disappoint him more often than we care to imagine. But the fact is, the awesome love of the Lord for all his disciples—past, present, and future—is unfathomable, undeniable, unconditional, indestructible, and incredible. Living by human ability and insight, we will disappoint him, but when we live by his strength and provision, we delight him and bring him great joy.

Becoming a Healthy Church

The context for healthy discipleship is a healthy church. We grow most effectively in environments conducive to our development. If this premise makes good sense, it's only natural that we take the principles of church health and translate them to the pew, the home, the workplace, the community, and the wider world.

In my previous book *Becoming a Healthy Church*,[1] I introduced ten traits of a healthy church. This list is the result of an extensive process of research, church visits, Bible study, prayer, dialogue with leaders, training, testing, and refinement. In summary, *a healthy church is prayerful in all aspects of church life and ministry, reliant upon God's power and the authority of his Word, and values the following:*

1. *God's empowering presence.* The healthy church actively seeks the Holy Spirit's direction and empowerment for its daily life and ministry. (Rom. 8:16, "The Spirit himself testifies with our spirit that we are God's children.")
2. *God-exalting worship.* The healthy church gathers regularly as the local expression of the body of Christ to worship God

in ways that engage the heart, mind, soul, and strength of the people. (John 4:23, "Yet a time is coming and has now come when the true worshipers will worship the Father in spirit and truth, for they are the kind of worshipers the Father seeks.")

3. *Spiritual disciplines.* The healthy church provides training, models, and resources for members of all ages to develop their daily spiritual disciplines. (James 3:17, "But the wisdom that comes from heaven is first of all pure; then peace-loving, considerate, submissive, full of mercy and good fruit, impartial and sincere.")

4. *Learning and growing in community.* The healthy church encourages believers to grow in their walk with God and with one another in the context of a safe, affirming environment. (Rom. 14:19, "Let us therefore make every effort to do what leads to peace and to mutual edification.")

5. *A commitment to loving and caring relationships.* The healthy church is intentional in its efforts to build loving, caring relationships within families, between members, and within the community it serves. (1 John 3:16, "This is how we know what love is: Jesus Christ laid down his life for us. And we ought to lay down our lives for our brothers.")

6. *Servant-leadership development.* The healthy church identifies and develops individuals whom God has called and given the gift of leadership and challenges them to become servant-leaders. (Eph. 4:16, "From him [Christ] the whole body, joined and held together by every supporting ligament, grows and builds itself up in love, as each part does its work.")

7. *An outward focus.* The healthy church places high priority on communicating the truth of Jesus and demonstrating the love of Jesus to those outside the faith. (Luke 19:10, "For the Son of Man came to seek and to save what was lost.")

8. *Wise administration and accountability.* The healthy church utilizes appropriate facilities, equipment, and systems to provide maximum support for the growth and development of its ministries. (Luke 16:11, "So if you have not been trustworthy in handling worldly wealth, who will trust you with true riches?")

9. *Networking with the body of Christ.* The healthy church reaches out to others in the body of Christ for collaboration, resource sharing, learning opportunities, and united celebrations of worship. (John 17:23, "May they [the church] be brought to complete unity to let the world know that you sent me and have loved them even as you have loved me.")

10. *Stewardship and generosity.* The healthy church teaches its members that they are stewards of their God-given resources and challenges them to sacrificial generosity in sharing with others. (2 Cor. 9:6, "Remember this: Whoever sows sparingly will also reap sparingly, and whoever sows generously will also reap generously.")

When I introduced these ten traits of a healthy church, pastors and leaders acknowledged them as principles that cut across all denominational affiliations and made sense to all who desire health and vitality in the context of their Christian community. They were written with multiple ministry styles in mind and represent a wide cross section of the body of Christ.

I have written the book you are holding on the basic premise that if two or more disciples of Jesus are pursuing the same priorities in life and service, they will have a very positive effect on the whole church. Disciple health and church health belong together, and when they are pursued in parallel fashion, the resulting transformation in the body of Christ is beyond measure.

If you are a disciple of Jesus Christ, it is incumbent upon you to see that you are growing to become more and more like him every day. If you are typical of the human race, you know that to accomplish this goal you need to understand your place within the body of Christ. We don't become like him in isolation; we grow in his image within the context of the church.

In his classic work, *Basic Christianity,* John Stott put it this way: "The Christian life is not just our own private affair. If we have been born again into God's family, not only has he become our Father but every other Christian believer in the world, whatever his nation or denomination, has become our brother or sister in Christ. But it is no good supposing that membership of the universal Church of Christ is enough; we must belong to some local branch of it. . . . Every Christian's place is in a local church . . . sharing in its worship, its fellowship, and its witness."[2]

Our roles as disciples of Jesus Christ make a difference in the health of the universal and local church. Our membership in the family of God leads us to take seriously the characteristics that need to be pursued by all of us who claim his name, his love, and his lordship. It is out of the core of our being in Christ that we exhibit faithfulness in every context of our lives. Focusing our attention on the "being" side of us more than the "doing" side will make for a more well-rounded approach to holistic Christian discipleship.

Becoming a Healthy Disciple

In the reading I have done over the years on the subject of discipleship, I have observed a common focus: Jesus is our example to follow, the ideal to achieve. Our tendency, however, is to focus on two primary attributes of Christ and his teaching—his prayer life and his evangelistic outreach to others in need. This gets translated in our day to the quiet time and the testimony. When our understanding of discipleship is wrapped up almost exclusively in these two areas, we tend to miss much of what Jesus said to his disciples in the first century and what he desires to say to us today.

The intention of examining the ten traits of a healthy disciple, therefore, is to broaden and strengthen our understanding of what it means to be a fully devoted follower of Jesus Christ. These traits include a variety of areas of personal life and service and require that we consider them systemically rather than linearly. In other words, when considered as an interrelated set of principles, we acknowledge that one feeds into another and impacts the whole. Each of the ten should be seen in light of Jesus' life and teaching, based on the Gospel of John and the relationship Jesus had with his disciples. The goal of healthy discipleship is to learn to love what God loves and practice his teachings in daily life. How will we ever discover what God loves? By becoming a friend of God, a beloved disciple.

The healthy disciple is prayerful in all aspects of personal life and ministry and reliant upon God's power and the authority of his Word. Specifically, the ten traits of a healthy disciple are as follows:

1. *Experiences God's empowering presence.* The healthy disciple understands the role of the Holy Spirit and lives daily with a fresh reality of his power and presence. (John 14:26, "The Counselor, the Holy Spirit, . . . will teach you all things and will remind you of everything I have said to you.")

2. *Engages in God-exalting worship.* The healthy disciple engages wholeheartedly in meaningful, God-focused worship experiences on a weekly basis with the family of God. (John 4:23, "The true worshipers will worship the Father in spirit and truth, for they are the kind of worshipers the Father seeks.")

3. *Practices the spiritual disciplines.* The healthy disciple pursues the daily disciplines of prayer, Bible study, and reflection in the quietness of one's personal prayer closet. (John 15:4, "Remain in me, and I will remain in you.")

4. *Learns and grows in community.* The healthy disciple is involved in spiritual and relational growth in the context of a safe and affirming group of like-minded believers. (John 21:6, "When they did [obey Jesus], they were unable to haul the net in because of the large number of fish.")

5. *Commits to loving and caring relationships.* The healthy disciple prioritizes the qualities of relational vitality that lead to genuine love for one another in the home, workplace, church, and community. (John 15:12–13, "My command is this: Love each other as I have loved you. Greater love has no one than this, that he lay down his life for his friends.")

6. *Exhibits Christlike servanthood.* The healthy disciple practices God-honoring servanthood in every relational context of life and ministry. (John 13:15, "I have set you an example that you should do as I have done for you.")

7. *Shares the love of Christ generously.* The healthy disciple maximizes every opportunity to share the love of Christ, in word and deed, with those outside the faith. (John 3:16, "For God so loved the world that he gave his one and only Son, that whoever believes in him shall not perish but have eternal life.")

8. *Manages life wisely and accountably.* The healthy disciple develops personal life management skills and lives within a web of accountable relationships. (John 9:4, "As long as it is day, we must do the work of him who sent me.")

9. *Networks with the body of Christ.* The healthy disciple actively reaches out to others within the Christian community for relationships, worship, prayer, fellowship, and ministry. (John 17:23, "May they be brought to complete unity to let the world know that you sent me and have loved them even as you have loved me.")

10. *Stewards a life of abundance.* The healthy disciple recognizes that every resource comes from the hand of God and is to be used generously for kingdom priorities and purposes. (John 12:24, "Unless a kernel of wheat falls to the ground and dies, it remains only a single seed. But if it dies, it produces many seeds.")

As you can see, this list of traits is more comprehensive than developing a quiet time and practicing your testimony. Don't get me wrong; a quiet time and a testimony are very important! I would contend, however, that they do not encompass the breadth, depth, length, and height of the discipleship Jesus promoted when he walked the earth, nor do they include all of what he would have for us today.

The world is desperate for a relevant gospel and an effective church filled with the healthiest of disciples. Our health as disciples has less to do with our physical, financial, or even emotional health. Our *spiritual* health is the priority of this book, and the way we conduct ourselves as Spirit-empowered people is what determines our health as Jesus' disciples. A physically disabled person can become a healthy disciple. A financially impoverished person can become a healthy disciple. An emotionally disenfranchised person can become a healthy disciple. That's the hope of the gospel. That's the joy of discovering Christ. That's the peace that he brings to our hearts and souls.

When our external (physical, financial) realities become our benchmark for discipleship health or when we pursue discipleship health in the hope that we will alter our external realities, we are headed in the wrong direction. The health of a disciple of Jesus Christ is marked by what happens *within* us first and foremost. Then, we will live our lives from the center of our hearts and souls, and we will give our lives away in loving, sacrificial ways.

A Healed Heart Is at the Core of a Healthy Disciple

When we discover that our hearts are broken and contrite, we come to the Lord with an earnest desire to repent of our sinfulness. It's out of this repentant heart that we find redemption in Christ. We are redeemed because of his sacrificial love on our behalf expressed in his death on the cross and his resurrection to eternal life. Because of his everlasting redemption, we are reconciled—brought into right relationship with God through Jesus Christ—and that reconciliation allows us to call God our heavenly Father. As new creatures in Christ, we walk through this life in the power of the Spirit as regenerate people—learning, growing, and becoming what he intends for us.

A healed heart becomes a renewed heart as we walk from repentance to redemption to reconciliation to regeneration. Our hearts are healed at the point of conversion, and they become healthy as we walk through life as Christian disciples.

The Beloved Disciple, Our Example

The biblical passages I've chosen to illustrate each of the ten traits come primarily from the Gospel of John. The commentary on the texts is from William Barclay's wonderful Daily Study Bible Series, which was written, in the words of Richard of Chichester's prayer, "to enable men and women to know Jesus Christ more clearly, to love him more dearly, and to follow him more nearly."[3] I chose Barclay not only because I appreciate his academic yet practical approach to biblical commentary but also because I agree with his summary of the authorship of John's Gospel and his assessment of the references to the "beloved disciple" throughout the text.

Barclay reviews the question of authorship alongside the debate about the identity of the beloved disciple. We know from early church writers that there were actually two Johns in the Ephesian church at the time the Gospel of John was written—John the apostle and John the elder. The elder John was so well loved that he was known as *The Elder.* He clearly had a unique place in the church. The Elder John was the penman of the Gospel. The mind and memory behind the Gospel was that of the aged John the apostle, whom John the elder always described as "the disciple whom Jesus loved."

> The more we know about the Fourth Gospel the more precious it becomes. For seventy years John had thought of Jesus. Day by day the Holy Spirit had opened out to him the meaning of what Jesus said. So when John was near the century of life and his days were numbered, he and his friends sat down to remember. John the elder held the pen to write for his master, John the apostle; and the last of the apostles set down, not only what he had heard Jesus say, but also what he now knew Jesus had meant. He remembered how Jesus had said: "I have yet many things to say to you, but you cannot bear them now. When the Spirit of Truth comes, he will guide you into all the truth" (John 16:12–13 [RSV]). There were many things, which seventy years ago he had not understood; there were many things, which in these seventy years the Spirit of Truth had revealed to him. These things John set down even as the eternal glory was dawning upon him. When we read this gospel let us remember that we are reading the gospel which of all the gospels is most the work of the Holy Spirit, speaking to us of the things which Jesus meant, speaking through the mind and memory of John the apostle and by the pen of John the elder. Behind this gospel is the whole church at Ephesus, the whole company of the saints, the last of the apostles, the Holy Spirit, the Risen Christ himself.[4]

Why is all of this so important? Because we look to the beloved disciple as an example of a person who lived close to Christ, fully attentive to his words and his ways, willing to sacrifice on his behalf, and desirous of reflecting his love and glory in his life of discipleship.

- The beloved disciple is at the Last Supper reclining close to Jesus (John 13:23–26).
- The beloved disciple is at the cross, and Jesus entrusts his mother to him (John 19:25–27).
- The beloved disciple runs with Peter to the open tomb and believes (John 20:1–10).
- The beloved disciple recognizes the Lord after his resurrection (John 21:4–7).
- The beloved disciple follows Peter and Jesus at a close distance (John 21:20–23).
- The beloved disciple is the eyewitness source of the Gospel of John (John 21:24).

Jesus is our focus, and John the beloved is a very fitting discipleship case study. Both are worthy of their place in our reflections on this important subject. John is a reminder that in order for us to become healthy disciples, we must draw near to Jesus in the most intimate way possible. It is by coming close to the Lord that we get to know his heart for us, hear his gentle voice, and serve him in response to his incredible love for us.

Becoming a Beloved Disciple

In answering the question "Who is a disciple?" Margaret Campbell writes,

A disciple of Jesus is a person who has decided to live in attentiveness to Jesus. We live in attentiveness in order to become like Jesus on the inside and, thereby, able to do what Jesus would do on the outside. As maturing disciples we progressively learn to live in attentiveness, adoration, surrender, obedience, and thankfulness to God, and all of this, without ceasing. Through the hidden work of transformation, God writes his good way on our minds and hearts and this is very good. By his grace, our hearts are divinely changed. We are progressively conformed to be like Jesus in mind and will and soul and word and deed. What we say and what we do more consistently reflect the glory and goodness of God.[5]

George Barna put it this way: "True discipleship is about a lifestyle, not simply about stored up Bible knowledge. Often, churches assume that if people are reading the Bible and attending a small group, then real discipleship is happening. Unfortunately, we found that's often not the case. Discipleship is about being and reproducing zealots for Christ. Discipleship, in other words, is about passionately pursuing the lifestyle and mission of Jesus Christ."[6] Living attentively to Jesus will create this kind of deeply committed discipleship. When we passionately pursue the heart of God through the person of Jesus and the power of the Holy Spirit, our lifestyle and mission become radically altered as we are transformed from the inside out.

A life of blessed discipleship is a life of discipline and grace. We discipline ourselves to develop the sweet relationship with Jesus to which he calls us when he says, "Come, pick up your cross, and follow me." We discipline ourselves to become more like him in our attitudes and actions. It is the balancing of discipline and grace that marks the life of a beloved disciple. Tipping the scales in either direction can lead to ill health or disproportionate legalisms that will destroy rather than empower us.

Jesus instructed his disciples to live a life wholeheartedly devoted to his teachings. He required his disciples to pay attention to the words they spoke, the decisions they made, the attitudes they expressed, the relationships they maintained, and the commission they fulfilled. Each of these aspects of their lives was to be in alignment with the purposes of God. In a similar way today, the ten traits of a healthy disciple are a refreshing reminder of the life we are called to discharge by his grace and under his lordship.

"To all who received him, to those who believed in his name, he gave the right to become children of God" (John 1:12).

Jesus calls us to himself in an intimate way. He invites us to become children of God. "The Word became flesh and made his dwelling among us. We have seen his glory, the glory as of the One and Only, who came from the Father, full of grace and truth" (John 1:14). Having heard the story and responded to the invitation, let's put our trust in him and follow his heart all the way to eternity. He promises to guide us every step of the way.

A Disciple's Prayer

Lord Jesus, as you called your first disciples into an intimate relationship as your children, I too respond to that call today. Help me along my life's journey to lean fully in your direction so that I may hear your voice calling me. As you invite me into a deeper relationship with you, give me the discipline and grace to respond in love and obedience. As you initiate on my behalf, give me the eyes to see your handiwork, the ears to hear your footsteps, the heart to know your unconditional love, and the hands to serve your watching world. I count it pure joy to be called your disciple-child. Lead me onward in healthy, life-producing ways. For your glory and for the expansion of your kingdom, I pray in your precious name, Jesus. Amen.

Ten Traits
of a
Vital Christian

1

Experiences God's Empowering Presence

The healthy disciple understands the role of the Holy Spirit and lives daily with a fresh reality of his power and presence.

The Counselor, the Holy Spirit, . . . will teach you all things and will remind you of everything I have said to you.

John 14:26

My promise was broken. My word was not trustworthy. My actions were evidence enough. It was her final game of the season, and I was in another state attending to the needs of other people for reasons that a brokenhearted ten-year-old didn't fully understand. "I'll make it right when I get home," I rationalized to myself. But the damage had been done, the game was now over, the trophies were handed out, and the memory was created without my presence to cheer, applaud, and celebrate. Could I really make it right?

Sure, my delightful ten-year-old daughter will forgive me. In time, she might even forget. The soccer trophy will collect dust and eventually be thrown into a box that will end up in the attic, and time will heal this hurtful, incomplete experience. "Many other dads miss times like this," I defensively responded to my family. "I'll watch the calendar more closely next time."

Thankfully for Rebekah, there were to be many more next times for me to make it up to her. I know the importance of being there for our children on special occasions. I remember when my parents were there for me. There was the Pinewood Derby in Cub Scouts, the Spartan Chorale and Winter Carnival in high school, the high school and college graduations and special awards ceremonies, birthdays, wedding, anniversaries, graduate school, ordination, installation services, etc. During those defining moments in all of our lives, there's something about having special people present without whom the experience is incomplete.

When God promises to be with us, his word is *never* broken. Not only on special occasions, but every day of life he's there to guide, protect, lead, and empower us by his Spirit's presence. His invitation is for us to "set our hearts at rest in his presence" (1 John 3: 19). As Immanuel—God with us—he will never leave us or forsake us. This word cannot be denied. Jesus' promise to his disciples that the Spirit would come and abide in their presence is fulfilled in our lives as well.

In general, the ministry of the Holy Spirit is misunderstood by the average Christian today. If you have a handle on the doctrine of the Holy Spirit, then you are above the norm. With more than three decades as a believer, as well as a master's and doctorate under my belt, I'm still growing in my knowledge and experience of the work and ministry of God's Spirit. However, we can rest assured his promised Spirit is always present. Always. It's not something that comes from head knowledge—it's a truth we can experience in every realm of our being. As we submit to God and invite him to reign supreme in our hearts, the Holy Spirit's presence is available to guide us in our decisions, enrich us in our relationships, and lead us in our hearts' desire to please and honor God.

In His Presence

There is fullness of joy in the presence of the Holy Spirit. Despite the circumstances of our lives, when we abide in his presence there is peace beyond measure, abundant life, and eternal hope.

The Spirit of God was also a vital presence in Jesus' earthly life. "Found to be with child *through the Holy Spirit*," Mary gave birth to a son, "'Immanuel,' which means 'God with us'" (Matt. 1:18, 23, italics added). He was spared the sword of Herod because of a dream whispered into the hearts and ears of his parents by the Spirit (Matt. 2:12). At his baptism the Spirit of God descended upon him like a dove and a voice from heaven announced, "This is my Son, whom I love; with him I am well pleased" (Matt. 3:16–17). When tempted in the desert by the devil himself, Jesus was ministered to by Spirit-empowered angels (Matt. 4:11). All throughout his earthly life, the Spirit's presence is acknowledged in the Scriptures as the listening ear, the protecting arm, and the guiding feet of Jesus.

The Spirit of God desires to be that same empowering presence to watch over and participate in our lives. Throughout John 14–16 we discover Jesus' promises to his disciples that he will send the Holy Spirit to live among them after he departs this earth. He loved his disciples and said, "I will not leave you as orphans" (John 14:18). Although not physically present with them after his death and resurrection, his Spirit's presence was sent for them and for us.

The roles the Holy Spirit plays in our lives are many and varied. The Spirit is the person of the Trinity who *convicts* us of our sin, turning our brokenness into joyfulness and faithfulness. The Spirit is sent to transform a broken heart and *converts* us from a life of oppression and self-absorption to a life of freedom and God-consciousness. Throughout our lives, the Spirit directs us in accordance with his will as he *counsels* us, healing our emotions, *comforts* us in the depths of our hurts and disappointments, and *consoles* us with his love and grace. Under the controlling auspices of the Spirit, we are called into a life of obedience to *cooperate* with the marching orders of the heavenly Father, birthing within us the hope and renewal that only he can provide. Then, as we grow in our lifelong journey of regeneration, the Spirit *continues* to quicken our hearts to remain in alignment with his love, Word, and ways. Ultimately, it will be the Spirit who *completes* the work in us so that when we go home to be with the Lord for all eternity, it will be the Spirit who empowered us to be recipients of the "well done, good and faithful servant" affirmation from our loving heavenly Father.

It is the work of the Spirit of God to convict, convert, counsel, comfort, console, cooperate, continue, and complete believers through his empowering presence in our lives. As followers of Christ, we need to have a *cross* experience daily, not just when we come to Christ initially, but as God's empowering presence brings us closer and closer to the heart of God and his purpose is lived out through us. The Spirit enables us to humble ourselves in his presence and to rely upon him in every circumstance of life.

Jesus wanted to make sure his disciples understood that there is plenty of room in his presence both here on earth and in heaven. "In my Father's house are many rooms," Jesus told his disciples (John 14:2). William Barclay comments on this passage: "An earthly house becomes overcrowded; an earthly inn must sometimes turn away the weary traveler because its accommodation is exhausted. It is not so with our Father's house, for heaven is as wide as the heart of God and there is room for all. Jesus is saying to his friends: 'Don't be afraid. Men may shut their doors upon you. But in heaven you will never be shut out.'"[1]

When we abide in his presence we stand amidst countless others, all of whom have plenty of room in his arms, on his lap, in the wideness of his heart. There is no overcrowding in the presence of God. There is plenty of room for all, not only in the everlasting kingdom of heaven but also here on earth.

Our Posture

As we enter God's presence and abide there throughout our daily routines, we are presented with a choice regarding our posture. Like all forms of basic communication, our body language tells more about the message we are seeking to convey than the words we speak and the tone of voice we use. So it is as we experience God's empowering presence.

When we wake up for a new day we are given the opportunity to be self-controlled or Spirit-controlled. Making the right choice each new day is critical to how our day begins and ends.

Suppose for a moment that I wake up and choose to be controlled by my self instead of the Spirit. I make up my own mind as to how I will use the day. I choose how to speak to my wife and children. I determine what agenda fits my personal needs first and foremost. I go about my day with *my* best interests in mind. If anyone gets in my way, I remind that person in one way or another that I don't appreciate the interruption. I am seeking my own agenda and the heck with everyone else.

On the other hand, when I wake up and start my day as a Spirit-controlled person, I am functioning in quite the opposite fashion. I start the day on my knees in prayer, reflecting on the Scriptures as my life-guide and anchor. I consider the needs of others more important than my own. I bend with agility toward the agendas of others while maintaining focus on the mission God has called me to fulfill. I choose to look for ways I can affirm others, building them up so their best interests are served. I function as a servant to God and others and find joy, peace, fulfillment, and hope in living life with such vitality.

The first example, that of living for my self, is a "clenched fist" posture. A clenched fist selfishly holds everything close to oneself, with no room for others and no interest in God. On the other hand, the example of the Spirit-controlled life is an "open hand" posture. An open hand is willing to receive from and submit to the Spirit of God, to look attentively toward the needs and interests of others, and ultimately to love, serve, give, affirm, and empower others to become the best God wants for them.

When we are truly walking through life in his presence we cannot help but see and feel the dramatic difference between those two distinct postures. The fact is that we wake up every day with those two basic options—self or Spirit?

The posture of the open, outstretched hand is ready to receive from the Holy Spirit the many joys of being in relationship with God—his calling to new birth in Christ, his empowerment for daily living, his filling and indwelling, his fruitfulness and gift-edness realized through us. This posture is reflected not only in outstretched hands but in open ears that hear the Spirit's still, small voice, in open hearts that are warmed by his abiding presence, and in obedient feet that are ready to move on a moment's notice into submissive service to God first and then to others as a reflection of our love for him.

Reflecting real love to Jesus is not always an easy thing. It is shown most fully in our loving and true obedience. "It was by his obedience that Jesus showed his love of God; and it is by our obedience that we must show our love for Jesus."[2] Jesus says to his disciples, "If you love me, you will obey what I command. And I will ask the Father, and he will give you another Counselor to be with you forever—the Spirit of truth. The world cannot accept him, because it neither sees him nor knows him. But you know him, *for he lives with you and will be in you*" (John 14:15–17, italics added). True obedience comes when we choose the posture of openness to the Spirit of God to work in our lives, guiding us in what to do and enabling us to do it. As we live in prayerful expectation for the Holy Spirit to work in and through us, he comes to empower us for a lifestyle of loving obedience.

Principle 1.1 Exemplify His Fruit

What does a healthy disciple look like while experiencing God's empowering presence? As we live in submission to the work of the Spirit each new day, we invite the Spirit's presence to be made known to us throughout our day and through our very lives.

In *Becoming a Healthy Church*,[3] I remind the reader that the plumb line against which we can measure whether we are abiding in God's presence is described by the apostle Paul as the fruit of the Spirit. "The fruit of the Spirit is love, joy, peace, patience, kindness, goodness, faithfulness, gentleness and self-control. Against such things there is no law. Those who belong to Christ Jesus have crucified the sinful nature with its passions and desires. Since we live by the Spirit, let us keep in step with the Spirit. Let us not become conceited, provoking and envying each other" (Gal. 5:22–26).

None of the nine lovely expressions of the Spirit can be fulfilled on our own strength or power. It is only when we are filled with the Spirit that these fruit can be exhibited. Therefore, it is a worthy discipline to pray daily that the Spirit would be so present in our lives that his fruit would be seen in us. Let's consider then the nine fruit of the Spirit one at a time and reflect on the meaning of each for our personal lives.

Love. The word for love used in this passage is the New Testament word *agape.* It is one of the four common Greek words for *love.* The best definition I have discovered for *agape* is "unconquerable benevolence." It means that no matter what people may do to us by way of insult, injury, or humiliation, we will never seek anything but their highest good. It is therefore a feeling of the mind as much as of the heart; it describes the deliberate effort—which we can make only with the help of God—never to seek anything but the best even for those who seek the worst for us.

Joy. The Greek word for joy in this passage is *chara*—the kind of joy based in a religious experience, not the kind that comes from our possessions and earthly pleasures. Nor is it the kind of joy we feel when we triumph over someone else in competition. The Spirit's joy has at its foundation our relationship with God. It doesn't need to be vivacious or overpowering; it can be a joy within one's heart that has no outward expression. Such genuine joy comes from the realization that our lives are held securely in God's hands.

Peace. The third fruit of the Spirit is peace, known in Greek as *eirene.* In the time of the apostle Paul, this word was commonly used to describe the serenity that a country would enjoy under a just and righteous leader. It was also used to describe the kind of law and order that existed in cities or villages because the "keepers of the peace" were doing their jobs correctly. Here it means the tranquility of heart and mind in the inner recesses of a Christian's soul that comes from the all-pervading consciousness that our lives are in the hands of almighty God.

Patience. The Greek word for the fourth fruit, patience, is *makrothumia.* Generally speaking, this word is used to describe patience with people rather than events or objects. We see it in the person who is slow to anger, even when tempted to fight back. This is often our most difficult attribute to reflect, which makes us all the more dependent on God to live through us in this regard. He has such unlimited patience that he bears with all of our sinning and chooses not to cast us off. That's an awesome truth. In our dealings with one another, we must reproduce this loving, forbearing, forgiving, patient attitude of God.

Kindness and goodness. The fifth and sixth fruits, kindness and goodness, are closely related terms that should be considered together. In fact, the Greek word for kindness is *chrestotes*, which can also be translated as *goodness.* The idea here is goodness that is kind. Kindness can be described as active helpfulness, while goodness can have the aspects of rebuke and discipline added to it. Jesus showed goodness toward the people in the temple when he cleansed it and drove out those who were making it a bazaar instead of a place of holiness and worship. He also showed kindness to the sinful woman who anointed his feet with her tears. In the life of the healthy disciple, we need the same goodness that expresses both kindness and strength of character.

Faithfulness. The fruit of faithfulness is also considered trustworthiness. The Greek word here, *pistis,* describes a person who is trustworthy, reliable, true to his or her word. Faithfulness is extremely important in the Christian community because there are few things worse than working with someone who has breached your trust. It takes time to become worthy of one another's trust, but as we live and minister together, seeing each other in our truest forms and working out the bugs of living in the community of faith, we build trust and confidence in one another.

Gentleness. The eighth attribute of the Spirit-empowered life is gentleness. The Greek word, *praotes,* has three distinct meanings in the New Testament. First, it means being submissive to the will of God. Second, it means being teachable or not too proud to learn. Third, it means being considerate of others. No matter what the conditions of life may be, no matter how great or unfortunate, gentle people know how to treat others with a tender word, action, or attitude and know how to control their anger. A gentle spirit turns away wrath and influences the tone of a faith community in a way that is compelling and beautiful. Gentleness is godly, not something to be shunned by the "macho" as a sign of weakness. It is a sign of inner peace and communion with God.

Self-control. The ninth and final fruit spelled out by the apostle Paul is self-control. He saved the hardest for last! The word in Greek is *egkrateia* and simply means "self-mastery." It is used elsewhere to describe the athlete's discipline of his or her body and of the Christian's mastery of sexual temptation. One who is self-controlled knows how to depend on the work of the Spirit to master one's desires, which makes a person fit to be the servant of others.

In essence, Paul is saying that for us to truly live out a Spirit-empowered life, we need a healthy self-mastery that is ready at a moment's notice to serve the needs of others. When we are self-absorbed, wanting to meet our own needs first, we are not walking with the Spirit or fully prepared to serve and give out of love. Self-control must affect every aspect of our being, including the use of our time, our bodies, our minds, our emotions, and our spirits. This is an ongoing process of growth under the lordship of Christ and the leadership of the Spirit.

To become healthy disciples, we must become people who abide in Christ and remain empowered by his Spirit. The apostle Paul tells us in Romans 6 that the Christian has died with Christ and risen again to a new, clean life in which the evil things of the past are done with and the lovely things of the Spirit are coming to fruition. Frankly, the more I have studied, taught, and reflected on the nine lovely fruit of the Spirit, the more I have become convinced that we cannot embody a single one of them without the empowering presence of God's Spirit. It is only through living in full submission to the work of the Spirit that the fruit can blossom and grow, and that requires daily prayer and obedience.

Principle 1.2 Embody His Thumbprint

In stark contrast to the Spirit of God is our life of flesh. Left to fend for ourselves, we will always have the tendency to lean away from what the Spirit wants and the Scriptures command. In fact, the leaning is so dramatic it is generally seen as outright disobedience to the will of God. This is called sin. This three-letter word, so small and nondescript, is actually the single most powerful force in opposition to a life of healthy discipleship.

Sin is not a popular subject today. In fact, it's one of the most blatantly avoided topics of our time. The defining lines between right and wrong, good and evil, truth and falsehood have been so blurred that the concept of sin has been taken out of public discourse and left in the hands of the theologian and the pastor. However, even within the circles of theological discourse and pastoral ministry, we aren't hearing a lot about sin. It's just not a subject that helps you win friends and influence people.

Since September 11, 2001, the concept of sin has become more front and center (without the word being used). We are more willing to speak of evil, especially when pointing a finger at despicable acts of barbarism and terrorism. That is blatant "sin," and we recognize it in a dramatic fashion.

Lest we neglect the three fingers pointing back at us as we point out the sins of others, what about the sinfulness that resides within us? In chapter 5, "Commits to Loving and Caring Relationships," we will address the sin that occurs in broken relationships with others, but here we must focus on what our sinfulness does to the heart of God and how it alters our experience of God's empowering presence.

Unless we are willing to wake up each day with a genuine heart's desire to come clean and confess our sins before God, we will not experience the richness of God's empowering presence and will continue to sin throughout the day. Upon our conversion, we do not become sinless human beings. Instead Christ invites his disciples to embody his thumbprint on our lives as we continually come clean of the sins that encroach upon us in thought, word, and deed.

Yes, even as we reside as sin-filled people in a sin-sick world, God offers us the Holy Spirit to watch over our lives in ways we don't expect or deserve. Inviting his empowering presence, however, is a matter of the will and a reflection of the heart. If we deliberately avoid or reject his presence, he will flee from us. It is our daily choice to invite him in—come, Holy Spirit.

As we invite God's Spirit to reside in our hearts, we can call upon his empowerment to forgive us when we sin and to restore and release us to deeper relationship with God and fulfillment of his will. It's like the natural patterns of breathing that bring us into his presence—inhaling choices to love and obey by the Spirit's presence and power, and exhaling his empowerment as we are released of our sinfulness and fully abandoned to his loving will.

When we recognize our daily—often hourly—need for his empowering presence, we can celebrate the life that he's given so freely and generously. When we fully embody his thumbprint, we express in word and deed the personality he has given to us. The focus moves away from our sinfulness and into our blessedness. As a blessed disciple of Christ, we rejoice in the life he has given to us and the person he has enabled us to become.

David Midwood, a colleague and friend in ministry, continually reminds me of the importance of watching for and listening to "God sightings" in our midst. Every day he journals about these sightings as a reminder of God's ever-present power at work in his life and in the lives of others. Where have you seen God today? Are you celebrating his life in you, redeemed from your sinfulness and destined for a great and marvelous mission to fulfill? Write it down today; it's all a part of the unfolding discernment of his unique thumbprint on your life.

Principle 1.3 Express His Gifts

An outgrowth of the embodiment of God's thumbprint is evidenced in the expression of his gifts. The Spirit has empowered each believer with gifts that grow beyond one's capacity to muster up abilities on our own strength or power. As the Spirit resides in the center of our heart, he fills us with himself and gives to us spiritual love offerings that are to be freely and generously given away to others. C. Peter Wagner defines them as "a special attribute given by the Holy Spirit to every member of the body of Christ, according to God's grace, for use within the context of the body."[4] They are part of the special gifting that the Spirit desires to implant within us for his purposes to be accomplished through the life of the healthy disciple.

Ruth has the gift of discernment. Paul has the gift of teaching. Joanna has the gift of intercession. David has the gift of mercy. Bob has the gift of evangelism. Tom has the gift of leadership. Pat has the gift of hospitality. Ted has the gift of speaking in a spiritual tongue (spiritual prayer language). Brian has the gift of prophecy. We can see these gifts in those around us, and when used for the glory of God, they are multiplied by the Spirit himself.

Discovery of our gift(s) is the first place to begin. Romans 12, 1 Corinthians 12, and Ephesians 4 are wonderful passages to read to see listings of the gifts of the Spirit. As we study and reflect upon such texts, we can begin to prayerfully seek the gifts of the Spirit or a deeper, fuller manifestation of the gifts we already have. Using materials like the *Network* curriculum from the Willow Creek Association,[5] participating in small group studies with others who are interested in discovering their gifts, and seeking the counsel of discerning believers can also affirm and help us understand the work of the Spirit in us.

After we discover our gifts, we need to hone them in order that they become more and more effective. Ruth's gift of discernment is honed as she participates in counseling with and praying for others. Paul grows in his teaching gift as he practices with groups of all ages and in varieties of teaching settings. Joanna develops as an intercessor both in the quietness of her prayer closet and as an active member of the healing prayer team. David becomes more effective in his ministry to underprivileged children as he extends mercy to them throughout all seasons of the year. Bob's evangelism gift is put to the test each time there is a divine appointment with a seeker. Tom becomes a more effective leader as he harnesses the energy of his ministry team and develops new resources for multiplying their work in the local church. Pat practices hospitality naturally, but when put to the test with increased numbers of people at the events for which she is responsible, she realizes her need for a team to assist with the growing numbers of attendees.

Our spiritual gifts are harvested for the glory of God when we give them away in service to others. The apostle Peter reminds us, "Each one should use whatever gift he has received to serve others, faithfully administering God's grace in its various forms. If anyone speaks, he should do it as one speaking the very words of God. If anyone serves, he should do it with the strength God provides, so that in all things God may be praised through Jesus Christ. To him be the glory and the power for ever and ever. Amen"

(1 Peter 4:10–11). What greater motivation or higher calling than to exercise the gifts of the Spirit for the glory of God?

Principle 1.4 Envision His Call

A natural spiritual outflow of the expression of his gifts is in the envisioning of God's call upon our lives. Another way of saying the same thing is through the term *vision*. What is the Spirit of God calling us to passionately pursue as his disciples? What is our long-term dream for the years ahead? Into which pathway is the Spirit of God leading us as individual members of the body of Christ?

Vision is best depicted by the phrase "preferred future." It's the direction of our lives that propels us forward in fulfillment of his call. Paul's strong sense from the Lord was that his spiritual gift of teaching, his love for various people groups around the world, combined with his passion for international missions and travel equaled a call out of a single ministry setting into an international leadership training mission. There the embodiment of the fruit of the Spirit, expressed in his unique personality and mix of gifts, is now being evidenced in the passionate vision he has for the future. He is fulfilled in his work because of the near perfect melding together of each of these elements.

The reflection of 20/20 vision is nearly impossible except when it's a vision that comes from the Spirit of God. Prayerfully seeking God's vision and obediently following after it makes for an energizing experience as a disciple of Christ.

To envision the call of God is to understand that in this life we are destined to fulfill a piece of his overall vision for the world. We may not make it into the history books of the Christian church, but each of us has an important part to play in God's elaborate encyclopedia of humanity. We are not here on earth by mistake or without reason; in his infinite wisdom he has called us to participate in the grand design of humanity. He desires to reveal through that still small voice his visionary purposes for us—yes, even us. We will cover this in more detail in chapter 8, "Manages Life Wisely and Accountably."

Principle 1.5 Experience His Presence

If we are ever to fully embrace a lifelong experience in God's empowering presence, we must live dependent upon God's Spirit, trusting his plan and purpose for our lives each and every day. The difficulty is that we love our independence and would rather live out our days in our own self-righteousness and under our own auspices rather than through the indwelling work of the Holy Spirit.

When we practice the presence of God, however, we acknowledge that he is here with us always—throughout every moment of every day. His omniscient (all-knowing), omnipresent (ever-present), omnipotent (all-powerful) influence over our lives is now and always. The psalmist put it beautifully:

> You know me.
> You know when I sit and when I rise;
>   you perceive my thoughts from afar.
> You discern my going out and my lying down;
>   you are familiar with all my ways.
> Before a word is on my tongue
>   you know it completely, O LORD. . . .
>   You have laid your hand upon me.
> Such knowledge is too wonderful for me,
>   too lofty for me to attain.
> Where can I go from your Spirit?
>   Where can I flee from your presence?
> If I go up to the heavens, you are there;
>   if I make my bed in the depths, you are there.
> If I rise on the wings of the dawn,
>   if I settle on the far side of the sea,
> even there your hand will guide me,
>   your right hand will hold me fast.
>
> Psalm 139:1–10

God's empowering presence is a fact for every Christian disciple. The first step toward healthy discipleship is affirming his presence, living in it daily, and lapping up the blessings he freely and generously gives to all his children. Keep your eyes open, your ears attuned, and your heart sensitized to the work of his Spirit. Your life will never be the same again.

A DISCIPLE'S PRAYER

Spirit of the living God, fall afresh on me. Melt me, mold me, fill me, use me. Spirit of the living God, fall afresh on me. These simple words of praise are my words today, dear Lord. I long to live in your empowering presence, refreshed in the reality of your Spirit, embracing the fruit of the Spirit, and exhibiting the gifts of the Spirit.

I open up myself to the fullness of your Spirit's power so that I am released to embrace your vision and call. May my daily experiences of life be marked with your abiding presence. And may your power reside within me as I trust you today as my empowering Master and King. All for your glory and in the reflection of your Son's love, the Lord Jesus Christ. Amen.

For Reflection and Renewal

The healthy disciple understands the role of the Holy Spirit and lives daily with a fresh reality of his power and presence.

1. Which aspect of the ministry of the Holy Spirit needs further clarification for you today? Which aspect was most striking to you in this chapter and why?
2. How will you focus your heart and mind on the fruit of the Spirit in the coming week? Memorize the nine lovely fruit of the Spirit and place them in written form prominently before you in one or more creative locations in your home or office.
3. What gifts of the Spirit are you most thankful for today, and how will you hone this gift in the days ahead? What gifts can you affirm in others?

4. Write out a prayer that speaks to how the Spirit is nudging you today to practice living your life in his empowering presence.

5. Share one or more highlights of this chapter with someone you trust, and commit to praying for one another for the faithful embodiment of this trait of discipleship health.

2

Engages in God-Exalting Worship

The healthy disciple engages wholeheartedly in meaningful, God focused worship experiences on a weekly basis with the family of God.

The true worshipers will worship the Father in spirit and truth, for they are the kind of worshipers the Father seeks.

John 4:23

The world rings with praise—lovers praising their mistresses, readers their favorite poet, walkers praising the countryside, players praising their favorite game—praise of weather, wines, dishes, actors, motors, horses, colleges, countries, historical personages, children, flowers, mountains, rare stamps, rare beetles, even sometimes politicians and scholars. I had not noticed how the humblest and at the same time most balanced and capacious minds praised most, while the cranks, misfits, and malcontents praised least. I had not noticed either that just as men spontaneously praise whatever they value, so they spontaneously urge us to join them in praising it: "Isn't she lovely? Wasn't it glorious? Don't you think that magnificent?"[1]

Worship that enlivens the spirit and expands the truth of God within the believing community is becoming more and more rare. There are more "cranks, misfits, and malcontents" in the pews of churches today than we care to admit. We may in fact be looking at one in the mirror as we prepare for worship each Sunday morning. "Not me," you might say, when most certainly there exists within each of us that propensity to miss the praise and the joy of God because we enter worship for all the wrong reasons, reflecting attitudes that kill worship rather than enhance it.

I hate to admit that on occasion I too am one of those "cranks, misfits, and malcontents." There have been far too many Sundays when the last place I wanted to be was in a pew (or even a pulpit!), and my attitude was about as distant from *spirit and truth* worship as possible! Like the time I raised my voice at my son as we were driving into the parking lot of the church moments before worship, forgetting that my unrighteous indignation would spoil the morning for the entire family. Or the time I saw a fellow "crank, misfit, and malcontent" in the hallway prior to the service and proceeded to fill his mind with my tale of woe about the church. Or, worse yet, the day I arrived at church with absolute disgust toward that person who days earlier had hurt my wife with an unkind word and was now sitting in the pew behind us.

Those are the times when we stink up the church with attitudes that destroy worship. Unfortunately those times happen every week in every church on every continent of this planet. And, yes, even you have been a part of creating this mess!

Yet it doesn't have to be that way when we gather to worship almighty God. You and I can make choices that will help lead the people of God into genuine, God-exalting worship—the kind the Father seeks.

The word *worship* literally means "to attribute worth" to someone or something. When we gather for congregational worship we are attributing worth to God in ways that express our earnest desire to praise him for his mighty deeds, all-powerful presence, and life-transforming Word. Entering into worship requires that we come expectantly so that the spontaneous presence of God is invited and experienced from the depth of our being. As we give ourselves to God, we do so with heart, soul, mind, and strength.

Spirit and Truth Worship

True worshipers "worship the Father in spirit and truth, for they are the kind of worshipers the Father seeks," Jesus reminded his disciples (John 4:23). Friendship and intimacy with God is the goal of this kind of worship, and it is something the Father desires in relationship with his children. Love, obedience, devotion, commitment, and profound loyalty to the priorities of God emerge out of this kind of worship.

Jesus, in this same passage, contrasts the intimacy of spirit and truth worship with that of the Samaritans. He calls their worship ignorant worship. Since they only knew and revered the Pentateuch (the first five books of the Old Testament), they had a truncated understanding of biblical truth that led them to a truncated worship of God.

The Samaritan's form of worship was not founded on love and knowledge but on ignorance and fear. It was more superstition than true worship, as seen in the historical record when they brought their own gods with them to dwell in Samaria (2 Kings 17:29). They created for themselves a false worship, the opposite of what Jesus was promoting to the disciples.

What does false worship look like? According to the commentator William Barclay, false worship is first of all a *selective worship.* It chooses what it wishes to know about God and omits the rest.[2] The Samaritans took as much of the Scriptures as they wished and paid no attention to the rest, which created a one-sided religion. Jesus reminds us that total truth worship is to be our sole desire, not snatching at fragments of truth that happen to suit our own positions.

Second, false worship is *ignorant worship.* Religious experiences are far more than merely the strenuous exercise of the intellect, but today a very large part of religious failure is due to intellectual sloth. Our faith is built on hope, but it is hope with reason behind it (1 Peter 3:15). Worship ought to be the approach to God of the whole person, in the context of the whole body of Christ. We must exercise our minds in worship as well as our hearts, souls, and strength.

False worship is third a *superstitious worship.* It is worship that is given not out of a sense of need nor out of any real desire but basically because a person feels it might be dangerous not to give it. Just as so many of us refuse to walk under a ladder, don't want a black cat to cross our path, believe in luck, or are uncomfortable with the number thirteen, so there are those of us who go to worship out of fear of what might happen if we leave God out of our lives. This is not genuine worship, for true worship is not based on fear but on the love of God and our gratitude for all God has done on our behalf.

Our worship is not to be selective, ignorant, or superstitious; instead, it should mirror the true worship Jesus taught and exemplified as he walked with his disciples. Because God is spirit, our gifts to God in worship must be gifts of the spirit. In this way truth and spirit are married to one another in all genuine acts of worship. As healthy disciples, this is the form of worship to which we should aspire in all our experiences of God-exalting worship.

Love-Based Worship

Early on in the Gospel of John, the beloved disciple points us in the direction of Jesus' miracles, beginning with his first miracle at the wedding at Cana in John 2:1–11. John's intent in sharing the details of this miracle was to celebrate what happens when Jesus comes into a person's life. There comes a new quality of life for the worshiper that's likened to the turning of water into wine. "Without Jesus, life is dull and stale and flat; when Jesus comes into it, life becomes vivid and sparkling and exciting. Without Jesus, life is drab and uninteresting; with him it is thrilling and exhilarating."[3]

We see this response to Jesus in the seven miracles of the Fourth Gospel:

Wedding feast at Cana (John 2:1–11)
Healing the official's son (John 4:46–54)

Healing the lame man (John 5:1–15)

Feeding the five thousand (John 6:1–15)

Walking on water (John 6:16–20)

Healing the blind man (John 9:1–41)

Raising Lazarus from the dead (John 11:1–44)

Jesus is the miracle worker, and when he enters the hearts of his disciples, worship erupts and he receives all the praise. In essence, that's the kind of genuine, love-based, spirit and truth worship that the Father longs for from his disciples. That is also what healthy disciples express from the depth of their hearts in response to the miraculous feats that Jesus has done on their behalf.

When we become friends of God, there is a stark contrast between our true worship as members of the believing community and the false worship of others. Accounts of Jesus' early miracles describe the great faith and following that Jesus stirred up among the people. But, as time goes on, the chief priests and Pharisees try to bring it all to an abrupt end. By chapter 11, a plot to kill Jesus has been crafted by the Sanhedrin. "What are we accomplishing?" they asked. "Here is this man performing many miraculous signs. If we let him go on like this, everyone will believe in him." Love-based worship was an affront to these leaders and they sought to bring it all to an end.

At Lazarus's home in Bethany, we note a dramatic contrast between genuine and false worship:

Six days before the Passover, Jesus arrived at Bethany, where Lazarus lived, whom Jesus had raised from the dead. Here a dinner was given in Jesus' honor. Martha served, while Lazarus was among those reclining at the table with him. Then Mary took about a pint of pure nard, an expensive perfume; she poured it on Jesus' feet and wiped his feet with her hair. And the house was filled with the fragrance of the perfume.

But one of his disciples, Judas Iscariot, who was later to betray him, objected. "Why wasn't this perfume sold and the money given to the poor? It was worth a year's wages." He did not say this because he cared about the poor but because he was a thief; as keeper of the money bag, he used to help himself to what was put into it.

"Leave her alone," Jesus replied, "It was intended that she should save this perfume for the day of my burial. You will always have the poor among you, but you will not always have me."

John 12:1–8

In this passage, Jesus encouraged the love-based form of worship displayed by Mary. In a parallel Gospel account, he said, "She has done a beautiful thing to me" (Mark 14:6). What is this beautiful thing? An appropriate, worshipful response to Jesus out of sincere gratitude for all that he has done on her behalf. Why didn't Judas respond in kind? Because his heart was hardened and he was preoccupied with selfish gain.

Mary's worship of Jesus was reckless. The expensive perfume she poured on Jesus' feet was an expression of her costly love in appreciation of his sacrificial, unconditional love for her. It was risky, daring, and out of her comfort zone, but its spontaneity provides the beautiful picture of intimate identification between Mary and her Lord. This form of love-based worship toward Jesus was not at all offensive to his friends (disciples), but was greatly misunderstood by the skeptics, onlookers, and unbelievers in their midst.

In the same way, we see love-based worship come forth from those who were touched dramatically by each of the miracles Christ performed. As the movement of Christ-followers was mushrooming, many lives were transformed by his saving mercy and power. Those who had the eyes of their hearts opened by God were delighted to express their love-based worship in response.

The crescendo was reached on that day of triumphal entry into the city of Jerusalem on the back of a young donkey (John 12:12–19). The street was filled with a great crowd that had come for the feast and heard that Jesus was on his way into Jerusalem. They took palm branches and went out to meet him, shouting, "Hosanna! Blessed is he who comes in the name of the Lord! Blessed is the King of Israel!" The euphoria of that moment must have been spectacular to experience. The crowd continued to spread the word about his miraculous powers, and many came out to meet him.

But the Pharisees were not at all happy. "See, this is getting us nowhere. Look how the whole world has gone after him!" (John 12:19). It was soon thereafter that Jesus predicted his death, knowing that his days of earthly ministry were coming to an end. "The hour has come for the Son of Man to be glorified," he told his disciples. There's something significant about love-based worship. It's beautiful to behold by the heart of a genuine disciple and an affront to those who refuse to allow their hearts to be touched by the loving hand of God.

In our day love-based expressions of worship toward God receive a similar response from the Sanhedrins, Pharisees, or Judases in our midst. While some in the believing community enjoy more expressive forms of worship, others may not. Those who prefer a more liturgical style and those of a more contemporary free form of worship can be poles apart. People of different denominations and theological persuasions will approach love-based worship in a variety of styles. Regardless of the style, however, when is the last time you expressed your love-based worship of God in a similar manner to those we observe in these passages? Are you willing to bring your very best as a "beautiful thing" before the Lord?

Love-based worship in our congregations can occur when men and women, young and old, are willing to bring their very best into worship. When parents come forward to dedicate or baptize their children, they offer their best. When people invite Christ to be Lord and leader of their lives, they offer their whole heart in loving devotion. When youth come back from a life-transforming missions trip, they worship with immense gratitude for the fabulous service they've experienced as a team. As the living Christ is made evident in our lives and ministries, we can't help but incline our hearts fully in his direction and offer praise and thanks for the life of worship he invites us to enjoy.

The choice is left in our hearts. What will we choose? A life of love-based worship or a life void of the joyful privilege of worshiping God with heart, soul, mind, and strength? It's up to you.

Lord Jesus, I confess that my love and worship of you is more stingy than extravagant. I worry more about how others will perceive me if I become more expressional toward you in my worship. Help me to come out of myself and become more like Mary in the freedom she experienced as she exalted you in worship.

Our congregational worship experience would be that much richer if all of my brothers and sisters were free to worship you in spirit and truth, grateful for your love and lordship over our individual lives and our shared life together. Lead me into a deeper sense of true worship in the context of my own prayer closet so that when I enter into worship with my believing family, I may be a catalyst for God-exalting worship through my openness to the Spirit's work in my life and in our midst.

It is out of profound appreciation for your love for me that I offer my heart, soul, mind, and strength to you in worship now and always. In the name of the Father, Son, and Spirit I pray. Amen.

Total Worship

When my friend David Midwood teaches on the subject of God-exalting worship for the healthy disciple, he talks about worship as a "total" exercise—engaging the mind, emotions, spirit, and body. The scriptural backing for such a comprehensive experience is amazing. You may wish to reflect on the following outline as you think through your personal experiences in worship.

1. We worship with *our renewed mind* (Phil. 2:3–5)
   a. All heart, soul, mind (Matt. 22:37)
   b. Praying with the understanding (1 Cor. 14:15)
   c. Praising with the understanding (Ps. 47:6–7)
2. We worship with *our revived emotions* (Rom. 12:11–15)
   a. Zeal, fervor, spirituality (Rom. 12:11–15)
   b. Shouting and clapping hands unto the Lord (Ps. 47:1)
   c. Praising him aloud with the congregation (Ps. 47:1)

   d. Rejoicing and expressing thanksgiving (Ps. 100:1, 4; Phil. 4:4)

   e. Whatever you do, working at it with all your heart (Col. 3:23)

   f. Being silent before the Lord (Ps. 46:10; Hab. 2:20)

 3. We worship with *our regenerated spirit* (Ezek. 36:26; John 1:13)

   a. Worshiping in spirit (John 4:23–24)

   b. Praying in the spirit (1 Cor. 14:14)

   c. Singing spiritual songs (1 Cor. 14:15; Eph. 5:19; Col. 3:16)

   d. Giving thanks "well" by the Spirit (1 Cor. 14:16–17)

 4. We worship with *our rededicated body* (1 Cor. 6:19–20)

   a. Presenting our whole bodies to God as a living sacrifice (Rom. 12:1)

   b. Exercising ourselves into godliness (1 Tim. 4:7–8)

   c. Bowing down/kneeling in worship (Ps. 95:6; Phil. 2:9–10)

   d. Waving hands in praise (Ps. 63:4)

   e. Lifting hands (Pss. 63:4; 141:2; 1 Tim. 2:8)

   f. Standing before the Lord in awe (Ps. 4:4 KJV)

   g. Clapping hands (Ps. 47:1)

   h. Playing instruments (Pss. 33:2; 92:3; 98:6; 144:9)

   i. Shaking tambourines and playing percussion instruments (Ps. 150:4–5)

   j. Dancing before the Lord (2 Sam. 6:14; Pss. 30:11; 149:3; 150:4)

   k. Bowing our heads (Gen. 24:26, 52; Micah 6:6–8)

   l. Lifting our heads and eyes (Pss. 3:3; 123:1; Heb. 4:16)

   m. Praising; singing and shouting for joy (Pss. 32:11; 47:6; 59:16; 66:8; 69:30; 98:1; 100:1–2)

   n. Being silent before the Lord (Ps. 46:10; Hab. 2:20)

In several places in the Word of God we see the people of God engaged in worship with heart, soul, mind, and strength. That is to be our goal as well as we participate in the lifelong process of becoming a healthy disciple. As we engage fully in the worship experience within our congregation, we contagiously assist others in becoming free to be involved in silence, serenity, songs, and even shouts of joy! As the truth of God's Word is richly proclaimed and the Spirit of God rests supremely in your gathered place of worship, each disciple becomes a worshiper, wholeheartedly giving ourselves to God. Worship is that simple—a genuine expression of love and gratitude from our hearts to his.

Worship Praxis

The context of God-exalting worship is the setting of "Sabbath rest" for the believer, the believing family, and the local church. What is the priority of Sabbath rest within the life of a healthy disciple and the family/church context? Sadly, it seems that we have lost the meaning of Sabbath by cramming our Sundays full of activities that leave no room for meaningful reflection on the worship we experience with the family of God. Isn't it time we reclaim the gift of rest as outlined so thoroughly by God in the Ten Commandments? Max Lucado, in his best-seller *Traveling Light,* reminds his readers of the poignancy of God's command for the Sabbath:

> Of the ten declarations carved in the tablets, which one occupies the most space? Murder? Adultery? Stealing? You'd think so. Certainly each is worthy of ample coverage. But curiously, these commands are tributes to brevity. God needed only five English words to condemn adultery and four to denounce thievery and murder.
>
> But when he came to the topic of rest, one sentence would not suffice. "Remember the Sabbath day by keeping it holy. Six days you shall labor and do all your work, but the seventh day is a Sabbath to the LORD your God. On it you shall not do any work, neither you, nor your son or daughter, nor your manservant or maidservant, nor your animals, nor the alien within your gates. For in six days the LORD made the heavens

and the earth, the sea, and all that is in them, but he rested on the seventh day. Therefore the LORD blessed the Sabbath day and made it holy" (Exod. 20:8–11).

God knows us so well. He can see the store owner reading this verse and thinking, "Somebody needs to work that day. If I can't, my son will." So God says, *Nor your son.* "Then my daughter will." *Nor your daughter.* "Then maybe an employee." *Nor them.* "I guess I'll have to send my cow to run the store, or maybe I'll find some stranger to help me." *No,* God says. *One day of the week you will say no to work and yes to worship. You will slow and sit down and lie down and rest.*

A century ago Charles Spurgeon gave this advice to his preaching students: Even beasts of burden must be turned out to grass occasionally; the very sea pauses at ebb and flood; earth keeps the Sabbath of the wintry months; and man, even when exalted to God's ambassador, must rest or faint, must trim his lamp or let it burn low; must recruit his vigor or grow prematurely old . . . in the long run we shall do more by sometimes doing less.[4]

How about the disciple of Christ in search of health and vitality? The Sabbath is a call to us as well—yes, even in the twenty-first century. Consider afresh the priorities of God as they relate to rest and refreshment of body, soul, heart, and mind. The experience of God-exalting worship will be all the richer as a result of our choosing to reclaim the wider context of our worship—Sabbath rest.

If, therefore, our goal is the obedient expression of extravagant love in the context of engaging, God-exalting worship, then how is this to be expressed in our weekly experiences with the family of God? The following principles are benchmarks for consideration and application in the practice of worship as disciples in pursuit of Christ-honoring spiritual health and vitality.

Principle 2.1 Preparation Begins on Monday

How do you prepare for worship with the family of God each week? "Why should that be my concern?" you might wonder. "Isn't that what the pastor's supposed to do?" Certainly the pastor is expected to plan the weekly worship service, but every member of a healthy church needs to see that they are fully prepared to engage in worship, adding their heart, mind, and voice to the worship celebration.

This kind of preparation is what we do in the quietness of our prayer closets each day preceding Sunday. In essence, our preparation for worship begins on Monday morning as we approach God's throne of grace, utilizing the Scriptures, prayer, and reflection as our primary spiritual disciplines (the subject of our next chapter). When we each come into corporate worship having fully prepared ourselves via our personal worship experiences, we enhance the congregational worship for all.

"As a pastor, when I have a member of the congregation come to me before the service saying he or she has been praying, studying, and anticipating the upcoming worship hour, I know this person will gain so much more from each element of the service," remarked my pastor friend. "And I am certain that this same person will have much more specific feedback after the service as to how he or she sensed God's presence in a particular way, heard the Lord speak, or felt the message or music blended with what he or she had been praying about that prior week. It's amazing how differently the prepared worshiper engages in the experience as opposed to the unprepared."

The healthy disciple enters worship with the family of God in an attitude of expectation buoyed by the presence of God's Spirit and prepared through personal experiences with him. Entering into corporate worship in this manner is dramatically different from being one of the masses who come with no preparation, who bring very little to the shared worship encounter with the congregation. Imagine how different *your* worship will be if you come prepared—starting on Monday morning.

Principle 2.2 Participation Begets Fulfillment

How often have you heard one of the following remarks?

"I didn't get anything out of that worship service."
"I didn't get a thing from the pastor's message today."

"I don't understand why the choir thinks they need to sing those classical pieces."

"What was the point of that story? I just don't get as much out of that approach to our missions emphasis."

Any of these sound familiar?

The common thread of each statement is one of *getting* something out of worship. Where did the notion of *getting* emerge in an activity that the body of Christ shares week after week that's designed with *giving* in mind? Aren't we supposed to be worshiping the Lord in a posture of giving—our lives, our hearts, our family, our service, etc.—back to the Lord who gave us these gifts in the first place?

We go to worship to give, not get! Yet in our giving, we certainly receive. It's like the prayer of St. Francis: "It is in giving that we receive; it is in pardoning that we are pardoned; it is in dying that we are born to eternal life." The primary motivation of the worshiper should be to come into the sanctuary to give all we are and have back to God out of gratitude, love, and obedience.

Unfortunately, this notion of worship as an act of giving has been displaced by the consumer mentality of those who occupy the pews of churches all across this land. We have needs, and we come to get those needs met. We have opinions, and we come to get them massaged (certainly not challenged!). We have limited time, and we come to make sure that time is well spent. We have expectations, and we come to have them exceeded. We have relational dysfunction, and we come to see others affirm that it's okay. We come to worship for a variety of reasons, most of which are to get something out of God, the pastor, or one another.

This mentality, however, must be tipped upside down or, better yet, upside right! Let's get it right once and for all and begin to realign our posture for worship in a manner befitting the Lord whom we worship. Remember Mary at the feet of Jesus giving her most expensive perfume, pouring it out on the feet of Jesus, and wiping it with her hair and tears (John 12:1–8)? Was that a posture of getting? Certainly not, but in her reckless abandon of worship she received the extravagant grace, love, and kindness

of God. When it comes right down to it, this is truly the best and
only way to come into God-exalting worship—humbly, receptively,
lovingly, and with an attitude of giving. That's the kind of worshiper the Father seeks.

Principle 2.3 Proclamation Styles Reflect Diversity

In the book *Becoming a Healthy Church,* I confess to my readers
that I am an EpiscoBaptiPentaGationalist! I admit that the diversity of worship styles represented by those four groups is what I
have grown to appreciate in congregational worship settings. I
enjoy the liturgy of the Episcopalians, the Word-centered worship of my Baptist-oriented home church, the Holy Spirit focused
expressions of the charismatic community, and the rootedness of
my Congregational church upbringing. In essence, I have become
rather eclectic in my appreciation of the varieties of worship styles
available in a large number of churches today (most likely because
the ministry I led for over fourteen years, Vision New England,
serves churches from more than eighty denominations!). And
over my twenty-five years of ministry I have become convinced
that I am not alone.

What about you? Are you so stuck in one worship style that
to participate in any variation of that style would wreak havoc
on your expressions of love, praise, gratitude, and obedience to
God? Or are you one of a growing number of Christians who
are frustrated that your church is stuck in a worship rut? What
is your opinion of those who worship in ways that are different
from your preferred style?

There are huge variations in worship styles within the Christian community. In order for you to fully engage in worship it's
important that you give fully of yourself—heart, soul, mind, and
strength—regardless of the selected style in your local church.
You should also honor those who approach weekly worship in
ways that differ from yours in style and variety out of respect for
the diversity of the body of Christ.

Frankly, the healthiest disciple is able to engage in worship no
matter what the style as long as the substance of worship is not

compromised. Far too often we form opinions about substance by what we see in style, but it is important as a healthy disciple to be more discerning than that. Style is the expression of substance and should be treated accordingly.

The fact that the church believes in the lordship of Jesus Christ, the love of the Father, and the presence of the Holy Spirit is the best place to begin when dealing with substantive worship matters. From that basic Trinitarian backdrop, we move into areas such as preaching, prayers, songs and hymns, confession of sin, baptism, communion, giving tithes and offerings, etc. to formulate our opinion on substance in worship. When I'm more enamored by the candles, robes, symbols, or sounds than I am by the Word, prayers, and focus on Christ, then I've prioritized style over substance. Be open to various styles, but never sacrifice substantive worship—it's far too important for you as a disciple and for your congregation as the family of God.

Principle 2.4 Protection from Distraction

I find that I am easily distracted in worship. As a family man, I am cognizant of my wife and children sitting near me, aware of their every breath and movement. As a friend, I see people across the sanctuary with whom I would like to talk after the service. As a man of God, I am mindful of the needs of others as they stroll to their pews. As a disciple, I am aware of the program of the morning, reading the insights about church life in the newsletter that accompanies today's bulletin. There are plenty of reasons for me to be distracted as I enter into worship. How do I handle such distractions?

Whether you are a member of a church of twenty, two hundred, or two thousand, the goal is to listen to God's voice in the cacophony of voices (and faces, needs, circumstances, etc.) all around you. This is especially true in the proclamation of the Word as the Scriptures are read, sung, and preached. Prayer is the only way I know of dealing with any distractions from hearing the voice of God.

Prayer is a relationship discipline that needs to be cultivated in our personal prayer times, our times with others in small and large group settings, and also here in the collective gathering place of worship. When prayer permeates our worship experiences with the congregation, the Spirit of God quiets our hearts to become more receptive to his presence, Jesus becomes the focus of our worship, and God's love guides us into a deeper understanding of his direction for our lives as a result of meeting him in worship.

Prayerfulness is a posture that defines God-exalting worship, for it reminds us of our utter and complete dependence on him for our very being. In worship we come into direct contact with God and, as a result, our lives are realigned around his priorities for us as he transforms us more and more into his image.

So instead of being distracted by my family members beside me, I need to pray for them. Scanning the sanctuary for friends, my priority shifts to prayers on their behalf. The crying needs of others get melted away as their heart-wrenching stories are placed at the foot of the cross in prayer. As I review the bulletin, I recognize that I need to hold off on reading the accompanying newsletter until later and instead simply pray.

The worship experience in the life of the congregation will be enhanced significantly by this one choice—remain in prayer. Only then will the healthy disciple fully engage in God-exalting worship!

Principle 2.5 Prescription for Enhancement

A friend recently sent me an e-mail entitled "Why Go to Church?" (author unknown). It read:

A churchgoer wrote a letter to the editor of the local newspaper and complained that it made no sense to go to church every Sunday. "I've gone to church for 30 years now," he wrote, "and in that time I have heard something like 3,000 sermons. But for the life of me I can't remember a single one of them.

So I think I'm wasting my time and the preachers are wasting theirs by giving sermons at all."

This started a real controversy in the "Letters to the Editor" column, much to the delight of the editor. It went on for weeks until someone wrote this clincher: "I've been married for 30 years now. In that time my wife has cooked some 32,000 meals. But for the life of me, I cannot recall the entire menu for a single one of those meals. But I do know this: They all nourished me and gave me the strength I needed to do my work. If my wife had not given me those meals, I would be physically dead today. Likewise, if I had not gone to church for nourishment, I would be spiritually dead today!"

Thank God for our physical and spiritual nourishment. And thank God that we have a church to call our spiritual home week after week, year after year.

Many, however, have been traveling from house to house, eating meals in dining room after dining room, not staying with any one family for more than a month or a season. There are far too many vagabond disciples out there today, and even though they've enjoyed the "meals" offered in the local church, they have gone to more dining tables than one can count.

We don't condone such activity among families because it is important to remain committed to and share life with our own family—in the good and in the hard times of life. So it is within the Christian community. The longer we stay in one church family, the more we give and receive from that family.

Membership, commitment, solidarity, longevity, partnership—all these values within church life are important priorities. They affect our shared life in ministry and in the context of worship. You want an enhanced experience in worship? Then become a regularly committed member of the family. Don't run from house to house, dining room to dining room for your spiritual nourishment. Make a commitment to the family of God and stick with that commitment over the long haul. If it becomes necessary for you to leave one church for another, do so with dignity befitting of Christ himself.

A DISCIPLE'S PRAYER

Lord, I ask that starting this coming week I will become more of the kind of worshiper you desire and long for—one who is willing to become far more extravagant in my expressions of love to you than I have ever given before. Help me to lean fully in your direction as I worship you this week so that when I enter the sanctuary I will do so in a posture of prayerful anticipation. May the love that I have for you as one of your disciples be reflective of the love you have for me, so that I may contribute positively to the worship we celebrate together as the family of God. May the words of my mouth and the meditations of my heart be acceptable in your sight, oh Lord, my Rock and my Redeemer. In the mighty name of Christ I pray. Amen.

For Reflection and Renewal

The healthy disciple engages wholeheartedly in meaningful, God-focused worship experiences on a weekly basis with the family of God.

1. What is the "beautiful gift" you can give to God in worship this next week? How will your approach to congregational worship be different than it has been before?
2. In what ways can you encourage full engagement in God-exalting worship among the members of your congregation in the days ahead?
3. What is your potential for distraction in worship, and what choices can you make to radically alter the manner in which you approach worship fully focused on God rather than the needs and opportunities all around you?
4. Are there one or two things you can do this coming week that will encourage a deeper level of commitment among members of your local church?

5. With which of the five worship praxis principles do you resonate the most and why?

6. How can you reclaim the priority of Sabbath for yourself and your family? What will this mean regarding the activities that tend to engulf and consume any sense of consistent, weekly Sabbath rest?

3

Practices
the Spiritual Disciplines

The healthy disciple pursues the daily disciplines of prayer, Bible study, and reflection in the quietness of one's personal prayer closet.

> Remain in me, and I will remain in you.
>
> John 15:4

As an anchor for her soul on the heels of her husband's sudden and untimely death, the discipline of practicing the presence of God became critical to the spiritual health of Joanna Mockler. Psalm 16 became for her the lifeline to wholeness,

> I have set the LORD always before me.
>   Because he is at my right hand, I will not be shaken.
> Therefore my heart is glad and my tongue rejoices;
>   my body also will rest secure,
> because you will not abandon me to the grave,
>   nor will you let your Holy One see decay.
> You have made known to me the path of life;
>   you will fill me with joy in your presence,
>   with eternal pleasures at your right hand.
>
> Psalm 16:8–11

Joanna is one of the most lovingly disciplined women of God that I have ever met. She exudes inner peace and contentment as a child of God. She has endured hardship and personal pain with grace and joy in the Lord. She ministers to others through her generosity of heart, prayer, and love for those who are much less fortunate than herself. When asked how she finds strength for each new day, she quickly replies, "The overriding discipline is to choose to live by faith rather than by one's feelings. And this does take a lot of discipline!"

In conversation with Joanna, one learns the secrets of her depth of character and commitment to Christ. "The disciplines of choosing to live by faith and practicing the presence of God lead naturally into the disciplines of living a life of gratitude, a lifestyle of forgiveness, and the ongoing willingness to wait patiently for God to work in our lives in ways that please and honor him." Her depictions of this life of faith are grounded in the Word of God. (For example, when she articulates her life of gratitude, she quotes from Philippians 4:6–7 and 1 Thessalonians 5:18; regarding forgiveness, her favorite passage is Colossians 3:13–14; and her discipline of waiting is based on Psalm 130:5 and Isaiah 30:18.) This life of devotion is based on the Scriptures, and the results of her life speak for themselves—God has richly blessed and multiplied ministry through this faithful disciple of Christ.

For example, in her community Joanna has led countless weeks of Bible studies for women. In her church she has held leadership positions in women's ministries, prayer ministries, Sunday school classes for seekers, and care and compassion ministries. She has also ministered through volunteer staff positions and has led an informal network of encouragement to scores of individuals and families. In the region she has served on boards of major ministries and a local seminary. Outside the region she serves on the board of an international relief and development agency. She is involved in the lives of her children, grandchildren, extended family, community groups, and many friends. She lives life out of the center of her soul, for it's in the quietness of her daily time with Christ that she understands and then fulfills the call of God. What an inspiration!

If we are to become healthy disciples, the practices of developing one's spiritual disciplines need to be honed on a daily basis. These are not to be occasional or sporadic habits, for if the soul is to be cultivated in a manner befitting Christ, then it certainly must find great joy and deep satisfaction in the daily presence of God. It's out of this cultivated soul that we discover our mission for life.

Abiding in Christ

What then is a disciple? It is a person who is on a lifelong journey of loving with heart, soul, mind, and strength everyone and everything that Jesus loves. In order for this journey to be properly cultivated, it takes a daily abiding in Christ on behalf of the disciple. The key, however, is to begin by receiving for oneself the love of God—a gift to be welcomed with an open heart since it cannot be earned.

Practicing the spiritual disciplines of prayer, Scripture reading, and reflection may feel at times like we are earning God's love. However, his amazing love and grace are an unconditional gift that he extends freely and generously toward us as his disciples. It is in the daily choosing of spiritual disciplines that we show our gratitude and cultivate our relationship with him.

God loves us despite the condition of our hearts—whether inclined in his direction or in utter disobedience toward him. That's the amazing truth of his love. When understood in its deepest sense, the agape love of God is a *no matter what* kind of love! No matter what we may say, think, feel, or do, God loves us unconditionally in return. We have a hard time comprehending this kind of love because many of us have never experienced an ounce of this in our lives. We grew up with a *yes it certainly does matter* kind of love in which performance, proficiency, and possessions outweighed anything that would smack of being unconditional. It's what we did, how we acted, or the manner in which we related that became grounds for being loved. It's not that way with God, and that's not how it should be between his disciples.

God doesn't delight in our sin, but he finds great joy in our lives. He deals with our sin in the wider context of his love, grace, mercy, and forgiveness. As we disappoint and disobey him, he wraps his loving arms around us and whispers in our ears how much he enjoys forgiving us. We often don't hear these words because we are taking so much time and energy covering up our sin, unwilling to acknowledge it and purposefully or inadvertently avoiding the reality of it. Why is it that we play this game of cover-up when in fact he knows all about it anyway?

As we come to grips with the reality of agape love, we bask in its glory and relish every moment of discovering its depths for ourselves. We quickly acknowledge that there is no way we can humanly muster up this kind of love toward God or others unless God empowers us with this fruit of his Spirit (as discussed in chapter 1). The amazing reality is that God delights in showering his children with this kind of extravagant love. In the quietness of our prayer closets we can discover the significance of this gift for ourselves.

The spiritual disciplines are in many ways a hearing test for us. Do we listen intently for the voice of God? It's not necessarily an audible voice, but when we press the pause button of our active lives long enough, we hear him in the stillness of the moment, through the pages of the Scriptures, and in the beauty of his creation. He longs to communicate his love toward each of his children, and it's incumbent upon us to stop long enough to listen. The key to discovering his abiding presence is to become anticipatory, alert, and attentive to his voice, his love, his grace, and his deliverance from sin as he fills us with new life. This is what it means to truly abide in Christ.

Remaining in Him

My heart was the heaviest it had ever been. I was in a season of spiritual drought as I dealt with the death of my father, coped with a forthcoming major surgery for my son, and managed the heartache of a lifetime in ministry. As I cried out to God, I sought his face and listened carefully for his voice, yet I struggled to see or hear either one. Where was he? Didn't he care? Is he there only in the good times? I wanted more than anything to feel his touch and know his tender care, and instead I found myself in one of those "dark nights of the soul."

In the midst of this difficult season of life and ministry, Ruth and I were scheduled to go to Quebec City for a long weekend. We looked forward to getting away for some time of solace and renewal together. Our destination was merely across the border, but it felt to us like a distant, foreign land. Little did I know that on that long weekend away I would begin to hear the voice of God once again. I thought he had abandoned me, but I discovered that was not true at all.

In the early morning hours I took long walks in the Plains of Abraham, a park along the river that ran through the city. These were delightful times of exercise and reflection. I found great strength from the hours spent in this discipline. It was here that I regained perspective, renewed hope, and reconnected with the God of the universe who loves me with an infinite, matchless love.

On Sunday morning I was startled awake earlier than usual with my heart pounding with a fresh vision of God's grace, peace, and truth and my mind racing with thoughts and ideas about future ministry pursuits. I grabbed the small notepad and pencil provided by the hotel, went into the bathroom so as not to disturb Ruth's sleep, and began to write down all that filled my heart and mind. After nearly four pages of notes and a graphic image depicting my thoughts and renewed zeal for God, I left earlier than usual for my walk.

I found myself crying out to God in a much bolder fashion. Had I heard from him that morning in a renewed manner? Were the thoughts and ideas I had written out that morning from his heart to mine? What was I to do with the emotions I was feeling and the sense of his presence I was experiencing? I was listening with intensity, alert to his abiding peace and love.

I kept walking and praying until I reached a section of the park where there were several benches circling a small turnabout with a flagpole in the center surrounded by lovely flowers and shrubs. The sun was shining brightly on that early morning setting along the river. I found myself looking heavenward, praying openly and fervently, asking the Lord for his confirmation that indeed he was the source of the whispering in my ear earlier that morning, the sounds of which I had not heard with clarity for such a long time.

Without realizing it, I was crying out to God with a simple prayer, "Are you here, Lord?" and as I looked down at the base of the flagpole, the manicured shrubbery below spelled out the greeting *"Bonjour!"* In that simple French greeting, it was as if he was responding to me with his answer. "Hello! Good day! Yes, I am here," said the Lord, and "Yes, I love you, am attentive to the cries of your heart and the needs of you and your loved ones, and I hold your future securely in the palm of my hand." It wasn't audible, but it was so very obvious. In the bushes (although not ablaze with fire!) was the gentle reminder of God's presence. All I needed to do was remain in him long enough to hear him speak, and when he did, his voice was clear.

I walked back to our hotel with buoyancy! I was filled with joy in the Lord through this simple spiritual encounter with almighty God. He had heard my deepest appeal and had reminded me gently and clearly of his love. He had never left me, and in my genuine longing for God, I found myself wandering back into the center of his wide-open, welcoming arms of love. I was reawakened to the prayerful reality of God's abiding presence and grace on that early Sunday morning, and the result was renewed joy in Christ, deeper fellowship with my heavenly Father, and everlasting peace amidst the storms of life.

When I returned to the hotel more than an hour later, Ruth was amazed as she listened intently to my story. She confirmed the work of God in our midst and celebrated this encounter with affirmation and tears as she too cried out to God for a deep sense of his abiding presence. The message we both received that day was Christ's reminder, "Remain in me, and I will remain in you" (John 15:4).

What I have discovered over the years is that practicing the spiritual disciplines is not for the purpose of knowing more data about God, more facts about his Word, or more information about the Christian life. Instead, the disciplines are for the purpose of knowing and experiencing the richness and vitality of a relationship with God—a relationship that begins with the

Lord's expression of intimate love for us. His earnest desire is that we relish this truth at the deepest recesses of our being. By coming before him with ears, eyes, hands, and heart open wide, we remain in him long enough to hear his voice and make choices aligned with his will.

Zephaniah 3:17 says it best: "The LORD your God is with you, he is mighty to save. He will take great delight in you, he will quiet you with his love, he will rejoice over you with singing." His presence (God is with you), his power (mighty to save), his passion (delighting over you; rejoicing over you), and his peace (quieting you with his love) are the gifts God grants freely and generously to his people. When is the last time you experienced him in the fullness of such richness?

Listening for the love language of God toward you, his disciple, begins with the recognition that God longs to be in relationship with you, initiating his love toward you continuously throughout the day. The key for us is to become anticipatory, alert, and attentive to God's voice and his love, grace, and deliverance from our sin. He fills us daily with the abundance of his love so that we can live for Christ under the divine inspiration of God.

Fullness of Joy

John the Baptist's testimony about Jesus brings greater lucidity to the notion of remaining in Christ for every healthy disciple. "The friend who attends the bridegroom waits and listens for him, and is full of joy when he hears the bridegroom's voice. That joy is mine, and it is now complete. He must become greater; I must become less" (John 3:29–30). When we hear the bridegroom's voice, we can't help but shout for joy!

The joy we discover in the intimacy of our walk with Jesus begins with a celebration of all that he is. Consider from the Gospel of John the great "I am" passages as you reflect on the ministry of Christ. Jesus said:

I am the Bread of Life (6:35)
I am the Living Water (4:14; 7:37–39)

I am the Light of the World (8:12)

I am the Door of the Sheepfold (10:7)

I am the Good Shepherd (10:11, 14)

I am the Resurrection and the Life (11:25)

I am the True Vine (15:1)

I am the Way, the Truth, and the Life (14:6)

Knowing how Jesus chooses to manifest himself in our lives and in this world is great cause for joyful exuberance. Such joy leads his children to celebrate in a grateful chorus of praise and adoration. When we begin our personal worship in this way, we reflect an attitude befitting the glory of God. It is here that we begin the process of abiding in Christ, remaining in him for the time we practice our disciplines of the heart—prayer, Scripture reading, and reflection. And we remain in him as we reenter our respective worlds of family, work, and witness.

Scattered throughout the Gospel of John are appeals to come close to Jesus and "remain in him." In John 15, Jesus uses the analogy of the vine and the branches—created to intertwine and remain connected for life-giving, life-enhancing reasons. Barclay reminds us that over and over again in the Old Testament Israel is pictured as the vine or the vineyard of God. "The vineyard of the LORD . . . is the house of Israel" (Isa. 5:7 RSV). "Yet I planted you a choice vine" is God's message to Israel through Jeremiah (Jer. 2:21 RSV). Ezekiel 15 likens Israel to the vine, as does Ezekiel 19:10. "Israel is a luxuriant vine," said Hosea (Hosea 10:1 RSV). "Thou didst bring a vine out of Egypt," sang the psalmist, thinking of God's deliverance of his people from bondage (Ps. 80:8 RSV). The vine had actually become the symbol of the nation of Israel. It was the emblem on the coins of the Maccabees. The vine was part and parcel of Jewish imagery, and the very symbol of Israel.[1]

When Jesus calls himself the true vine (John 15:1), he contrasts himself with the people of Israel. The people of God run wild as a branch when they are not connected to the true vine. Barclay comments, "It is as if Jesus said: 'you think that because you belong to the nation of Israel you are a branch of the true vine of God. But the nation it is; a degenerate vine, as all your prophets saw. It is I

(Jesus) who am the true vine. The fact that you are a Jew will not save you. The only thing that can save you is to have an intimate living fellowship with me, for I am the vine of God and you must be branches joined to me.'"[2] Jesus was making it clear in this passage that God's salvation was not obtained through lineage but only through faith and a genuine relationship with Jesus. No external qualifications suffice in setting a man right with God; only friendship with Jesus Christ can do that. This kind of friendship only develops through time spent with him on a daily basis through one's center of quiet and the practice of spiritual disciplines. Jesus himself practiced these disciplines, and so must the disciple who desires intimacy with God. "I have told you this so that my joy may be in you and that your joy may be complete" (John 15:11).

Out of the completeness of our joy in Christ, we are chosen to "go and bear fruit—fruit that will last" (John 15:16). What is it that we are chosen for? Barclay says we have been:

- Chosen for joy—however hard the Christian way is, it is, both in the traveling and in the goal, the way of joy.
- Chosen for love—we are sent out into the world to love one another.
- Chosen for friendship—Jesus tells his followers that he does not call them slaves any longer; he calls them friends.
- Chosen for partnership—we were not called out or set apart for a series of tremendous privileges, we have been called to partner in the work of leading the world to God.
- Chosen for ambassadorship—we have been chosen to in turn be sent out to represent the King of Kings in this world.
- Chosen for advertisement—we are chosen to go and bear fruit that will stand the test of time, to show the world the fruit of the Christian life.
- Chosen for family membership—so that whatever we ask in his name the Father will give to us as his beloved children.[3]

Therefore, out of incredible gratitude for the call of God on our lives, we are compelled by grace to be transparent with our

Maker as we come to him daily. Come clean, rest secure, and trust completely. He knows you inside and out, and he loves you with the depth of eternal and unconditional love that only he can provide.

Cost of Discipline-ship

The high cost of our discipleship begins with the cost of discipline-ship—being willing to devote a portion of each day in solitude, silence, and complete surrender. In the midst of the stresses and strains of our lives, the pauses and punctuation marks along the way become even more significant. We don't become healthier disciples of Christ by osmosis—it won't happen by wishful thinking!

Instead, the disciplines of a heart that longs after God's heart are the lifeblood of our calling to remain in Christ. Growing in godliness requires the exercising of the soul that leads to a wholesome agility that can sustain the stresses and strains of a busy life. When we don't have this kind of centeredness in Christ, our active lives become empty of purpose, meaning, and significance. Of course, we don't develop our spiritual strength and agility by looking at a poster or reading about a person with godly muscles—we have to get down on the floor and exercise ourselves!

Philip Yancey, in one of his regular columns in *Christianity Today*, talked about his fifty-year spiritual checkup in this way: "When I turned 50 this year, I underwent a complete physical checkup. Doctors poked, prodded, x-rayed, and even cut open parts of my body to assess and repair the damage I had done in half a century. As the new millennium rolled around, I scheduled a spiritual checkup as well. I went on a silent retreat led by a wise spiritual director." In those days of silence and reflection, several issues arose that Yancey wanted to change in order to keep his soul in shape. Here is a sampling of the steps he felt led to take:

- Come to God with your own troubles, as well as the world's.
- Question your doubts as much as your faith.

- Do not attempt this journey alone. Find companions who see you as a pilgrim, even a straggler, and not as a guide.
- Allow the good—natural beauty, your health, encouraging words—to penetrate as deeply as the bad.
- For your own sake, simplify. Eliminate whatever distracts you from God.
- Find something that allows you to feel God's pleasure.
- Always "err," as God does, on the side of freedom, mercy, and compassion.
- Don't be ashamed of the gospel.
- Remember, those Christians who peeve you so much—God chose them too.
- Forgive, daily, those who caused the wounds that keep you from wholeness.

"My spiritual checkup offers one clear advantage over my physical checkup," Yancey continues. "From my doctor, I learned that no matter what I do my body will continue to deteriorate. At best, a good diet and exercise routine will slow that deterioration. Spiritually, however, I can look forward to growth, renewed vigor, and improved health—as long as I continue to listen, and then act on what I hear God saying."[4] That is the key—continue daily to listen to God, and then be sure to act on what you hear!

It's impossible to ride the coattails of a godly friend or family member into the kingdom of God, nor is it possible to ride the wave of another's spiritual journey. You won't make it to heaven because of the faith of your spouse or parents, nor will you grow in God's grace due to their devotion to Christ. Eventually every disciple pursuing spiritual health and well-being will be confronted with this reality. It's the choice of the disciple to select the manner in which the basic disciplines are practiced and incumbent upon that same disciple to act accordingly.

Author Rueben Job writes, "One cannot live on borrowed faith alone. No one can hitchhike on another's spiritual journey. We can have companions along the way, but ultimately each person must live and die by his or her own faith experience. Touched by

God's grace, we are never quite the same, even when the absence of God seems stronger than the divine presence. Martin E. Marty has observed that 'the religious person and community cannot dip into the endowment and live off the interest and the principal of a spiritual capital in which they did not invest.'"[5] Daily investments of time with God, practicing the disciplines of the Spirit-filled life, will reap great fruit this side of heaven and for all eternity.

Spiritual Transformation

A life of blessing is a life of discipline and grace—well balanced, properly understood, and gratefully lived in the grace of God. Dallas Willard, speaking at the inaugural Pastors Convention in early 2001, had the following to say about spiritual formation:

> Spiritual formation is shaping the inner person in such a way that the words and deeds of Christ naturally flow from us. It is the inward transformation of the self that makes it easy and natural to do the things that Jesus said. Christian spiritual formation is the process. What we call spiritual formation in Christian circles now, is really spiritual transformation. Formation has already happened and that is a major part of the problem. We have already been formed spiritually and we need to be transformed. It is holistic; it applies to all of us. It is not just a matter of changing the center part. It is a matter of the transformation of the self so that now your body is going to be set to do righteousness, as previously it was set to do what was wrong.[6]

Spiritual transformation is a lifelong process of becoming more like Christ, reflecting more and more of his image in every aspect of our lives. It grows out of our soul's affections and leads toward a life inclined in his direction, resolved to embody words, emotions, and actions that have been transformed by the grace of God. Jonathan Edwards, the great eighteenth-century Puritan preacher and leader of the Great Awakening, did a weekly self-check, summing up how he was doing and seeking God's help in the process of a growing number of personal resolutions. At the age of seventeen he penned twenty-one resolutions by which he would live his life. He kept adding to this list until, by the time of his death, he had seventy such resolutions![7]

It doesn't take seventy resolutions to live a spiritually trans-formed life. However, it certainly requires that we resolve to daily attend to the state of our souls and pursue the following principles and practices.

Principle 3.1 Prayer: ACTS and Relate

Writer Christopher Lydon memorialized Sarah Small in an article that appeared in the *Boston Globe* in 2001.

> At the University of Massachusetts in Boston for 30 years, Sarah Small was the campus minister who had never gone to college. She had been the fighting soul of the civil rights movement in the Little Mississippi town of Williamston, North Carolina—endlessly arrested, jailed, and threatened in the early and mid-1960s. With Martin Luther King Jr.'s encouragement she came to Boston in 1970 to preside over the openly Christian community at Packard Manse in Roxbury. She was a pillar of the prayer life of the Twelfth Baptist Church, where the pastor, the Rev. Michael E. Haynes, observed: "She probably could be described as a little bit of Harriet Tubman, Mary McLeod Be-thune, Melnea Cass, and Aimee Semple McPherson, all rolled up into one. She was bold, proud, humble, simple, wise, loving, generous and sold out to the Lord Jesus Christ." Sarah Small's day would normally begin between 4 and 5 in the morning, with prayer calls to and from people who needed a word of encouragement or direction.[8]

The life of Sarah Small can best be described in one word: *prayer.* She was a firm believer in prayer as the top priority of the Christian. "It's about a plan," she'd say, "The mission is to get in tune with the Lord."[9] In essence, that is the purpose of prayer. Sarah Small focused on this from the early morning hours and throughout her day. To know Sarah was to see a life fully devoted to prayer and sold out to the notion that God cares enough about his children to reveal his mission and shower his children with untold numbers of blessings and joys.

What does it mean to "pray at all times" (1 Thess. 5:17 TEV) or "pray without ceasing" (NRSV)? Is this a feasible goal for the healthy disciple?

Prayer is a pilgrimage into the intimacies of a love relationship with God. As Juan Carlos Ortiz reminded his listeners, "Another word for prayer is romance."[10] We need to treat prayer with the same kind of tenderness and thoughtfulness we would give to our most intimate lover. As our lover preoccupies our hearts and minds throughout our days, all the more should the Lover of our souls capture our hearts and minds as we stay focused on how to adequately express human love in return for the sacrificial and unconditional love that's expressed toward us by God moment by moment, every breath of every day of our life!

The disciplined life of prayer is open to the progression of prayer that's outlined so simply in the word *ACTS*—Adoration, Confession, Thanksgiving, and Supplication. It's an acronym that believers of all maturity levels can use to assist them in deepening their prayer experiences, and it's one that I promote for those who are committed to becoming healthy disciples.

The more time we spend in prayer, the more we discern how easy it is to get out of touch. Therefore, the call of God is to develop life patterns that prioritize the importance of prayer. To "pray without ceasing" in essence is to remain prayerful throughout our days, mindful of the abiding presence of God's Spirit, who beckons us to come closer to the heart of God. As we approach his throne of grace, we are reminded of the stark contrast between God and us.

Adoration. The natural place to begin each prayer is to adore God for all he is, all he has done, and all that he promises to do in our lives and throughout the world. Adoration and praise is the starting point—"romancing" him with our words, thoughts, and actions in awe and worship of the amazing God we serve!

Confession. As we spend time adoring God in prayer, we begin to see our own inadequacies and idiosyncratic, even sinful, behavior. As we consider his power, knowledge, grace, kindness, mercy, and love (just to name a few of his attributes), we begin to see the stark contrast between him and us. Out of adoration we are led into confession of our sinfulness, and we cry out with desperation for his unconditional love and forgiveness. One may remember hearing that "confession is good for the soul," and indeed that is true. Not only is it good, it is essential for the health of the soul.

In *Becoming a Healthy Church*, I remind the leaders of the church to be sure confession is integrated into the experience of the worshiping community of faith, because it is so often overlooked or ignored. As individuals seeking to become healthy disciples, we also remember the significance of confession in the cleansing of the soul and the preparation of the heart for a life of joy and faithfulness. Unless we are willing to genuinely confess sin, there will not be health and vitality that springs forth from the depths of the soul. The psalm King David wrote after being sought out by God through the prophet Nathan and finally confessing his sin is replete with words of heartfelt repentance:

> Have mercy on me, O God,
>   according to your unfailing love;
> according to your great compassion
>   blot out my transgressions.
> Wash away all my iniquity
>   and cleanse me from my sin.
> For I know my transgressions,
>   and my sin is always before me.
> Against you, and you only, have I sinned
>   and done what is evil in your sight,
> so that you are proved right when you speak
>   and justified when you judge.
> Surely I was sinful at birth,
>   sinful from the time my mother conceived me.
> Surely you desire truth in the inner parts;
>   you teach me wisdom in the inmost place.
> Cleanse me with hyssop, and I will be clean;
>   wash me, and I will be whiter than snow.
> Let me hear joy and gladness;
>   let the bones you have crushed rejoice.
> Hide your face from my sins
>   and blot out all my iniquity.
>
> Psalm 51:1–9

The psalm continues with an appeal for a clean and pure heart, which is the result of the purifying influence of repentance and confession of sin. Confession is essential in developing a genuinely intimate relationship with almighty God. David's heart cry is, "Create in me a pure heart, O God, and renew a steadfast spirit within me" (v. 10). When we follow David's example of confession, we can experience afresh the joy of the Lord that indeed is our strength and our song, our source of sustenance for living out each new day.

Thanksgiving. Out of adoration and confession, we move into a time of prayerful thankfulness for the grace of God evidenced in our lives. Who among us doesn't enjoy hearing the words "thank you"? How much more important, therefore, to speak heartfelt words of thanks to God. A thankful heart is one that is filled with deep and abiding joy as we find more reasons to be grateful than there are words to speak or time adequate for the full expression of our thankfulness. If we tried to list the people, experiences, and possessions for which we are thankful, we would not have enough paper available to count them all. In prayer, as we become more and more thankful for God's many blessings, our hearts are filled to overflowing and the spill over into our human relationships is enormous.

Supplication. After a season of prayer that includes adoration, confession, and thanksgiving, we can then move into supplication—praying specifically for the needs of people, churches, communities, ministries, national and international issues, and a host of other concerns that weigh deeply on our hearts. As we can see here, praying for specific requests comes at the end of our prayers, even though these needs often occupy the forefront of our minds as we enter into times of prayer. It takes discipline to begin our prayers focusing on adoration, confession, and thankfulness before we launch into asking God to meet the needs of those we love (including ourselves). As we approach prayer in this way, however, we begin to see with spiritual eyes what truly matters most to God—the captivation of our hearts, in alignment with and freshly attuned to his heart.

Prayer is a massive subject, one that has been covered elsewhere in far greater detail than is feasible in this book. As we mature in our faith and desire to go deeper into this subject, it would be advisable to read extensively on this subject, consulting such contemporary authors as Richard Foster, Dallas Willard, Henri Nouwen, John Piper, Eugene Peterson, Brennan Manning, Ken Gire, Jack Hayford, Chuck Swindoll, Bill Hybels, Stuart and Jill Briscoe. There also is a plethora of historical figures who are giants in this subject such as C. S. Lewis, Dietrich Bonhoeffer, St. Augustine, John of the Cross, Teresa of Avila, Ignatius of Loyola, and Madame Jeanne Guyon (just to name a few).[11] There is enough literature on the subject of prayer to last the rest of our lifetimes. Begin with the experience and expression of prayer, continue to read on this subject, and turn daily to the Scriptures in informing the key components of prayer outlined here—adoration, confession, thanksgiving, and supplication—and your relationship with God will be significantly enhanced.

Principle 3.2 Scripture: Read and Discover

The second and even more important discipline for the healthy disciple to pursue is the daily reading of God's Word. Scripture is undeniably the most significant daily nutrient for the health of the soul—a discipline as important for the soul as bread and water are for the body. For it is in the pages of Scripture that we prayerfully discover the God of our past, present, and future. In the Bible we begin to see more clearly into the heart of God, the mind of Christ, and the movement of the Spirit. The Triune God is contained within every page of Scripture, from Genesis to Revelation. It is here that we find our greatest joy, comfort, inspiration, guidance, love, and awe. Realizing that God loved us so much as to reveal his heart to us in this manner should cause us to praise and adore him.

The place to begin in reading the Scriptures is by praying through each selected passage, inviting the Spirit to bless, inform, and enlighten our hearts and minds to the things that matter most to God. When we read his Word with a prayerful, open attitude, ready to be edified, encouraged, and electrified by his truth, we discover new insights every time. Our receptivity to the Scriptures will directly impact the fruit of our discipline. Coming to the Bible with an earnest desire to meet with God and hear from him through his Word, we discover how much he longs for this fellowship with us—an incredible truth to contemplate.

When I first came into personal relationship with God as a junior in high school in the early 1970s, my hunger for the Word was vigilant and urgent. As I studied and reflected on God's Word, the vistas of my world opened up before me in a dynamic fashion, and the Bible began to come to life for me. The more I read, the more I wanted to read, and the more I understood, the more I began to apply. The more I began to apply, the more I realized how far I had to go, and the more I moved forward, the more I came to realize that this was a lifelong journey. The more I realized that it was a lifelong journey, the more I enjoyed this uniquely intimate experience with God through the prayerful reading of his Word and the depth of our growing relationship of love.

Then, somehow, I got the idea I could slow up the pace, and I began to get sloppy in my disciplines of study and prayerful re-flection on God's Word. The more I skipped days of reading the Bible, the more I allowed myself the privilege of filling my days with "more important" activities, and the more I filled my days with activity, the further away I got from the heart of God. The further away I got from God, the more I began to make my own decisions, and the more I made my own decisions, the deeper I got into a lifestyle that was unbecoming of Christ. The more I was unbecoming of Christ, the more I dishonored his name, the reputation of Christianity, and the cause of Christ. Interesting how the downward cycle leads to a life of sinful self-centeredness and how profoundly and diametrically opposed this is to a vibrant, God-centered existence.

I'm not generally known to be a legalist, nor do I pride myself in pharisaical practices, but this one thing I do know—the daily discipline of reading, studying, and prayerfully reflecting on God's Word will change your life. It will transform your heart and will lead to attitudes and actions that reflect the kind of Christlike behavior that God deems most important for every healthy disciple. What better discipline to be made a daily priority than this?

Once we've made up our minds that Scripture is a daily priority, how much is enough? This is where any potential legalism breaks down, for it truly doesn't matter if we read one book of the Bible, one chapter, one paragraph, one sentence, or one word. It's healthiest when we've grown to the place where we can meet God in any of these ways. There have been times when I couldn't put the Bible down and read for an extended period of time, covering many chapters in a book of the Bible. There have also been times when I've been arrested by a single word (such as *joy, contentment, sin, Savior, creation,* or *forgiveness*), prayerfully contemplating that word during my quiet time, journaling about its meaning, and reflecting on its application all day long. The important point here is that the opening of the Scriptures in the quietness of time spent alone with God should be maintained as a daily priority between ourselves and God. Entering into that time with a sense of joyful anticipation is where it all begins. The amount of material to be covered is less important than the fact that we take the time to read and prayerfully contemplate the implications of the Word for the life of the disciple *today.*

Take the time; find a quiet place; begin with prayer; open the Word; dive in as deep as God leads; reflect with pen in hand; study additional texts for deeper meaning and insight; consult Bible dictionaries, commentaries, study/prayer guides, and other helpful resources; and go forth with insight to apply to relationships, decisions, and activities yet to unfold. Then start fresh as you commence the cycle the next day. Where we begin doesn't really matter (although with our emphasis on the Gospel of John, this would be an ideal launching point and well worth consideration by the earnest disciple). The daily accumulation of wisdom will shape a life beyond anything we could ever ask or imagine! "Trust in the Lord with all your heart and lean not on your own understanding; in all your ways acknowledge him, and he will make your paths straight" (Prov. 3:5–6).

Principle 3.3 Reflection: Review and Preview

Finding the time for prayer and Scripture reading in the context of a lifestyle and culture filled with hurry-sick lives can be our greatest challenge as we become healthy disciples. However, there is no other alternative for growing in our love relationship with Christ. There are no alternative activities that can be substituted for these disciplines. How they are cultivated and enriched along our journey is crucial for believers.

As we hop off the treadmills of our lives in order to practice the spiritual disciplines, it's incumbent upon us to reflect on the occupations and preoccupations of our heart. What is keeping us from living a vibrantly healthy life in Christ? To whom are we listening more than the Holy Spirit? How are our personal study of the Scriptures and our disciplined life of prayer being enhanced each new day? If we were given the opportunity to relive the last twenty-four hours, what decisions would we remake or relationship blunders would we repair or needs would we respond to differently? These are sample questions that embody the priorities of the discipline of reflection.

The mystics of old were known by the adage, "Action without reflection is meaningless action." I have thought long and hard about this simple phrase, and the profundity of it amazes me. Truly, if we go through our days without sensing the need to reflect on what we've observed, experienced, felt, or heard, we miss the rich meaning of our daily walk. There is so much to say about what we see, hear, touch, taste, and smell about life—and the discipline of reflection exposes all of this in a healthy, life-giving way.

The Puritans called this "preview and review." The practice of *preview* is an encouragement to begin our day with our Bible, journal, and calendar, focusing on the day ahead, inviting Jesus to walk with us in our day, and surrendering to the plans of the Lord in the hours to follow. The practice of *review* encourages disciples to spend an equal amount of time at the end of the day with our Bible, journal, and calendar, looking back on our day, noting the highlights and disappointments of the day, and praying over situations or relationships that need follow-up prayer or action.

In the practice and exercise of the discipline of reflection—through *previewing* and *reviewing* our days—we learn the significance of our silence before God and the end result of submission to his love and lordship. As we learn to recognize God's work in our days, we begin to see with greater clarity how his grace, power, presence, and blessing are woven throughout each new day. God is at work in every relationship and every experience we have as we abide in Christ. *Preview* and *review* teaches the disciple to anticipate with God the many ways he delights to show himself to us as his children. As we keep our eyes and ears open to his work in our midst, we celebrate his divine intervention in others' lives as well as in our own.

Principle 3.4 Proactivity: Rhythm and Rhyme

Jesus was proactive and intentional in making it a priority to pull away from the crowds to practice his spiritual disciplines. "Very early in the morning, while it was still dark, Jesus got up, left the house and went off to a solitary place, where he prayed" (Mark 1:35). "After leaving them, he went up on a mountainside to pray" (Mark 6:46). "But Jesus often withdrew to lonely places and prayed" (Luke 5:16). "One of those days Jesus went out to a mountainside to pray, and spent the night praying to God" (Luke 6:12).

If this intentional act of prayer was such a priority for Jesus, how much more should it become a proactive discipline for us. The spiritual disciplines are what keep us focused on the Word and prayer. They remind us of God's great grace, extended generously in our behalf. When the disciplines are treated with this healthy balance—this rhythm and rhyme—then we don't err on the side of legalism ("I must have my seven minutes with God today or his judgment will rest upon me") or teeter onto the opposite side of absolute sloppiness ("It doesn't really matter if I've skipped my daily devotions for the past six months; God loves me anyway").

The spiritual disciplines of prayer, Scripture reading, and reflection are best treated in a balanced fashion, and they are most fruitfully experienced in our lives when we know with certainty that there is discipline to the experience of God's grace and there is great grace in the celebration of our disciplines. The trek toward discovering this balance is what a lifetime of discipleship is all about. Be sure to enjoy the rhythm and rhyme of your love relationship with Christ—it makes all the difference.

Principle 3.5 Accountability: Family and Friends

When our son's physician spent over an hour with Nathan at his sixteenth birthday checkup, we were absolutely amazed. Dr. Palant showed paternal love to Nate unlike any other doctor has ever shown. He treated Nate to a fatherly talk about sex, drugs, and alcohol and gave him his business card and even his home telephone number. He told Nate to call him any time day or night if ever there was a need to talk about a problem, temptation, or concern he had about any aspect of his physical or emotional well-being. This kind of support from a doctor is something every parent would be delighted to have. His love for our son, expressed in this tangible way, is something we will never forget. Our loyalty to this doctor went through the roof on that memorable afternoon, at a critical time in the growth and development of our son. What more could we have asked for?

In our journey of faith as God's disciples, there is a growing need for one-on-one and small group accountability. One-on-one is better than a small group, and a small group is better than a large one. Jesus had a small band of followers in whom he invested, and so should we. As we are held accountable to walk the talk and not just talk the walk, it certainly helps to have trusted mentors, advisors, and friends who will walk beside us and help us along the way.

Our family and friends begin to play an even more important role in our lives as they stand alongside us to encourage our faithfulness to the call of God and to keep us focused on the disciplines of the heart that matter most to our spiritual health and well-being. When Leighton Ford chose to move from mass evangelism to becoming a soul friend to leaders, his life was dramatically reshaped from revival evangelist to spiritual director. He has become a third person in the relationship between an individual and God—a spiritual guide and friend who helps others hear what God is saying to them.

It's only when we are held accountable in a loving way that we receive the gift of such profound friendship. After Nathan experienced the love of his physician, there was no hesitation in picking up the phone and calling Dr. Palant. For those being mentored by Leighton Ford, the spiritual friendship runs deep, and the fruit of such relationships is multiplied beyond measure as those he befriends touch the lives of others. Who will you invest in as a spiritual friend, and to whom are you being held accountable in your own spiritual life?

A DISCIPLE'S PRAYER

Lord, I know that you call me to yourself in order to reshape my daily spiritual disciplines by your grace and realign them to your priorities. I long to rediscover the freshness of my relationship with you and recommit myself to practicing the daily disciplines of prayer, Scripture reading, and reflection. May this kind of discipline-ship mark my life in the depths of my inner being, and may the choices I make each new day bring me back in step with your heart for my life.

May my love for you be like that of your beloved disciples, and may I be counted among this generation's disciples who discover the vitality and vigor of a life of abundant grace, realized in my prayer closet as I seek your face and draw near to your loving voice. You call me to yourself; help me to heed that call, and in return may my life be multiplied in my love for the souls of others who are near and dear to your heart and mine. By your grace and in your strength, I submit to the practicing of these disciplines. For your glory and honor, in the precious name of my dear Savior, Jesus. Amen.

For Reflection and Renewal

The healthy disciple pursues the daily disciplines of prayer, Bible study, and reflection in the quietness of one's personal prayer closet.

1. In the Gospel of John there are several places where Jesus demonstrates his priorities for his disciples through his life and his teachings. Note the following references in John 14–17 that highlight his role as spiritual mentor to his disciples. As you prayerfully read through each passage, begin to identify ways in which his priorities are applicable to the life of a healthy disciple today.

   - In John 14:1–10 Jesus guides his disciples to the Father.
   - In John 14:15–17 Jesus points them to the Holy Spirit.
   - In John 14:1–3 and 14:27 Jesus encourages them with hope for tomorrow.
   - In John 15:18 and 16:1–4, 32–33 Jesus speaks honestly of the messiness of the real world.
   - In John 16:8 Jesus tells the truth about the human heart.
   - In John 16:13 Jesus creates readiness for the already present activity of the Holy Spirit.
   - In John 17:1–26 Jesus practices the ministry of prayer for his followers. His attention to their spiritual growth does not end when their time together is over but continues onward through prayer.[12]

2. What spiritual disciplines are you in need of reprioritizing in your life, and how will you accomplish the goal of maintaining these disciplines in your daily walk with Christ?

3. Who do you need to invite into your life as a spiritual friend to hold you accountable for the practicing of your daily disciplines? Who around you needs this same kind of loving attention, and how will you prayerfully offer yourself for this purpose in his or her life?

4

Learns and Grows in Community

The healthy disciple is involved in spiritual and relational growth in the context of a safe and affirming group of like-minded believers.

When they did [obey Jesus], they were unable to haul the net in because of the large number of fish.

John 21:6

My wife, Ruth, and her friend Bev first met each other in the lunchroom at our children's school. It was a chaotic time for the volunteers on that particular day. The school year was still very young, and they were using makeshift space for the lunch hour (due to a construction project). On this particular September day the crowded lunchroom was abuzz with activity. All the helpers were scurrying about fulfilling their assigned responsibilities. They struck up a few lively conversations among themselves, but Ruth found herself very preoccupied. The previous day she had heard the news that our brother-in-law had suffered a cardiac arrest while on the racquetball court (an incident that would eventually take his life a few weeks later).

So, when Ruth and Bev's cars collided in the parking lot after lunchroom duty came to an end, they both apologized profusely for not seeing each other. Both women were mortified by the experience. They assessed the damage and determined it wasn't worth making any claims. They were each more interested in how the other was feeling than in the condition of the cars.

Little did they know on that day how God would orchestrate their "bumping into each other" in a much more meaningful way one year later. It was the following September when the women's Bible study groups were being assigned to each of the core leaders. Ruth was looking forward to meeting the women she would have the privilege of leading for that season. She was delighted to see Bev's name on the list.

Bev was a part of Ruth's core group for that following year and was an active participant in each week's study. In fact, one year later, Bev agreed to colead the group with Ruth. This divine appointment of two lives intersecting at a critical time for each has been a joy to behold. The love these two women have for each other has emanated out to all the other women in their group.

Bev notes, "I know with certainty that God led me to come alongside Ruth to keep her lifted up in prayer. Not only has it been clear that God brought Ruth and me together for this purpose, but God also orchestrated the exact persons to join us in the group. These women have been handpicked by God so that they could minister to one another during this specific season in all of our lives.

"It's like we are underneath the everlasting arms of God when we are together," she continues. "In a large group, while you can receive input on the Scriptures from a gifted teacher, you can get lost and feel very anonymous. But, when you get into a healthy small group, the Word comes alive and penetrates the soul. As our comfort level with one another has grown, and the trust has deepened for the sharing of life's most intimate details, the result has been a deeper work, a deeper healing in each of our lives."

This group of disciples longs for growth and maturity in Christ, which makes it a great place to openly raise issues that they legitimately wonder about as they read the Scriptures and reflect together on the meaning of God's truth as applied to their daily lives. It's a terrific place for them to share about their personal lives, family concerns, health issues, dreams for the future, and spiritual pilgrimages. In fact, it's such an important part of their lives that they carve precious time out of busy schedules to be together, offer prayers on each other's behalf, and study the Word with intensity and determination. They all long to grow as healthy disciples, and they love the context for learning that this group provides.

This is but one of thousands of other such groups that are in existence today within the body of Christ. They come in all shapes and sizes—from evangelistic Alpha study groups, to women's and men's early morning prayer groups, youth ministry Bible studies, children's Sunday school classes, Pioneer Clubs and Awana, couples clubs, small groups, accountability partners, missions prayer groups, choir prayer triads, intergenerational gatherings, and a host of other Christian community-building ministries that are offered within the church and throughout the wider context of the city, workplace, and neighborhoods we represent.

These groups have various purposes and embody a myriad of needs. They have become increasingly more important, especially for those who live such scattered and overloaded lives. Those who make a commitment to participate fully in such gatherings find their lives are enriched beyond description, and the fruitfulness of involvement is undeniable and incalculable.

Yet not every group is a healthy group. That's where the concept begins to deteriorate for many. An unhealthy community experience can have exponentially worse ripple effects and can actually lead a person either down an inappropriate pathway or even away from the faith completely. Why is this so? Because many groups today are focused on the narcissistic needs of the participants rather than on the Bible, prayer, and the most effective application of truth into the lives of those who gather together to study, reflect, learn, and grow.

Diana Bennett, our resident expert on small groups here in New England, describes an unhealthy small group experience this way:

A group is unhealthy when there is a lack of intentional leadership and where the leadership style resembles the laissez-faire attitude of "let it all just happen." This occurs when there is inadequate prayer and preparation, little understanding of the purpose of the time together, neglect in approaching the Scriptures with integrity, the inability to create effective discussion, no attention to the basic stages of growth in the life cycle of a group, and little knowledge of how to deal with difficult personalities. In these settings, it's the unhealthy dynamics which dominate and where members get discouraged. As a result, members do not make the small group a priority, trust level disintegrates, which prevents intimacy and accountability, and the group flounders and eventually dies.[1]

Far too often it's the unhealthy groups that we hear more about, which keeps many away from the prospect of creating and participating in groups that breathe life and health into our spiritual lives. When we are learning and growing in community with one another, we are gaining deeper insights into God's Word, applying it in our daily lives, celebrating God's work in and through one another, and multiplying the influence of the group in the hearts of those we love and serve in every area of life.

Jesus' Disciples in Community

In contrast to what we experience today in our small groups, note well how Jesus' disciples learn and grow in the context of their community. The selection from the Gospel of John for this trait is chapter 21, particularly verse 6: "He said, 'Throw your net on the right side of the boat and you will find some [fish].' When they did, they were unable to haul the net in because of the large number of fish." Here in this important story of postresurrection connection with his disciples, Jesus once again dramatically enters their community experience and reinforces the central message of the gospel in the hearts of his followers.

The story is a description of the risen Christ appearing to the disciples during their nighttime fishing adventure. With their blazing torches as their guide, their boat glided over the calm sea, and the men on board were keenly alert to their potential prey in the waters below them. When the fish would appear, they were ready to quickly spear their catch or fling their prepared nets overboard. However, on this particular night their nets were empty and their spears were left unused—until the man onshore instructed them to alter their approach.

He asked them, "'Friends, haven't you any fish?' 'No,' they answered. He said, 'Throw your net on the right side of the boat and you will find some'" (John 21:5–6). They must have thought the man either crazy, sarcastic, or absolutely correct. In fact, it was the latter. He was acting as a guide. It wasn't necessarily written here as a miracle story, for this kind of thing happens frequently on the lake. Remember, the boat was only about a hundred yards from land.

> H. V. Morton describes how he saw two men fishing on the shores of the lake. One had waded out from the shore and was casting a bell net into the water. "But time after time the net came up empty. It was a beautiful sight to see him casting. Each time the neatly folded net belled out in the air and fell so precisely on the water that the small lead weights hit the lake at the same moment making a thin circular splash. While he was waiting for another cast, Abdul shouted to him from the bank to fling to the left, which he instantly did. This time he was successful. . . . Then he drew up the net and we could see the fish struggling in it. . . . It happens very often that the man with the hand-net must rely on the advice of someone on shore, who tells him to cast either to the left or the right, because in the clear water he can often see a shoal of fish invisible to the man in the water." Jesus was acting as guide to his fishermen friends, just as people still do today.[2]

Why then was this strange story included in what appears to be an added chapter to an already complete Gospel? Well, the first reason is so Jesus could be seen once again as the risen Christ. He needed to demonstrate once and for all the reality of the resurrection. "There were many who said that the appearances of the Risen Christ were nothing more than visions which the disciples had. Many would admit the reality of the visions but insist that they were still only visions. Some would go further and say that they were not visions but hallucinations. The gospels go far out of their way to insist that the Risen Christ was not a vision, not a hallucination, not even a spirit, but a real person. They insist that the tomb was empty and that the Risen Christ had a real body which still bore the marks of the nails and the spear thrust in his side."[3]

This story goes even further than that. "A vision or a spirit would not be likely to point out a shoal of fish to a party of fishermen. A vision or spirit would not be likely to kindle a charcoal fire on the seashore. A vision or spirit would not be likely to cook a meal and to share it out. And yet, as this story has it, the Risen Christ did all these things."[4] Yes, in this story the reality of the resurrection is made crystal clear to the disciples in the context of their true community experience as real-life fishermen.

The story has a second great meaning as well, and that is the universality of the church. The disciples followed the instructions of Jesus, and by casting their net on the other side of the boat, they were unable to haul in the net because of the large number of fish! In fact, the Gospel writer is precise in the head count of those overgrown guppies—153 *large* fish to be exact. What a breakfast this must have been—bread and fish cooked over a charcoal fire with their hero, fisher-of-men, Jesus. Can you even imagine what that must have been like?

Why 153 fish? Barclay outlines a few different theories for the precise count.

> It has indeed been suggested that the fishes were counted simply because the catch had to be shared out between the various partners and the crew of the boat, and that the number was recorded simply because it was so exceptionally large. But when we remember John's way of putting hidden meanings in his Gospel for those who have eyes to see, we must think that there is more to it than that. Many ingenious suggestions have been made, such as:
>
> • Cyril of Alexandria said that the number 153 is made up of three things: the 100 are the fullest number and rep-

resent the fullness of the Gentiles who will be gathered
in to Christ. The 50 stands for the remnant of Israel who
will be gathered in. The 3 stands for the Trinity to whose
glory all things are done.

- Augustine says that 10 is the number of the Law, for
  there are ten commandments; 7 is the number of grace,
  for the gifts of the Spirit are sevenfold; now 7 + 10
  makes 17; and 153 is the sum of all the figures, 1 + 2
  + 3 + 4 . . . up to 17. Thus 153 stands for all those who
  either by Law or by grace have been moved to come to
  Jesus Christ.

- The simplest of all explanations is that given by Jerome.
  He said that in the sea there are 153 different kinds of
  fishes; and that the catch is one which includes every
  kind of fish; and that therefore the number symbol-
  izes the fact that some day all men of all nations will be
  gathered together to Jesus Christ.[5]

However we may interpret the significance of the number 153,
suffice it to say that this huge catch was gathered in one unbro-
ken net. The deeper meaning, no matter how you interpret the
count, is that the net stands for the church of the risen Christ.
There is room in that net for all people of every nation. No matter how many that will be, there is room for all who respond to
the invitation of Christ to come and follow him. No selectivity
and no exclusivity—the embrace of God's church is as wide as his
arms can reach. And his love that binds us together transcends
generations and nationalities because it's the love of the resur-
rected Christ.

The experience of the disciples on that postresurrection morning around the breakfast fire of love was a dramatic portrayal of
what happens when the people of God come together to fellowship
with the Master. They came in the company of the committed, sat
at his feet, listened to his Word, and encouraged one another to
listen for and pursue the ongoing call of God to be fishers of all
men and women. The drama of that early morning at the edge
of the sea is one that can be similarly replicated in homes, offices, classrooms, and churches worldwide. It's a drama waiting

to unfold before those of us who long to be in community with others, learning and growing in Christ together.

The concluding paragraph of the Gospel of John (John 21:15–25) features Peter being set apart as the great shepherd (and John as the great witness to Christ). Peter's honor was in fulfilling the mandate of Christ to shepherd the sheep of Christ. This is where we too can follow in Peter's footsteps. Each of us, as disciples of Christ, can guard someone else from going astray, and certainly all of us can feed the lambs of Christ with the eternal food of the Word of God. Peter's mandate is ours as well, and it is best fulfilled when we are in community relationships within the body of Christ, learning and growing together as brothers and sisters in the Lord, listening to him speak with clear instruction, and then responding with love and obedience.

Someone Else Will Lead You

Peter was challenged with a new thought in this same passage. "I tell you the truth, when you were younger you dressed yourself and went where you wanted; but when you are old you will stretch out your hands, and someone else will dress you and lead you where you do not want to go" (John 21:18). Jesus was reminding Peter of a truth that is worthy of our reflection as well.

Here Jesus articulated his vision for spiritual maturity. His view is quite the opposite of what the world says (i.e., "When you grow old you will be able to make your own decisions, go your own way, and control your destiny"). Instead Jesus says that maturity "is the ability and willingness to be led where you would rather not go. Immediately after Peter has been commissioned to be a leader of his sheep, Jesus confronts him with the hard truth that the servant-leader is the leader who is being led to unknown, undesirable, and painful places. The way of the Christian [leader] is not the way of upward mobility in which our world has invested so much, but the way of downward mobility ending on the cross. . . . The downward-moving way of Jesus is the way to the joy and peace of God, a joy and peace that is not of this world."[6]

How will Peter get to this level of maturity? Well, it begins with a vital relationship with Jesus Christ, but it is enhanced in the fellowship of a believing community that encourages one's growth to maturity. It is this same Peter who later penned the books of 1 and 2 Peter and wrote, "Like newborn babies, crave pure spiritual milk, so that by it you may grow up in your salvation. . . . You also, like living stones, are being built into a spiritual house to be a holy priesthood, offering spiritual sacrifices acceptable to God through Jesus Christ. . . . You are a chosen people, a royal priesthood, a holy nation, a people belonging to God, that you may declare the praises of him who called you out of darkness into his wonderful light" (1 Peter 2:2, 5, 9).

Peter's life was dramatically redirected by the influence of Christ. He became a new person through and through. His impulsivity was refined and refocused on intentionally serving Christ with vigor, love, and enthusiasm. His mark upon the early church was dramatic, and his influence upon the deepening of community—the care for the sheep, the chosen people who belong to God—was remarkable. His life was lived in full obedience to Christ even though it meant that he had to suffer at the hands of the unbelieving world that sought to destroy the work of God. Peter, the other disciples, and the entire early church were knit together as one in Christ, and the impact of their community of love will have eternal consequences.

What about your community of faith? How will you and your church family continue the legacy of the earliest believers in the ways you learn and grow together in Christ? As you mature in your faith, who will be there to lead you into unknown, undesirable, and painful places? We normally don't want this to be the purpose of any group. However, in the most effective small group experiences there will be that nudging influence of the Spirit, spoken of through the Scriptures and articulated in words of challenge and encouragement by members of your community. In the healthiest communities we entrust our lives into the care of others who will help us discern the call from God to love and serve others in ways that are not of this world. It is the way to Christ, for his call is one of sacrifice and service (see chapter 6), and it grows out of our experience in community—learning, growing, and maturing in our discipleship together.

Jesus longs for us to cast our nets on the other side, for it is there we will discover a new way of life. For our Christian community experience to be the very best possible, we will need to come before God with an earnest desire to help others grow in maturity as we open ourselves up to their input into our lives as well. For many this is casting our nets on the other side because it contradicts our normal way of living independently, devoid of any input from others. However, the healthy disciple is involved in spiritual and relational growth in the context of a safe and affirming group of like-minded believers.

What Is Community?

The process of growth to Christlike maturity is one through which we need to patiently walk in the context of community because it is impossible to experience any kind of significant growth on our own. If we are going to experience the richness of learning and growing in community, then we need to be in a covenant group with people we trust and with whom we can share our lives through thick and thin.

When we enter into a covenantal relationship, we make an unusual commitment to one another. We say in essence, "I want to grow up in Christ with you. I want to play with you, laugh with you, cry with you, pray with you, share with you, study with you, and grow with you, and I hope you want the same." We are committing to each other with the willingness to live out all the "one anothers" of the Scriptures, such as:

- Love one another (John 13:34–35; Rom. 13:8; 1 Peter 1:22; 1 John 3:11, 23; 4:7, 11–12).
- Confess your sins and pray for one another (James 5:16).
- Care for one another (1 Cor. 12:24–25).
- Greet one another (1 Peter 5:14).
- Bear one another's burdens (Gal. 6:2).

- Encourage and build up one another (1 Thess. 5:11; Heb. 3:13; 10:25).
- Submit to one another (Eph. 5:21).
- Bear with one another and forgive one another (Eph. 4:2; Col. 3:13).
- Admonish one another (Col. 3:16).
- Serve one another in love (Gal. 5:13).
- Spur one another on toward love and good deeds (Heb. 10:24).

When we are in covenantal fellowship with a small group of like-minded and like-hearted believers, we will discover that when the hard times come our way, we are not left to stand alone. In crisis moments when it feels as though our world is spinning out of control or the bottom is dropping out, we can cling to one another and find hope and joy for the journey. That is what the Christian community is supposed to look like. Is that your experience in the context of your local church?

The healthy disciple understands that the "one anothers" are not optional for the Christian life. They are community-building mandates from God to his people. His longing is for us to live in such vibrant Christian community that we can't help but shine brightly in juxtaposition to how others live in this world. However, for many North American Christians the "one anothers" are foreign teachings. We are nervous about pursuing or participating in such in-depth relationships. Our response to going deep in community relationships can be summarized by these questions:

"What will others think of me?"

"Will I be misunderstood or treated differently if they *really* know what I am thinking about or how I am living my life?"

"Can I really trust others with my true self?"

As a result of these (and many other) piercing questions, we choose instead to keep to ourselves, with maybe one or two close friendships, and miss out on true community.

Granted, there is room for caution in Christian community relationships. We've all been in disappointing relationships with others, and there is a natural reticence among many Christians to participate in ever-deepening relationships. However, our experiences in the past should not deter us from every possible community-based group in the future. As hard as it may be, and as simplistic as it may sound, it may be best for us to forgive others who have not been worthy of our trust (one of the subjects of the next chapter) and move forward into new relationships that will birth life, health, and vitality into our learning and growing in Christ.

In what contexts do we find healthy disciples learning and growing in community? They can be summarized in two categories:

- mentoring relationships
- ministry partnerships

In *mentoring relationships* there is give and take in the learning process. Usually there is a leader or teacher who comes prepared to speak to the group. Yet there are also times in these relationships when the peer-to-peer input is very strong and can supercede the role of the defined leader. These mentoring relationships can be defined as follows:

a. Pastor and member(s)—in which the pastor is the defined leader and members are present for the sake of learning and discovering truth; more need-based and topical in approach.
b. Teacher and student(s)—in which the teacher comes prepared to teach a lesson and the students interact with each presentation; more deductive in approach.
c. Leader and group—in which the leader facilitates the learning process and leads with insights, questions, and oversight of the group; more inductive in approach.

   d. Mentor and mentees—in which the mentor is available
      to listen to the needs of others and asks questions, prays
      for, and disciples others out of the context of the mentor's
      maturity and wisdom; more directive in approach.
   e. Peer-to-peer accountability—in which the group is formed
      for the sake of peers sharing their journey areas of both
      common and individual interest or concern; a more loosely
      held "mutually mentoring" approach.

For healthy *ministry partnerships* to congeal in community,
there is usually a missional priority to the group. In such contexts
there are people with whom we enjoy spending time and one
or more that are challenging to the group and the leader. Once
when I complained to my ministry mentor about a certain ministry partner, he said, "If he wasn't in your life or a part of your
ministry team today, how would you be growing as a leader?"
We grow in partnership with one another as we work through
the difficult relationships as well as enjoy the positive ones. In
ministry partnerships:

   • We grow as we serve and give to others.
   • We learn as we experience ministry together.
   • We discover how best to learn and grow as we wrestle with
     truth as it is applied to life and life-change within and around
     us.

The key to all of these relationships is summed up in the word
safe, which is the focus of the key principles stated below. Any
community that is not safe is a pseudocommunity, for these
principles of safety are basic to the healthy disciple's experience
in a genuine community of faith. Jesus' disciples knew all about
"safety nets," and in John 21 they worked hard to safeguard the
quality of their nets in order to haul in the big catch! Safety in
community means that we are free to be who we are while at the
same time growing to become all that God intends.

Diana Bennett put it this way: "When small groups are grounded
in prayer and proper preparation, when they are well facilitated
and allow ownership and high trust levels to develop among

members, then the members experience meaningful community, care, and connection with God and one another. It's out of that time together that spiritual growth becomes evident, life change occurs, and healthy disciples of Jesus Christ are formed."[7] In the context of a safe community experience, the growth process is greatly enhanced. If safety is at all compromised, however, growth is stilted and often abandoned.

How then do we proceed in developing healthy community experiences that birth the learning and growth for which each of us longs as Christ's disciples-in-process?

Principle 4.1 Safe Place to Share

Jesus' disciples shared their lives, even their vocations, with one another. A rather rough-and-tumble lot of men, their intimacy with Christ and one another led them into sharing spiritual highs and lows. Each of the Gospels is replete with examples of how these highs and lows drew the disciples closer to one another and into more intimate fellowship with the Savior.

By far the best environment for faith development is when our faith is most challenged. It is in such places where we wrestle with the truths of God's Word, ask all of our hardest questions, and seek prayerfully for direction and support that we become empowered to go forth into the world to love and serve Christ. Where would we be if we didn't have family, friends, mentors, and peers with whom to learn and grow throughout our lives as children, youth, and adults? Since we don't outgrow the need for learning, this lifelong pursuit after holiness demands that we maintain a safe place to share our life story. In the sharing of the story, we rediscover how God is present to care for our every need and leads us deeper into the fulfillment of his longing for us as his children.

Finding a safe place to share our story requires that we be transparent with one another and learn to hold in confidence all information shared with us. If confidentiality and trust is breached, then community begins to deteriorate. In my small group experiences, I have learned to trust that my friends will not abuse the information I've shared with them. I've taken the risk to share, and the fruit of strong community relationships has deeply enriched my personal life and growth. How about you?

Principle 4.2 Safe Place to Pray

Gathering around a charcoal fire with the risen Christ (John 21:9–10) was reminiscent of the disciples' times alone with him in service, sacrifice, and prayer. They saw in Christ their model prayer warrior, and they were destined to portray that same example before others. This was an especially poignant moment for Peter because his recollection of charcoal fireside encounters with Christ must have reminded him of the day he denied Christ. It was by an earlier fire that two servant girls and a few bystanders recognized Peter as a follower of Christ, but he denied their claim. After the cock crowed, Peter realized the significance of what he had done (John 18:15–18, 25–27). The pain of that moment is something with which we can all empathize as Christ-followers, for we too have denied him access into the deepest recesses of our soul. As a result, we are called to pray for forgiveness, restoration, and newfound freedom in the Spirit.

When we find ourselves involved in healthy community groups, the depth of insight into a life of prayer can be greatly enhanced. In one of my community groups, we share in reading and praying through the same devotional, using Rueben Job and Norman Shawchuck's *A Guide to Prayer*.[8] When we are unable to meet together, we can e-mail each other comments about what we're reading that week and how certain thoughts and prayers bring one another to mind. Then when we are together, the richness of our fellowship is enhanced by this common prayer experience. This is merely one idea of many to bring depth into community through the safety net of prayer with and for one another.

The health of every effective community group experience is based on the centrality of the Word of God, a dependence on the Spirit of God, and a commitment to share in the prayers of the people of God. Prayer is one of the most important ingredients of spiritual growth for every healthy disciple. Come close to the charcoal fire and remain there in prayer to experience a fresh encounter with the Savior—in both the times of repentance of sin and in the joy of grateful fellowship.

Principle 4.3 Safe Place to Process

Imagine the breakfast conversation between the disciples and Jesus as they began to eat the fish together. Read beneath and beyond what the Scriptures reveal—wow, you can just about imagine what they had to process and learn at the feet of Jesus! Their transformational experience of throwing the nets to the other side of the boat was only a glimpse of things to come after hearing his voice and responding to his leadership in their lives. They had so much to talk about in the days following this fresh encounter with the risen Christ. Little did they realize at that time the impact their theological reflection would have upon future generations of Christ's followers.

We learn so much when we are together in community, sharing common experiences and being stretched in new areas of life and service. Jesus and his disciples shared many intimate moments like the lakeside breakfast in John 21. As a result, the disciples found a safe place to ask their questions and listen to wise truths at the feet of the Master. They had so much to process and needed to know that Jesus would be there for them every step of the way.

If it weren't for the many groups I have had the privilege of either leading or joining over the years, I'm confident my spiritual depth would be far shallower today. Processing important information, sharing the journey of life with one another, making important vocational decisions, determining family priorities, working through significant theological truths, praying together, and holding one another accountable to grow and learn are just a sampling of the fruit that has emerged. I'm committed to this process and look forward to how God will use the lives of other healthy disciples to assist me in my growth. How about you?

Principle 4.4 Safe Place to Care

You will definitely get to know someone deeply when you spend large blocks of time together. The disciples were on one massive retreat with Jesus for a few years, and they grew in their love for him and for one another. They were all equals when it came to their day-to-day needs, and they were there to care for each other even when they fought for center stage in Jesus' affection.

In the same way, a safe place to care for one another today grows out of understanding each other's needs and being there for each other during times of both struggle and joy. Ruth and I will never forget the times when community members were there for us during the twelve surgeries our son, Nathan, has experienced over the past seventeen years. We'll never forget the meals, baby-sitting, flowers, phone calls, or prayers of the saints. Our community of friends also pulled through with both tangible and intangible expressions of love and support when both of my parents were dying. This is the fruit of healthy community, and it's something we all long to experience.

The tangible signs of care come in the form of meals, financial assistance, acts of mercy, and meeting specific needs. The intangible gifts of love are embodied in grace-giving, joy-sharing, and unconditional expressions of support. True love within community is a caring love for another person no matter what that person may say or do to you. When we are living in vital community with fellow believers, the acts of love come naturally, freely, and generously from the heart and are a genuine reflection of our love for Christ and his bride, the church.

Principle 4.5 Safe Place to Grow

The disciples were always "on the grow"—for good and not for ill. They were on the pathway of growth, becoming healthy disciples each day they traversed the Holy Land with Jesus. It seems the beloved disciple, John, and his counterpart Peter had the most to learn, for they became central players in the formation of the "new community" being established by Christ.

That new community ultimately became the early church. The Book of Acts tells us all about how the church multiplied beyond itself and began to conquer the world with the life-changing message of Jesus. The small group of Jesus' first disciples were multiplied in their lifetime, and the growth of disciple making worldwide has continued in full force ever since. The goal of the first group was growth, and that goal should be ours as well.

Often growth requires change. In order for us to experience genuine growth, we may have to say some fond farewells, welcome new members into our community, and even divide so that we can multiply our effectiveness. In addition, we don't grow as individual disciples by staying in the same place spiritually—we too must always be on the grow. As seasons of our life experience change, so also do groups within the Christian community. Often we don't embrace such changes, and we long for the "glory days" when things stayed relatively the same and we knew everyone in the group intimately. Yet we must be prepared for such transitions. When proactively handled, leaders and members of small groups experience the richness of the here and now while anticipating what's yet to come.

Changes in the composition of our community can actually enhance our lives and add color and flavor to our learning and growth in Christ. Celebrate the community of which you are currently a part, and look forward to new community being forged in the days ahead. You won't be disappointed if you wait with faith-filled, open, outstretched arms to receive from Christ and his people every new season of this journey we call *life*. In the arms of Christ is the safest place on earth.

A Disciple's Prayer

Lord Jesus, you and your disciples experienced the richest form of community known to mankind. As I look at the Gospels in light of that intimate community in which life-transforming learning and growth occurred, I can't help but ask for a similar expression within the context of my church. I long to be involved in a vital relationship with you, and I'm confident that my small group experiences will in fact draw me closer to you.

Help me reach out to others in my faith community who may be desirous of the same learning and growth opportunity. May I speak freely of my desire to know your Word, to become dependent upon your Spirit, and to embody your life here on earth. May I generously share my journey with others of like heart and mind, and may the richness of our fellowship come directly from your heart to ours. Build within our combined lives a sense of your empowering presence so that as we read your Word, join hearts and hands in prayer, and encourage one another to trust you, we may in reality find our common roots and affirm your love as evidenced in our lives.

May the close walk you had with your first disciples be replicated in my life, in our community, and for generations to come. You are the Lord of my life, and I gladly submit to your love and leadership throughout all the growing and learning days of my journey of faith. For the love of Christ. Amen.

For Reflection and Renewal

The healthy disciple is involved in spiritual and relational growth in the context of a safe and affirming group of like-minded believers.

1. Read through John 20 and 21. Note all the ways Jesus appeared after his resurrection. What were some of the themes of these encounters with the risen Christ, and how did his followers learn and grow in community as a result? Spend some time in these chapters, reflecting prayerfully on the life-changing impact that occurred as a result of faith communities coming into direct contact with Christ. How should these experiences impact your own community in the days ahead?

2. Are the small groups within your local church healthy? If not, how can you encourage health in these contexts of learning and growth? Are you in a small group? If not, why

not? If so, are you contributing positively to the health of that group?

3. How do you define the word *safe* in relation to small community groups? Do you concur with the five principles above, and would you add any additional principles to the list? If there are groups within your fellowship that are no longer safe, what can you do to help bring health and vitality back into those groups?

5

Commits to Loving
and Caring Relationships

The healthy disciple prioritizes the qualities of relational vitality that lead to genuine love for one another in the home, workplace, church, and community.

My command is this: Love each other as I have loved you. Greater love has no one than this, that he lay down his life for his friends.

John 15:12–13

Jimmy and I grew up on the same street and were best of friends for most of our childhood years. We rode bikes together, played kick ball in the street, went swimming, hiking, running, and shoplifting together. Wait a minute, did I say shoplifting? What I meant to say was "shop-borrowing" together.

Actually, shop-borrowing was only an occasional antic of this wild twosome. In fact, when the drugstore manager caught us carrying out our favorite pack of gum, and then a second time when he stopped us at the door with a few pencil erasers in our pockets, we decided we'd better stop. We lived across the street from one another and our mothers seemed to know everything about everyone, so we figured out they would most likely learn about this too. (Surprisingly enough, they both went to their graves unaware of their sons' escapades. Maybe not, says every mother reading this book!)

One of the most notable events of our friendship came when Jimmy and I were riding our bikes around the block on a hot summer day, shirtless and shoeless on our banana-seat stingrays. (Mine was the bright orange one with the silver seat.) We had just hopped out of his above-ground swimming pool and decided to dry off by taking a spin on our bikes.

After turning the final corner of that memorable lap, I wiped out on the sand-covered corner of Myopia and Sherwood Roads. Jimmy kept riding as I lay there in pain, blood dripping from my left leg, now full of gravel from the road that had never been cleaned since winter. My bike tire was up against the car tire of an elderly woman who thankfully came to a complete stop before riding over my favorite stingray (never mind my leg!). The tears started to flow, and the shock began to set in. Where was Jimmy?

Well, this devoted friend had deserted me. Actually, he panicked and rode his bike home, only three houses away from the accident scene. He ran into his house and locked himself in his bedroom out of fear that his friend had been seriously hurt and he was responsible for this awful accident. Apparently he didn't reemerge from his bedroom until the ambulance left our street corner with his buddy in the back. I didn't find this out until later in the day when he came to visit—or, as I vividly recall, when he came to see the big bandage on my leg.

Jimmy wasn't the only one to disappear quickly from an uncomfortable scene. One day the two of us were playing a friendly game of tossing rocks across the street, apparently to see who could throw the farthest (go figure!). Well, I guess I won that game because my largest rock landed in the back window of Jimmy's dad's new Chevy Impala. It was then that I discovered how a big piece of glass shatters quickly into a billion pieces.

This was my turn to run. In fact, I ran straight to my bedroom and stayed there crying out of disbelief and remorse over my actions. It was only moments later that Jimmy's dad arrived at our front door. He wasn't there to scold or humiliate but to offer a word of comfort and consolation. Here I had done the dumbest thing, and Mr. P. was there to offer grace. I didn't deserve it, but he knew me almost as well as my own father did, and he knew it was an accident that I'd never forget. He also knew that offering grace was far better than dishing out a pound of shame. He ushered me—arm in arm—out to the back of his car, where we scoped out the broken glass. He assured me that it would soon be fixed, he was glad neither Jimmy nor I had been hurt, and he hoped we had learned a lesson. I discovered more about friendship that day than about consequences, and I've never forgotten his forgiving and restorative love.

Jimmy and I had many such experiences together. We were best of friends, and freely sharing love and caring came naturally for us. We shared dinners at each other's homes—my mom always had the well-balanced meals, so we tended to migrate more often to his house where his mom would make us dinners of nothing but homemade French fries. (Sorry, Mom, but what young boy cares about needing a green salad, two vegetables, a starch, glass of milk, and small dessert?) We shared walks to Robin Hood Elementary School. We shared girlfriends, homework, shaving cream, and much, much more. After all, what are friends for?

Great Commandment

My friendship with Jimmy didn't come close to the kind of love Jesus had for his disciples. In fact, when he issued his command, "Love each other as I have loved you," he was preparing them for his example to them that "greater love has no one than this, that he lay down his life for his friends" (John 15:12–13). Jesus in fact did exactly that—he laid down his life for his first clan of disciples, and he did it for us as his twenty-first-century disciples. What will be your response to his sacrificial love for you? Are you willing to share it with others?

When I get into my envisioning mode, I find myself dreaming about all the *what ifs* of the Christian life. For example, what if Christians were truly known for their love? What if the world saw only love when they looked our direction? What if all the world heard was loving conversation coming from our lips? What if all our relationships were motivated by true love? What if our tough love was more loving than tough? What if our love for the lost overpowered our love for self? What if our churches were known exclusively for their love for God and one another and for giving love away to others? What if our love was filled with gratitude, grace, and generosity?

That's exactly the kind of love Jesus blessed and the kind of love he longed for his disciples to exemplify. The contrasts between that kind of love and what was evidenced so often around him were startling. Consider, for example, the following story from the Book of John. We've looked at it once already in relation to worship, but let's look at it again to find out what it has to say about love.

Six days before the Passover, Jesus arrived at Bethany, where Lazarus lived, whom Jesus had raised from the dead. Here a dinner was given in Jesus' honor. Martha served, while Lazarus was among those reclining at the table with him. Then Mary took about a pint of pure nard, an expensive perfume; she poured it on Jesus' feet and wiped his feet with her hair. And the house was filled with the fragrance of the perfume.

But one of his disciples, Judas Iscariot, who was later to betray him, objected, "Why wasn't this perfume sold and the money given to the poor? It was worth a year's wages." He did not say this because he cared about the poor but because he was a thief; as keeper of the money bag, he used to help himself to what was put into it.

"Leave her alone," Jesus replied, "It was meant that she should save this perfume for the day of my burial. You will always have the poor among you, but you will not always have me."

John 12:1–8

What a fabulous tribute to extravagant love. Here Martha, Mary, and Lazarus were hosting Jesus. He not only was residing in their home but also had made residence in their hearts. The setting was typical to these three loving individuals, who knew Jesus was the long-awaited Messiah and who weren't afraid to shower him with the love he deserved. Martha was the hostess par excellence, Lazarus was grateful beyond comprehension for the miracle of new life granted to him by Jesus, and Mary was positioned once again in a posture of humility and worship.

Mary's heart was overflowing with love for Jesus. A pint of pure nard, worth a full year's wages, was destined for the feet of Jesus. She wiped the perfume with her hair, and not only did that intimate act of love fill her heart anew, it also enveloped the entire house. The fragrance was beautiful beyond description, enjoyed by those who shared Mary's love for the Master and yet despised by those whose hearts were cold and indifferent.

In response to the extravagant love of Jesus, Mary demonstrated at least three qualities of her love in return. First of all, we see her heart of *gratitude* in this act of worship. Mary's love for Christ is unself-conscious! She gives love back to Jesus out of profound thankfulness for the outpouring of his incredible love that she has received. The fact that Mary wiped Jesus' feet with her unbound hair showed that she didn't care about her reputation (respectable women in Palestine would never do such a thing). No, she never even thought of that. While many others would have been much more self-conscious, Mary was living in a world all her own—a world of extravagant love.

One can only imagine the quality of Mary's relational strength beyond what we see here at the feet of Jesus. From observation of many such "Marys" over the years, one can certainly assume that this Mary's human relationships were loving and caring, a natural overflow of her love for Christ.

Expressing thanks to God for the gift of his relationship with us leads naturally into thanking the Lord for all of our relationships. The quality of our relationships with family, friends, work associates, church, and community should reflect our extravagant love for Jesus. Be sure to tell God how grateful you are for these people, and take the time to express gratitude to those who are within your relational web of connections. It's the relationally healthy thing to do, even when some of those relationships are stressed and strained!

Second, we see in Mary a *grace*-filled response to Jesus' love. The humility of pouring expensive ointment on the feet of Jesus shows not only the grace of Christ but also the response of grace by his loving disciple. Mary knew he wasn't looking for honor, prestige, or recognition of his kingliness—no, Jesus was most interested in reigning supreme in her heart. He had captivated her by his awe-inspiring love, and her graceful response is a wonder to behold. True love is humble love, and it is exemplified in graceful servanthood (the subject of our next chapter).

To whom do you need to extend grace in your circle of relationships? Is it your parent, spouse, sibling, friend, roommate, or colleague? Most likely there are one or more individuals within your relational sphere who need to receive the gift of grace from you. Prayerfully consider that need and determine now to make it right with that person, shower him or her with the grace of Christ (most likely you can't muster it up on your own strength), and begin to mend the broken heart within through the life-transforming power of God. The Lord wants your relationships to be healthy, and many times it must begin with your own initiative. Don't wait any longer—you don't want it to be too late for any of your key relationships.

Third, we see here a *generous* love. Mary took the most precious thing she possessed and spent it (wasted it according to Judas) all on Jesus. Love is not love if it neatly calculates the cost. No, it gives all, and its only regret is that it has not still more to give. O. Henry, the master of the short story, wrote a moving tale called "The Gift of the Magi." Barclay summarizes the love story:

> A young American couple, Della and Jim, were very poor but very much in love. Each had one unique possession. Della's hair was her glory. When she let it down it almost served as a robe. Jim had a gold watch, which had come to him from his father and was his pride. It was the day before Christmas, and Della had exactly one dollar eighty-seven cents to buy Jim a present. She went out and sold her hair for twenty dollars; and with the proceeds bought a platinum fob for Jim's precious watch. When Jim came home at night and saw Della's shorn head, he stopped as if stupefied. It was not that he did not like it or love her any less; for she was lovelier than ever. Slowly he handed her his gift; it was a set of expensive tortoise-shell combs with jeweled edges for her lovely hair—and he had sold his gold watch to

buy them. Each had given the other all there was to give. Real love cannot think of any other way to give.[1]

What better love to give away than a generous, extravagant love? Our generosity gives rise to generosity in others. When I talk with my friend Pablo and hear the many ways he generously loves others in Jesus' name, I am challenged within my heart to generously love in Jesus' name also. It's contagious and effervescent and oh, so honoring to the Lord. Surprise someone you feel called to love today in a specific way—and do so generously and whenever possible invisibly, so that God is glorified and receives all the praise.

Commandment Broken—Opportunity Lost

Judas, on the other hand, turned coldly away from the extravagant love of Jesus. His warped understanding of Jesus' mission led to his demise. Instead of seeing Mary's act of surpassing loveliness as a sign of her heart of love and gratitude, he saw this drama as an absolute waste. Since he was such an embittered man, he had an embittered view of life. The eyes of his heart had never truly been opened to the love of Jesus, and he was unable to see the beauty of the moment.

A person's eyesight depends on what's going on inside, in the inner recesses of the soul. "We see only what we are fit and able to see. If we like a person, he can do little wrong. If we dislike him, we may misinterpret his finest action. A warped mind brings a warped view of things; and, if we find ourselves becoming very critical of others and imputing unworthy motives to them, we should, for a moment, stop examining them and start examining ourselves."[2] This was indeed Judas's problem. His heart was cold, and he ascribed ulterior motives to Mary.

Not only did Judas complain about Mary's wastefulness of expensive perfume, but he also painted himself as a philanthropist to the poor and impoverished. When was Judas ever known as caring for the poor? Jesus knew Judas's heart, and he spoke right into it when he reminded Judas and all who were present that the poor would always be with them. Jesus' time, however, was limited. The time had come for Jesus to head for Calvary's cross, and it was urgent that his disciples express their heart's devotion to him then and there. Judas missed this grand opportunity, and his eternal doom was now assured.

Failure to act *now* in a loving manner brings bitter remorse *later.* Mary's act of extravagant love was in response to the unconditional love of Jesus. She couldn't help but show her deepest thankfulness for his love. She couldn't stop herself from expressing her grace and humility, keenly aware of her profound need for Jesus' love and forgiveness. She didn't care that the perfume was worth a year's salary as she spontaneously poured it out on his feet. How beautiful and radiant was her love. She didn't miss the opportunity, and her eternal joy was sealed forever.

Ever had a Judas appear in your life? A ministry friend of mine never thought he'd have one, and then all of a sudden, early one spring, his Judas showed up in the garb of a partner in ministry. He had known this person for over twenty years as a friend and confidant, yet almost overnight he felt the anguish of this same person stabbing him in the back and making his life as miserable as possible. Trust and confidence were broken, and the relationship of so many years came unraveled. Harsh words were voiced and injustice emerged. Truth telling was out the window, and grace, generosity, and gratitude were nowhere to be found. It took several months for my friend to rediscover emotional equilibrium, found in the presence of Christ and in the company of a few special friends in the faith who held his hand and fed his soul with the realities of God's grace to restore and renew his broken heart.

The capacity for "Judas the relationship destroyer" is within each of our sinful hearts. Having experienced a Judas myself, I pray I won't become one to others, and I trust I won't be blindsided when it occurs again. Having seen the destruction of a Judas, I hope that the tornado funnel of rage won't litter relational clutter in other significant ministry settings in the days ahead. *Lord, may it never be so in our relationships, and may your love reign supreme in the hearts and lives of those we are called to love in Jesus' name.* May this be your daily prayer as well.

No Greater Love Than This

Jesus' commandment is very simple: love. Love one another as Jesus has loved you. It begins with loving Jesus and works its way outward into every sphere of your relationships—home, work, school, neighborhood, community, and church. Yes, all areas of personal life and relationships are to be highlighted by love. This is our calling, and this is to become our greatest earthly joy.

The kind of love that Jesus commands is *agape*—unconditional love. There is really no greater love than this. It's that kind of love that God showers on us each day, and it's the kind of love he wants us to share with one another in order to reach the world with the gospel of love. It's love that's given no matter what another person may do or say to us. It's love that's birthed in our hearts and radiates outward to all who cross our path. In the context of the body of Christ, it's the natural overflow of our community and fellowship as brothers and sisters in the Lord. Is that your experience today?

For many believers the sin of pride and self-absorption stands in the way of loving, caring relationships. When it's all about me, it's virtually impossible to think first of the other person's needs and reach out in loving compassion and concern. I don't know about you, but I despise seeing pride eek its way out of me.

I have vivid recollections of one such day when my pride stood in the way of loving and caring for my son, Nathan, then sixteen years old. It was a Saturday afternoon, and I had reluctantly agreed to drive him to the house of one of his friends. I had other tasks to attend to and was a bit agitated by this "interruption."

When we were getting into the car, I asked Nathan if he had turned off the lights in our house and locked the front door. When he fumbled his unconvincing answer to what I thought was a very clear question, I went back to the house and was disgusted to find the front door unlocked, all sorts of lights left on, and the back door swung wide open. This was a major crime after all, because of course *I* would never leave the house this way. When I got back to the car, I let my tongue do the lashing about this and every other offense known to mankind that Nathan had ever done or could have imagined doing. I went on and on as if I were some perfect person who never forgot a single responsibility. Needless to say, I would have never won a fatherhood award for the way I handled that one.

We drove away from our home in cold silence after my tirade ended. Twenty miles later when we got to his friend's house, I dropped Nathan off without a farewell, zoomed *so maturely* out of his friend's driveway, and tore my way back home. By the time I got home, I was overwhelmed with guilt and shame. Standing in front of the mirror, I could see the word *pride* in neon lights across my chest.

Pride, that oh-so-awful hindrance to loving and caring relationships. It's the root of many other relational illnesses—such as focusing on the failures of others, having a critical spirit, looking down on others, being self-sufficient, controlling and manipulating others, always needing to be right, never admitting error, shaming, blaming, and name-calling. Do any of these shoes fit you?

In order for disciples in pursuit of health to lovingly care for one another, we must be willing to be broken and contrite over the things we do that kill relationships. In your family or circle of friends, who's the first one to say "I'm sorry"? Or is that completely absent from your relational vocabulary?

The moment I returned to our house after blasting Nathan on that Saturday escapade, I realized I was to blame. I was totally disgusted with myself. I knew I was wrong and needed to make it right. Since we'd been down this road before, I knew I had to apologize once again for blowing it big time. Did I want to apologize? Absolutely not. Was I called to do so? Positively. Was it humbling and humiliating? You bet. Did it enhance our relationship? Without a doubt. Would a similar incident ever occur again? Certainly. Would the same calling remain? Yes. Again and again and again, the need to say "I'm sorry; I was wrong; please forgive me" will reemerge in our relationships. Will you step up to the plate and take the lead in a God-honoring response? Go for it!

Relational Continuum

Often the quality of our relationships depends on where they fit into a very simple continuum. On one side of the continuum are the *independent* people in our lives. These are characterized by a closed-door approach to others. They firmly believe they have all the necessary ingredients to function effectively in this world without much assistance from others. These independent types are usually not the warmest people to get to know, and they tend not to participate in activities that require much relational skill. In one sense they present themselves as wholesome and healthy (and a tad mysterious), while the flip side is that these people are generally relationally impoverished and awkward. Building and maintaining healthy relationships with independents is a challenge because the door of their hearts is usually shut tight, bolted, and secured so no one can ever get a glimpse inside.

On the other end of the relational continuum are the *dependent* people. These generally have such an open-door approach to others that you'd prefer not to see any more. The relational dependents are individuals who have great difficulty making simple choices and are always looking for someone else to step in. They are usually quite burdened by life and continually need the assistance of others. They are needy, whiney, clingy, and difficult to satisfy. The dependent people in our lives are those who are high maintenance, constantly draining every ounce of our emotional energy because of their needy, narcissistic tendency to lean on others for support in most aspects of life. While we may not all have people in our lives that live in such an extreme state of relational poverty, many of us know someone who fits most of this profile.

In the center of the relational continuum are the *interdependent* people. These are by far the healthiest individuals with whom to maintain a relationship. They operate out of a swinging-door approach to others. Sometimes the door swings in, and there is openness to receive from others, while at times the door swings out in giving to others. The fact that the door of their heart swings both ways shows there is relational wholeness and vitality. Interdependent people understand that there are times when they need to work things out alone and times when they need to lean on others, and they can balance both with fluidity and flexibility. It's a pleasure spending time with those who understand interdependence and know the significant value of what they bring to the table while honoring and appreciating what others offer in the relationship.

Where are you in this continuum? Where are your primary relationships on this continuum? Where does there need to be some shifting and readjustment so that enough healthy relationships are being cultivated around you that will help you handle some of the unhealthy people in your life? Understanding this continuum will lead you to identify the strength and quality of your relationships and direct you toward greater health and vitality. The following characteristics are a few of the relational priorities of disciples of Jesus Christ who care deeply about the interdependent, interwoven nature of our lives as people of faith.

Principle 5.1 Agape Love

The baseline questions all disciples should ask of their relationships with others center on the concept of love: Am I loved? Am I capable of loving? Are my relationships safeguarded by love? When we can answer those questions affirmatively, we understand what love is all about. When we cannot answer them with a positive response, then we are deficient in life's most basic need.

Jesus continually reminds his disciples to love. In the Gospel of John we hear this repeatedly. "A new command I give you: Love one another. As I have loved you, so you must love one another. By this all men will know that you are my disciples, if you love one another" (John 13:34). "My command is this: Love each other as I have loved you. Greater love has no one than this, that he lay down his life for his friends" (John 15:12–13). When Jesus reinstates Peter in John 21:15–19, he repeatedly asks Peter if he loves him. The follow-up response from Christ is summed up in the mandate to feed and care for the sheep. Loving and caring relationships are Jesus' number one priority for all earthly relationships. So it must be for us.

Noted family specialist and author Gary Chapman, in his fabulous book *The Five Love Languages*,[3] suggests that each of us has a preferred language for receiving love from others. He proposes that if we take the time to learn the love languages of our spouse, children, family, and friends, we can communicate love far more effectively. His list of love languages is: words of affirmation, quality time, receiving gifts, acts of service, and physical touch. Expressing a commitment to loving and caring relationships begins with knowing the language of love most significant to each of our key relationships. What is your preferred love language? Do you know the language of those around you? If so, speak up and let your love shine through!

Principle 5.2 Absolute Joy

A pair of British researchers, a psychologist and a life coach, thought they had worked out a simple equation to quantify happiness that could put an exact figure on a person's emotional state. After interviewing one thousand people, the researchers concluded that happiness equals P + E + H. In the equation, P stands for Personal Characteristics (outlook on life, adaptability, and resilience), E for Existence (health, friendships, and financial stability), and H for Higher Order (self-esteem, expectations, and ambitions). Sunny weather, being with family, and losing weight were more of an influence on women's happiness, while romance, sex, hobbies, and victories by their favorite sports teams were important to men.[4]

While one may smirk at such a notion, many disciples today equate their joy with their happiness factors. Joy contains happiness, but happiness is not equal to joy. In fact, happiness is subservient to joy. In the truest sense of the biblical word, joy is rooted solely in God. Consider the psalmist's point of view: "Satisfy us in the morning with your unfailing love, that we may sing for joy and be glad all our days" (Ps. 90:14). Joy is exuberance over the unfailing love of God *despite* our happiness or lack thereof. In both good times and bad, when the joy of the Lord is our daily strength, we discover true joy as God carries us through.

World-renowned worship leader Graham Kendrick summarizes the significance of pure joy in his worship song "Consider It Joy":

Consider It Joy

Though trials will come
Don't fear, don't run
Lift up your eyes
Hold fast, be strong
Have faith, keep on believing
Lift up your eyes
For God is at work in us
Moulding and shaping us
Out of his love for us
Making us more like Jesus.

Chorus:
Consider it joy, pure joy
When troubles come
Many trials will make you strong
Consider it joy, pure joy
And stand your ground
Then at last you'll wear a crown.[5]

How far from the happiness equation is this description of joy? Immediately prior to his mandate for love among his disciples, Jesus talked about the fruit that would emerge in their lives if they clung to the vine. "I have told you this so that my joy may be in you and that your joy may be complete" (John 15:11). Joy comes to full fruition as we remain in Christ. In chapter 16, Jesus told his disciples that their forthcoming grief over his earthly departure would soon turn into joy, complete joy, something that no one can ever take away (vv. 20–24). For the disciple, pure joy is based on the fact that "Jesus, the author and perfecter of our faith, who for the joy set before him endured the cross, scorning its shame, and sat down at the right hand of the throne of God. Consider him who endured such opposition from sinful men, so that you will not grow weary and lose heart" (Heb. 12:2–3). Fix your eyes in his direction and joy will emerge within your heart and spill out onto all of your relationships. Wow!

Principle 5.3 Affirming Communication

Although words of affirmation may not be your preferred love language, each of us as Christ's disciples needs to learn how to communicate out of a heart of love. The goal of communicating effectively in our relationships is to be *empathetic*. If we are empathetic, we identify with and understand another person's situation, feelings, and motives. In loving and caring relationships, people make the effort to fully communicate with one another to the place where they can "walk in each other's shoes" emotionally. Building that depth of insight into each other is what becomes the work of relationships and is invaluable in making all of our interactions more healthy.

It takes more than words to communicate. In fact, words are the smallest percentage of the communication package. Believe it or not, it's our body language that most affects our ability to effectively communicate. When we don't look the other person in the eye or our arms are crossed, our fists are shaking, or our feet are tapping, we say far more to one another than any words that come out of our mouths. On top of that, our tone of voice, when added to our body language, speaks volumes to the person with whom we are communicating. Our words fade away when our bodies and tone of voice monopolize the conversation—especially when the latter two communication tools are loud and angry.

Don't believe me? Try this simple exercise: With a friend, say the words "I like you." First of all, look each other in the eye, hold each other's hands, sit with an open posture of relaxed acceptance, and say those three words with clarity, savoring each word with a reflective pause and a smile on your face. Then, try saying those same three words without looking at each other, no touch, a rigid posture facing away from each other, voicing the three words with a harsh tone and a brittle style. Which one meant the most to you? Which one was the most effective? Keep practicing, and when you get the point, move ahead with a heart to communicate with positive tone and body language every moment of your day.

Principle 5.4 Resolving Conflict

Unless you live in a bubble, you are guaranteed to experience conflict. We can't avoid it, nor should we. In fact the healthiest disciples embrace the opportunities to grow that are afforded in conflict situations. Unfortunately, the church is known more for its conflicts than for its grace. A church that's filled with disciples who are striving for health in their relationships of love and concern for one another will learn to resolve their besetting conflicts. These skills are teachable; the important question is, are we?

In the *Becoming a Healthy Church Workbook*,[6] I suggest several principles for church leaders to consider in dealing with conflict in the life of the local fellowship of believers. We as individuals need to determine how much we are willing to deal with the conflicting relationships that surround us. Are we willing, for example, to confess our sins to one another? Are we willing to participate in a free-flowing exchange of forgiveness between members of our immediate family and church family? These questions go to the heart of the matter with conflict. In essence, are we willing to step up to the plate ourselves in both learning the skills necessary for resolving conflict as well as owning up to the part we play in bringing it about?

When most people consider the goal of resolving conflict, there is the tendency to settle instead for compromise. For some, managing conflict means yelling louder and intimidating the other person to bend toward their will. For others, managing conflict means acquiescing to the stronger person in the relationship and quietly suffering in the pain of unresolved conflict. For still others, managing conflict means peace at any price as they work hard to satisfy the needs of everyone else, all the while living unfulfilled. Compromise is somewhere in between these last three options and full resolution. When we compromise, everyone accepts a bit of dissatisfaction and a bit of success. However, the goal of truly resolving a conflict is far superior to any of the other op-

tions. When we resolve a conflict, we find answers to the issues
before us that are not only satisfactory to each party involved but
in fact lead to deeper relationships and enhanced effectiveness
in service to others.

Whatever the cost, it's worth it to pay the price and strive
wholeheartedly to resolve every conflict that comes your way. If
needed, search the Internet or your church library for resources
to assist you in this process. Thankfully, there are many such
helps available to the body of Christ that will encourage you in
this strategic relational objective.

Probably the most challenging aspect of reconciliation, but
one that is crucial in healthy relationships, is forgiveness. In his
book *The Art of Forgiving: When You Need to Forgive and Don't
Know How*, Lewis Smedes summarizes the keys to forgiving in
the following way:

> Jesus was unequivocal on this point: As his followers, we are
> required to forgive those who sin against us (Matt. 6:15). But
> what if we don't feel like we've forgiven them? How do we
> know, then, if we have truly forgiven? The Holy Spirit, thank
> God, often enables people to forgive even though they are not
> sure how they did it. But forgiving, and knowing that we've
> truly forgiven, comes easier when we understand the realities
> of forgiveness:
>
> 1. Forgiveness is a redemptive response to having been
>   wronged and wounded.
> 2. Forgiveness requires three basic actions: first, we sur-
>   render our right to get even; second, we rediscover the
>   humanity of our wrongdoer; third, we wish our wrong-
>   doer well.
> 3. Forgiving takes time.
> 4. Forgiving does not require forgetting.
> 5. Ideally, forgiving leads to reconciliation.
> 6. Forgiving comes naturally to the forgiven.[7]

As forgiven disciples of Jesus Christ, may we be urged on to love
and forgive those who have breached a trust, spoken a harsh
word, performed an evil deed, or hurt our weakened hearts. Hold-

ing onto disappointment in another is crippling to our spirits, and we need the cleansing of the Holy Spirit in order to redeem the wrongdoing. You have my prayers for this task—one of the most difficult of all for every believer in search of spiritual and relational health.

Principle 5.5 Additional Time

When all is said and done, if we truly want to foster loving and caring relationships within the body of Christ and every one of our spheres of influence, it will take considerable time and energy. Time is the most precious commodity of the twenty-first century. We can have all the luxuries this world has to offer, but without time to enjoy life with those we love the most, the things of this world all wither away into nothing. If relationships matter significantly to you and yours, then time is the greatest gift you can give to one another. There's no time like the present to reprioritize your life around time spent deepening the health of your relationships so that at the end of your life you won't have to wish you could have spent more time with those you love.

Despite the myth that quantity of time doesn't matter as much as quality, I respectfully disagree. Both quantity and quality are important factors in moving relationships toward the goals we have covered throughout this chapter. Quantity + Quality = Quantum growth in relationships!

Later in this book we will deal with what it means to creatively manage one's time. We all have the same amount of time available to us as we fill each day and each week. It is wise to think through whom we are seeking to become as we make decisions regarding how we fill our calendars, with whom we spend our time, and what purposes we seek to achieve. Suffice it to say, if your goal is to deepen your commitment to loving and caring relationships, then *time* is your greatest available resource. Use it well and you will become a healthier disciple of Jesus Christ. He was the perfect example of time well spent here on earth with a quantum reach toward eternal significance for every moment spent with others. May it be so in our generation as well.

A Disciple's Prayer

Dear God, you know how I feel about the people you've sent my direction for these many years. I count each one as a precious gift from you. For the sake of the strained relationships I'm having today, I pray that you will bring healing and hope back into the center of our interactions with one another. For the healthy relationships I'm enjoying, help me to do my part in fostering deeper satisfaction and enhanced understanding.

You have modeled extravagant love for us, and those who knew you and loved you in return are role models for today. May my life embody some of those same characteristics so that I too can be a catalyst for extravagant love in my relational connections within my family, church, community, workplace, and circle of friends.

I long to be your vessel of agape love. I want to exhibit absolute joy. I desire to empathically affirm others in my communication with them. I need your help to contribute to the resolving of conflict. And, oh, how I lean in your direction for wisdom in managing my time so that I can give both quantity and quality to others. Envelop me with your love and care so that out of that vital spiritual experience with you I may joyfully share your love and care with all who cross my path. For your glory and in your name I pray. Amen.

For Reflection and Renewal

The healthy disciple prioritizes the qualities of relational vitality that lead to genuine love for one another in the home, workplace, church, and community.

An anonymous e-mail arrived via cyberspace that caught my attention. It's included here as an appropriate reflection exercise for contemplating the roots and models of our healthiest relationships.

Can you name the five wealthiest people in the world? The last five Heisman trophy winners? The last five winners of the

Miss America contest? Five people who have won the Nobel or Pulitzer Prize? Five Academy Award winners for best actor or actress? The last decade's worth of World Series winners?

Very few of us remember the headlines of yesterday. These are no second-rate achievers. They're the best in their fields. But the applause dies. Awards tarnish. Achievements are forgotten. Accolades and certificates are buried with their owners.

Consider another quiz. You are guaranteed to do better on this one!

1. List a few teachers who aided your journey through school.
2. Name three friends who have helped you through a difficult time.
3. Name five people who have taught you something worthwhile.
4. Think of a few people who have made you feel appreciated and special.
5. List five people you enjoy spending time with.
6. Name a half dozen heroes whose stories have inspired you.

A little easier than the first set of questions? The lesson here is that the people who make a difference in your life aren't the ones with the most credentials, the most money, or the most awards. They're the ones who care and love and pour courage into your heart.

Commit to becoming that kind of person *today*. Don't forget to complete the quiz above. In fact, you may want to add this list of key people in your life to your prayer journal. And by all means, be sure to write a note of thanks to as many of them as possible so they hear how they brought a commitment to loving and caring relationships to life for you!

Repentance exercise. With whom do you need to resolve a long-standing or short-term conflict? Pause and pray and ask God to direct you to specific ways you can approach this person with a genuine apology, seek their forgiveness, and restore the relationship with love and caring. Don't allow the Judas-in-you to cloud what God would desire most—Jesus-in-you!

6

Exhibits Christlike Servanthood

The healthy disciple practices God-honoring servanthood in every relational context of life and ministry.

I have set you an example that you should do as I have done for you.

John 13:15

When "Mama Nellie" Yarborough founded the Mt. Calvary Holy Church on Otisfield Street in Dorchester, Massachusetts, in 1962, she single-handedly created a tight-knit congregation that looks to her for moral, spiritual, and daily strength. "Mama Nellie won't reveal her exact age, but at 70-something, her strength and energy has not waned despite the hardships of inner city life," writes Christina Wallace. "This petite Southerner still has faith that one person can make a difference."[1] Today she is a bishop in her denomination, a school principal, and a community activist. To her colleagues and friends throughout greater Boston she is known as a faithful servant of Jesus Christ, which she has been since she was fifteen years old.

Mama Nellie has proven her servanthood over and over again. It only takes one phone call for her to rush to the side of an ailing parishioner. On most Saturday nights, she leads a neighborhood watch group and marches the streets scolding prostitutes and trying to drive them out of the Blue Hill Avenue high crime neighborhood. Every Thursday evening and Saturday morning she serves up hot meals to dozens of homeless people from the basement of her church, one of the longest-running soup kitchens in the city. She started a tutoring class for students who are failing in the classroom, organized a health workshop for women on the importance of breast cancer screening, started a neighborhood garden for people to pick up fresh produce in the summertime, and runs a drug treatment program throughout the year.

In addition, Mama Nellie has overseen the renovation of their well-worn church facility to accommodate a Christian elementary school that she founded in 1992. Instead of worrying about how the church will pay the heating bill, she forgoes a salary. "I don't take a salary. I'd rather pay the bills," says Yarborough. "It's hard, but it always works out. God has been good to me."[2]

She exudes a contagious optimism and believes it is the key to influencing lives, especially children's. Mama Nellie knows that there is always going to be a problem she can't solve or a sick person for whom her prayers won't be enough, but at least she can try. And try she does, for she exhibits Christlike servanthood toward all who cross her path daily. Nothing is too hard for her to take on. No neighborhood problem or social crisis is too daunting for this determined lady to tackle.

Mama Nellie's story brings to mind what the famous orchestra conductor, Leonard Bernstein, said when asked the question, "Mr. Bernstein, what is the most difficult instrument to play in an orchestra?" Without hesitating for a moment, he replied with quick wit, "Second fiddle. I can get plenty of first violinists, but to find one who plays second violin with as much enthusiasm or second French horn, or second flute, now that's a problem. And yet, if no one plays second, we have no harmony."

To exhibit Christlike servanthood is to be willing to play second to the needs and interests of others. Servants don't reside in the limelight of life and ministry but in the shadows of others.

To understand this truth is to comprehend what Jesus said to
his disciples when he called them to the lifestyle of a servant.
Healthy disciples who are determined to follow his example
will bring harmony to the body of Christ and effectiveness to
the ministry of the church of Jesus Christ.

The Royal Treatment

The dictionary definition of the word *servant* is "a person ar-
dently devoted to another or to a cause." When Jesus walked this
earth, his devotion was to the cause of his heavenly Father, and
his example was one of a faithful servant. He fulfilled his call with
faithful consistency, showing his disciples the fullness of his love
through many acts of servanthood.

By far one of the more dramatic expressions of Jesus' service to his disciples came during the Last Supper when he gave
them the royal treatment of washing their feet just prior to his
departure to the cross. In doing this he set an example of what
they should do for others (John 13:15). Few other incidents in
the Gospels reveal the character of Jesus and show so perfectly
his extravagant love.

"He knew that his hour of humiliation was near," writes Barclay,
"but he knew that his hour of glory was also near. Such a consciousness might well have filled him with pride; and yet, with the
knowledge of the power and the glory that were his, he washed his
disciples' feet. At that moment when he might have had supreme
pride, he had supreme humility."[3]

Bob Frederich, a pastoral mentor in New England, has been
an example of such servanthood to his beloved wife, Nona, for
all of the thirty-seven years of her increasingly debilitating illness. Bob will freely share that "as I'm doing for Nona the most
menial of tasks, I am mindful that I'm doing for her what Christ
gladly does for *his* bride, the church." Bob not only washes her
feet but cares for the most intimate needs of her daily care. To
see his face light up in talking about his beloved is to see the
face of a man who exhibits Christlike service with gladness and
singleness of heart.

Jesus knew that he had come from God and that he was going to God. He might well have had contempt for men and for the things of this world. He might well have been relieved that he was now nearly finished with the world, for he was on his way to God. However, it was just at this time, when God was nearest to him, that Jesus went to the depths of his service to his disciples. To wash the feet of the guests at a feast was the office of a slave. Why didn't the disciples think to do this first? The wonderful thing about Jesus was that his nearness to God, rather than separating him from his disciples, brought him nearer than ever to them.[4]

It is always true that the nearer we are to the heart of God, the nearer we will be to the people who surround us. Jesus dramatically displayed his heart for the Father through his servant heart for the disciples, and they were marked forever as a result.

In Luke's account of the Last Supper we find the tragic sentence, "a dispute arose among them as to which of them was considered to be greatest" (Luke 22:24). Even within sight of the cross, we find the humanness of the disciples oozing out of their most intimate of community experiences. It may very well have been their argument among themselves that led Jesus to perform such a dramatic act. The juxtaposition of his servanthood demonstrated with greater clarity the self-centeredness of the disciples. Maybe having their feet washed would wake them up to the reality of Jesus' expectations for them.

"It may well be that on the night of this last meal together they had got themselves into such a state of competitive pride that not one of them would accept the duty of seeing that the water and the towels were there to wash the feet of the company as they came in; and Jesus mended their omission in the most vivid and dramatic way."[5] He himself did what none of them were prepared to do. In fact, when disciples are so wrapped up in their own needs, it's difficult to see beyond the blinders and acknowledge others right there beside you. Jesus said to them, "Do you understand what I have done for you? . . . You call me 'Teacher' and 'Lord' and rightly so, for that is what I am. Now that I, your Lord and Teacher, have washed your feet, you also should wash one another's feet. I have set you an example that you should do as I have done for you. I tell you the truth, no servant is greater than his master, nor is a messenger greater than the one who sent him. Now that you know these things, you will be blessed if you do them" (John 13:12–17).

So often within the body of Christ, troubles emerge when someone is denied the "place" they believe they deserve. It happens when denominational dignitaries are offended for not receiving precedence befitting their title or office. It happens when a choir member is not given a solo and will not sing anymore. It happens when a player is one day benched from the roster of a team and then refuses to play anymore. Or when a politician is passed over for an office he thought he had a right to hold. Or when anyone else, for that matter, is given an unintentional slight and either responds with anger or broods for days afterwards.

When it's most tempting to think first of our rights or privileges, our prestige or our destiny, the picture of the Son of God with a towel girded around his waist and kneeling at the disciples' feet should wake us up to the reality of true servanthood. It's not all about our needs or our status or our position in life. No, true servants understand with great and growing certainty that it's all about *others,* and it's because of *him* that we center our lives around the service of Christ.

The royal treatment the disciples received was given by the King of Kings and Lord of Lords. His royalty was embodied in the attitude and actions of a servant rather than in pomp and circumstance. The simple act of foot washing was enough for Jesus to get his point across to those open to receive it.

It is not certain whether the meaning beneath the foot washing was ever fully internalized by each of the disciples. It definitely was not internalized by Judas, as he reclined at the table and had his filthy feet washed by the Savior. Judas's act of betrayal was fully and unquestionably accepted by Jesus, and the sheer cruelty of his disloyalty provided a brighter light to shine on the glory of Christ's fidelity.

It is this fidelity that we too are called to display as Jesus' disciples.

Some day these same disciples would take the message of Jesus out to the world. When they did, they would be nothing less than the representatives of God himself. An ambassador does not go out as a private individual, armed with only his own personal qualities and qualifications. He goes out with all the honor and glory of his country upon him. To listen to him is to listen to his country; to honor him is to honor the country he represents; to welcome him is to welcome the ruler who sent him out. The great honor and the great responsibility of being a pledged Christian is that we stand in the world for Jesus Christ. We speak for him; we act for him. The honor of the Eternal is in our hands.[6]

The selfless, sacrificial love of Jesus is portrayed within this simple story. His understanding and forgiving ways are difficult to fathom when placed beside our barrenness of heart and the self-centeredness of our lives. The Son of God desires to reside in the center of our broken hearts, and in his servanthood we too can find the fullness and vitality of life. Isn't it time his disciples gave the "royal treatment" to one another and to the world he has called us to serve in his name? Get down on your knees, take hold of a few feet, and show others the fullest extent of your love for them. That's what Jesus would do.

Thriving in Our Service

As a disciple in search of greater health and vitality, what is your response to the subject of servanthood? Are you thriving in an atmosphere of service to others, or are you stuck in the center of your own strivings? Many Christians today have replaced servanthood with "selfhood"—self-actualization, self-accumulation, self-satisfaction, self-fulfillment, self-this, and self-that, feeding the frenzy of "it's all about me" while at the same time denying what is happening within and around us. We've listened to the world's admonitions of "Have it your way," "Do yourself a favor," "You owe it to yourself," and "You deserve a break today," and the attitudes of Christian disciples look no different than those of the pagan next door.

Richard Foster, in his classic *Celebration of Discipline*, devotes an entire chapter to the discipline of service. He too focuses on the ministry of the towel and basin that defined Jesus' greatness before the disciples. He describes true service by contrasting it with self-righteous service, stating that "service enables us to say 'no!' to the world's games of promotion and authority. It abolishes our need (and desire) for a 'pecking order.'"[7] Distinguishing true service from self-righteous service helps us to understand and practice the kind of servanthood displayed by Jesus throughout his earthly ministry.

Foster continues his contrasting of self-righteous service versus true service in the following manner:

- Self-righteous service comes through human effort—true service comes from a relationship with God.
- Self-righteous service is impressed with the "big deal"—true service is unable to distinguish the small from the large service.
- Self-righteous service requires external rewards—true service rests contented in hiddenness.
- Self-righteous service is highly concerned about results—true service is free of the need to calculate results.
- Self-righteous service picks and chooses whom to serve—true service is indiscriminate in its ministry.
- Self-righteous service is affected by moods and whims—true service ministers simply and faithfully because there is a need.
- Self-righteous service is temporary—true service is a lifestyle.
- Self-righteous service is without sensitivity—true service listens with tenderness and patience before acting.
- Self-righteous service fractures community—true service builds community. It quietly and unpretentiously goes about caring for the needs of others. It puts no one under obligation to return the service. It draws, binds, heals, builds. The result is the unity of the community.[8]

As we have learned from Jesus and seen articulated so well by Richard Foster, service to others is much more than a list of things that we do—it is a way of living. The heart of the servant lives in the discipline of Christlike servanthood. The shapes, forms, colors, and designs of our service are formulated at the center of our loving hearts. When that occurs, the fruit of our service brings life, joy, and peace to all whom we encounter in our daily lives.

Foster helps us further by defining what this discipline looks like. For the Christ-follower, living in the discipline of service means we are comfortable in the service of:

- Hiddenness—giving anonymously and quietly
- Small things—consistently sharing the little things that bring such joy
- Guarding the reputation of others—not participating in gossip or slander
- Active helpfulness—going beyond the "I'll pray for you" into action
- Being served—allowing others the opportunity to serve you when in need
- Common courtesy—commonsense Christianity
- Hospitality—opening our homes and hearts to others
- Listening—allowing others the gift of being heard
- Bearing the burdens of each other—hurting with those who hurt
- Sharing the Word of life with one another—witnessing in word, thought, and deed; opening the Scriptures together, praying, and so on[9]

When all is said and done, if we desire to be servants we must submit to Christ in all of our thoughts, words, and deeds. In essence, it's learning a process of self-emptying—letting go of our own needs and agendas and embracing the concerns of those around us. The main problem in servanthood is to "be the way" without getting "in the way." When we can identify the obstacles that keep us from living out true service, we are cleaner, clearer vessels for the outflow of the love of Christ. When that occurs, we know with certainty that we are thriving in our service.

Why Feet?

In order for us to become cleaner vessels for the outflow of Christ's love, it will require that we reflect on our heart's attitude toward servanthood. When we read the story of Jesus washing the feet of his disciples, we may be repulsed with the thought of touching someone else's feet. I understand this completely, since I have one of the ugliest set of feet to walk planet earth. Not only do I not want to touch someone else's feet, but I certainly do not want someone to touch mine.

It's hard to admit such a thing—a Christian disciple not wanting to follow the example of Christ. In my nearly five decades of life, I've found more people like me who are uncomfortable with the thought of foot washing. Couldn't Jesus have come up with a better analogy for servanthood, such as back scratching? Or shoulder rubbing? Or hugging? Why all this talk of feet? What do our feet have to do with our hearts?

Well, in the days of Christ, dirty feet were the norm. The roads were dusty or muddy, the sandals were well-worn and susceptible to all the elements. At the entrances to most homes, there was a jug of water awaiting all guests, and at times there was a servant available to wash the tired feet of the traveler. Feet were known for being the dirtiest part of the body, and they required continual cleaning and attention. So, lest you be too hard on yourself for not liking the idea of washing feet, it was one of the most commonplace activities of Jesus' day.

Today our feet are usually covered, and our shoe selection is more like that of Imelda Marcos than Jesus. We have more sandals, dress shoes, athletic wear, and casual footwear than anyone in Jesus' day could ever imagine. In fact, we have so many shoes that we don't think about the need to wash our feet—they hardly get dirty enough in a given day. Yet since we still have such a fetish about having our feet touched by someone else, there may be a deeper meaning to this.

Quite possibly the reason we don't want to talk about feet or touch feet or think about the feet of another is that by enclosing ours in such garb we are hiding them. To reveal the status of our feet beyond a simple glance may in fact show something far deeper about the state of our hearts. What are we hiding that we don't want revealed or touched by another? Is there something about our protectiveness that shields us from such intimacy with another, or with God?

I'll never forget the first time I participated in a foot-washing ceremony. It was on the final night of my first mission trip to Haiti as a young pastor. We had worked well as a multiracial team for over a week serving children in a hospital, a clinic for the severely handicapped, a school, and an orphanage. We were intensely engaged in ministry from sunup to sundown. Our minds were stretched, our hearts were fully engaged, and after long days of serving, our bodies and our feet were tired.

There were moments during that trip when I couldn't wait to be home, and there were times when I thought I'd never want to go home. I fell in love with this impoverished land and her people. I was drawn to the desperate needs of the children and brokenhearted when at one point in the trip a mother held out her infant and asked me to please take her home to the States where she'd get a much better life. I was torn apart inside as one child after another flashed before my eyes, and their physical, spiritual, and emotional needs were more than any one of us could comprehend.

It was on the final night of that missions trip that our leaders decided to host a foot-washing ceremony. We filed into the room one at a time, not knowing what we were getting into. The ones who had gone before us were still lingering around the perimeter of the room, now prayerful on behalf of those who had just arrived. I was asked to be seated by Bill Matthews, one of the volunteers from our church who helped out on the trip. He quietly unlaced my sneakers, took off one sock at a time, held my two tired feet in his hands, looked up at my eyes, and started to share with me how much the trip had meant to him and how he had seen the love of Jesus living through me in a number of ministry settings. We had known each other from involvement in our local church children's ministry, and this trip had knit our lives together in a much deeper way. He talked about our shared experiences for what seemed like an hour but was in reality only a few choice moments in time.

My heart melted right then and there. I lost it and started to cry uncontrollably, weeping lavishly, overwhelmed by the power of the experience, the words that were spoken, the images of our past week of ministry, and the need for others to come along after us to serve the children of this nation who lived in such dire circumstances. The fact that Bill was holding and washing my feet was nothing in comparison to the service we had done together in Jesus' name in Haiti. All inhibitions were lost, there was no time to cover up or protect what was going on inside of me. The washing of feet brought out the state of my heart, and the worship that emerged from this incredible experience was unparalleled in my Christian walk.

When I realized what had happened so dramatically in our "upper room" that night, I determined to never worry again about who saw my ugly feet. It really doesn't matter, for the deeper meaning beneath the surface of the foot washing is to get under our skin and penetrate deeply into our souls regarding our willingness to embrace the posture of a servant. In many respects we simply need to serve others in the name of Jesus and allow them the same privilege of serving us in return. The life transformation we experience will undoubtedly change us forever. This is what Christ calls us to do for one another, and it's nothing short of humble, Christlike servanthood.

Principle 6.1 A Towel and Basin

Jesus showed his disciples the fullest extent of his love beginning with the foot-washing ceremony but culminating on the cross at Calvary. It was on the cross that he "made himself nothing, taking the very nature of a servant, being made in human likeness. And being found in appearance as a man, he humbled himself and became obedient to death—even death on a cross!" (Phil. 2:7–8). The cross brought closure to Jesus' life here on earth in a dramatic fashion. It became the symbol of his life and remains a symbol of

Christianity. There is nothing more significant for us as believers than to live in the awareness that on the cross our sins were paid for, once and for all, and the life he lived and death he died were so that we too could die to self in order that others can live. The lifestyle of the servant births life in others, and for that joyful privilege of participating in God's redemptive work here on earth we offer a hearty "Thank you, Lord!"

In Philippians 2 the apostle Paul urged all disciples of Christ to imitate his humility in all our acts of servanthood. "Do nothing out of selfish ambition or vain conceit, but in humility consider others better than yourselves. Each of you should look not only to your own interests, but also to the interests of others" (Phil. 2:3–4). Having been forgiven of our sins, reconciled into a right relationship with God the Father, and empowered to serve others by the Holy Spirit, we are fit to exhibit Christlike servanthood out of humble obedience. It is only when we are empowered by God to serve others that we are able to give ourselves fully in this manner.

Having an attitude of servanthood is the place where it all begins. We aren't inclined to pick up a towel and wash basin unless our hearts are attuned to God's purposes for us. During an intense week of missionary service in a foreign land, the atmosphere is conducive to such an attitude. However, in the daily grind of our personal lives and ministries, this attitude isn't as easily reflected. Ask God each day to give you his heart for serving others, and he will grant your request and open up opportunities to serve (towel and basin are optional!).

Principle 6.2 A Servant's Heart

Jesus had a heart for service. "Whoever wants to become great among you must be your servant, and whoever wants to be first must be your slave—just as the Son of Man did not come to be served, but to serve, and to give his life as a ransom for many" (Matt. 20:26–28). The paradox here is fitting—in his eyes, the greatest is really the least, the slave is considered first, and the servant is the priority posture for the disciple. Jesus lived this out over and over again in his consistent role as the servant to all, and he encouraged all his followers to do the same.

The ransom Jesus paid was his very life, and his call upon his disciples was the same—offer your very life and give to others from your heart. A true servant's heart is apparent in the words that are spoken, the attitudes that are reflected, and the actions that emanate outward toward all who come our way. The journey of servanthood is exhilarating, for the road holds many new twists and turns. When our hearts are inclined to Christ, we are ready at a moment's notice to respond in love to those who surround us.

For decades Mama Nellie Yarborough has been vulnerable in showing her heart of love and service to her church family and neighborhood community on a daily basis. As a result, her infectious heart of love spills out over countless lives that have been blessed by her obedient life of servanthood, and the fruit of her labors are evidenced in the changed lives of those she has been called to serve. All of Mama Nellie's service is for the glory of God, and all of it comes out of her loving, prayerful heart that has been given over to the purposes of God for this generation.

Principle 6.3 A Willingness to Give and Receive

Disciples of Jesus are called to be givers more than takers. Paul calls us to "share with God's people who are in need. Practice hospitality" (Rom. 12:13).

Coming home after a holiday vacation, our flight was delayed for several hours due to a snowstorm that had crippled the east coast. When we finally arrived at 1:45 A.M., it was such a joy to be greeted at the airport by our dear friends, David and Carolyn. They followed through on their commitment to meet us at baggage claim and taxi us home to our front door. They had unbegrudgingly waited at the airport into the wee hours of the morning after having shoveled out our long driveway and front walk earlier in the evening. Their acts of kindness were underscored when we discovered that they had just received word that same afternoon that Carolyn's father had passed away. There she was serving our family amidst the deep pain of her own personal loss. We were overwhelmed by their Christlike service in our behalf.

David and Carolyn have been godly examples of servanthood for more than two decades of friendship. Over and over again they have shown themselves to be givers more than takers. Their sacrificial service is done with an attitude of love and an earnest desire to give. Their willingness to consistently serve has provided a role model for us as disciples of Jesus Christ. They live out what St. Francis of Assisi prayed, "It is in giving that we receive." Their lives are ever the richer as a result of their giving hearts.

Giving to others is exhibited in numerous ways, such as:

- Investing time, energy, love, gifts, and guidance in another.
- Loving unconditionally, despite others' shortcomings and idiosyncrasies.
- Sharing our wisdom and insights so that others can grow and mature.
- Giving hospitality and companionship to the lonely and disenfranchised.
- Serving anonymously and in small, hidden ways, without need for recognition.
- Graciously and gratefully receiving the service of another.

When we give generously of ourselves, we do not need recognition or reciprocation. However, we should also learn how to graciously receive gifts of love and acts of kindness when they are given to us in return.

Principle 6.4 A Listening Ear

One of the greatest gifts we can offer to another is a listening ear. Romans 12:15 says, "Rejoice with those who rejoice; mourn with those who mourn." Thankfully, I'm blessed to have a wife who earnestly desires to listen to me—no matter the subject, the need, or even the time of day. Ruthie is there to rejoice when I rejoice, mourn when I mourn, offer perspective when I've lost my way, and harmonize when I'm in need of an alternative opinion. Her willingness to serve me through her listening ear has been one of her greatest gifts of love and service to me.

Far too often we disciples tend to talk more than listen, give an answer more than ask a question, think of a response more than request an opinion. Unfortunately, today's disciples of Jesus Christ are not known for our listening skills. We usually come across as know-it-alls instead of humble listeners, attending to the heart cries of those within our sphere of influence. We need to be available as listeners who are there for others no matter the need or situation, ready to speak words of hope and encouragement into their hearts.

Healthy disciples who are listeners more than talkers exhibit the following traits:

- Accept the other person's words, thoughts, attitudes, and expressions without need to correct or rebuke.
- Guard the reputation of the person by listening and maintaining confidences; never speaking inappropriately about another.
- Show common courtesy toward others simply by listening, praying, and offering counsel when appropriate.
- Desire of understanding the situation at hand so that quality guidance can be offered in the hope of remaining helpful and supportive.

Principle 6.5 A Life Well Lived

Jesus' disciples are called to be peacemakers rather than troublemakers. The apostle Paul wrote, "Do not repay anyone evil for evil. Be careful to do what is right in the eyes of everybody. If it is possible, as far as it depends on you, live at peace with everyone" (Rom. 12:17–18).

Early in my Christian pilgrimage, the man who had led me to Christ, Rich Plass, was deeply hurt by the leaders of our church. As a new believer and a high school student, I became bitterly angry toward the church for not trusting my new friend and his significant ministry. Not fully understanding the theological differences between a liberal church and my evangelical friend's theological stance, I became disillusioned with the church and its leaders. Rather than fueling that bitter fire, Rich chose to be a peacemaker instead of a troublemaker. He used this painful experience to teach me about the differences that existed between his beliefs and those of our church leaders. As a result, my deep disappointments were turned into prayers of forgiveness and restoration, and I grew because of his Christlike attitude.

How often are we faced with similar trials in our lives of faith, when it's easier to stir the pot of trouble between factions within the community rather than speak in a reconciling tone of compassionate empathy? The Christ-honoring servant will choose to be a peacemaker in troubled times and will turn a deaf ear to those who participate in fueling the fire of disagreement or disappointment. God's call is to always be peacemakers, and our motivation needs to remain purely focused on the needs of those we serve in the process.

In assessing our hearts as servants of Jesus Christ, we need to ask ourselves if the following impetus is behind our service as peacemakers:

- Am I desirous of the growth and maturity of others?
- Do I want to see them reconciled to God and one another?
- Will I lead them toward confession and forgiveness, marked by love, in the peacemaking process?
- Are humility and the ability to freely say "I'm sorry; I was wrong; please forgive me" the notable hallmarks of the peacemaking process?

If we are to become more like Jesus in our servanthood, we must be willing to wash the feet of others, reflect his heart, and exhibit a servant's lifestyle as givers more than takers, listeners more than talkers, and peacemakers more than troublemakers. Is this the posture of your life? It's not an impossibility for those who claim the name of Christ and lean totally on the Holy Spirit for their daily lives and service. The accumulation of days filled with small acts of servanthood, steadily and consistently offered to others, makes for a life well lived. May it be so for you and for our entire generation of healthy disciples.

Dying to Self

When you are forgotten, or neglected, or purposely set at naught, and you don't sting and hurt with the insult or the oversight, but your heart is happy, being counted worthy to suffer for Christ,
THAT IS DYING TO SELF.

When your good is evil spoken of, when your wishes are crossed, your advice disregarded, your opinions ridiculed, and you refuse to let anger rise in your heart, or even defend yourself, but take it all in patient, loving silence,
THAT IS DYING TO SELF.

When you lovingly and patiently bear any disorder, any irregularity, and impunctuality, or any annoyance; when you can stand face-to-face with waste, folly, extravagance, spiritual insensibility . . . and endure it as Jesus endured it,
THAT IS DYING TO SELF.

When you are content with any food, any offering, any raiment, any climate, any society, any solitude, any interruption by the will of God,
THAT IS DYING TO SELF.

When you no longer care to hear yourself in conversation, or to record your own good works, or itch after commendation, when you can truly love to be unknown,
THAT IS DYING TO SELF.

When you can see your brother prosper and have his needs met, and can honestly rejoice with him in spirit and feel no envy nor question God, while your own needs are far greater and in desperate circumstance,
THAT IS DYING TO SELF.

When you can receive correction and reproof from one of less stature than yourself, and can humbly submit inwardly as well as outwardly, finding no rebellion or resentment rising up within your heart,
THAT IS DYING TO SELF.

                                                      Author Unknown

A Disciple's Prayer

Lord Jesus, as I reflect on the principles of servanthood, I am not only reminded of your incredible example of service to all you met, but I am also mindful of how far I fall short of this priority in my own life. Forgive my self-centered pride that keeps me from loving, giving, listening, and reconciling. Release me from my continual preoccupation with my own needs, and open my heart up to the opportunities before me to offer myself in service to those within my family, church, workplace, and community.

When I pause in silence to consider the many heart cries of those around me, I am aware of many tangible and intangible gifts I can share with those whom you call me to love. May my willingness to gird myself with a towel and carry around a basin of grace and mercy be well received in both surprising and empowering ways. I long to thrive in my service to you and to all who cross my path. I want to be used of you to influence many for the sake and cause of Christ.

Do your cleansing work within me, I pray, so that I may become a clean vessel for your glory. This I pray in the all-powerful, loving, and tender name of Jesus the Servant of all. Amen.

For Reflection and Renewal

The healthy disciple practices God-honoring servanthood in every relationship context of life and ministry.

1. In this past week, how have others blessed you in their service in your behalf? List the many ways you've been served, and note especially the names of the individuals who gave of themselves for you. What can you do in this coming week to express your gratitude for their service?
2. As you read through the anonymous poem "Dying to Self," what images came to mind that reflect an embodiment of these principles within you and others in the Christian community? How are these examples of servanthood "God sightings" in your midst?

3. Read Romans 12:9–13. How does this paragraph reflect the servanthood principle of being "givers more than takers"?

4. Read Romans 12:14–16. How do these verses reflect the servanthood principle of being "listeners more than talkers"?

5. Read Romans 12:17–18. How do these verses reflect the servanthood principle of being "peacemakers more than troublemakers"?

6. How would you assess the status of your servant heart today? What cleansing and restorative work needs to be done within you in order for you to become a healthier servant of Christ, exhibiting his heart, attitude, and behavior in the coming week/month/year?

7. Write out a prayer to the Lord focusing on your thoughts from the above questions and reflections.

7

Shares the Love of Christ Generously

The healthy disciple maximizes every opportunity to share the love of Christ, in word and deed, with those outside the faith.

For God so loved the world that he gave his one and only Son, that whoever believes in him shall not perish but have eternal life.

John 3:16

Maria, Hector, and Collins are three very special friends of ours. In fact, they've become an important part of our family over the past few years.

Maria lives with her mother, grandfather, and two siblings. She loves to play volleyball, tell stories, and spend time with her friends. She regularly attends Sunday school and has participated in Vacation Bible School over the past few years. She's only seven years old, but her growth potential is incredible. Her dark, flowing black hair and beautiful eyes are sure to steal the heart of anyone who comes in contact with her.

Hector lives with his parents and six brothers and sisters. He's only four years old and enjoys playing with toy cars and neighborhood friends from sunup to sundown. His dad is often unemployed, and his mother spends all her time maintaining their modest home. Although Hector attends Sunday school on occasion, there are obvious needs emerging in his life that require prayerful attention and assistance. He has a look of curiosity and excitement in his eyes and a compelling attraction to our daughter, Rebekah, who wishes she could spend more time with this young boy.

Collins is turning the corner into adolescence, and his strapping good looks and dark complexion will most certainly draw a second glance from the young girls in his community. He lives on a farm with his mother and two siblings. He likes to help around the house, gathering firewood and assisting in the kitchen. Soccer and any other active sport are Collins's favorite outside activities. He's an average student who needs a lot of academic coaching in order to grow into a better student. He appreciates kind acts and responds with helpfulness. He has a heart for his family and a love for learning and life, so we are confident he will succeed in the years ahead of him.

Although Maria, Hector, and Collins appear to us on a day-to-day basis through their photographs that don the front of our refrigerator, in actual fact they live in Peru and Kenya. We have "adopted" them into our family through a relief and development agency, and they have captured our hearts as a result. Even though all we do is send them financial resources, letters, and photographs, they have come to know us as people who also offer many prayers and lots of love on their behalf. Having Maria, Hector, and Collins as a part of our lives provides a daily reminder of our need to share the love of Christ generously with others, and it has created an extension of our small family into two countries of our world that we have never visited.

So often we declare ourselves outwardly focused when in fact we are isolated to the writing of checks in support of what others are doing on our behalf. Sharing our financial resources is merely one (albeit *very* important) aspect of becoming a healthy disciple who sacrificially reaches out to another "with a cup of cold water in Jesus' name." What we do for Maria, Hector, and Collins is significant for them—and for us—but it's not the sum total of what Jesus is calling us to do as Great Commission disciples. His call for us is to participate in the dynamic process of making disciples—all over the world. Having invited them into the kingdom of God, we are then to see to it that they are baptized in the name of the Father, Son, and Holy Spirit, teaching them to live in faithful obedience to the Word and the will of God (Matt. 28:18–20). That's the joy of sharing the love of Christ!

This principle of discipleship health is embodied in a well-balanced approach to outreach. It means that:

- Within our family unit we are consistently living out Christ-honoring values in front of parents, siblings, children, and extended family members.
- Within our friendships, in our neighborhood, and at work we are striving to portray a lifestyle befitting Christ. This is evidenced in the words we speak, the attitudes we reflect, the decisions we make, and the actions we fulfill, working through issues, circumstances, and relationships in a manner that honors God and reflects his priorities.
- In our urban (as well as an increasing number of rural) centers, we are ensuring that time, talent, and treasure are extended to those in need—the homeless are provided for, the poor are prayerfully cared for, and the indigent are sacrificially considered priority within the mix of societal woes.
- Around the globe, those who are working feverishly to spread the Good News of Christ are supported, affirmed, thanked, visited, and prayed for on an ongoing basis. They are on the front lines of some of the most difficult work, confronting the powers of darkness and proclaiming the light of Christ in desperate corners of our globe.
- Most importantly, the children and families of this world who suffer from AIDS, malnutrition, famine, war, and gross poverty are reached with practical, humanitarian, emotional, and spiritual sustenance.

Sharing the love of Christ generously touches on our need to be involved at one level or another in:

- evangelism with neighbors, friends, family, and work associates
- social action in needy rural communities and urban centers
- international missions endeavors
- worldwide relief and development

It's overwhelming to consider the needs of our world today. They are growing in every community and on every continent. No place is immune to having needs. Therefore, it's incumbent upon us as Christian disciples to discern and meet needs wherever possible and by whatever means we have within our grasp. However, the meeting of such needs only comes to fruition out of a heart that's been penetrated with the love of Christ and overwhelmed by the opportunity to reach out to those who are lost and in need of a Savior—and all along the way, offering a cup of cold water in Jesus' name.

Jesus and Nicodemus

Let's consider the following passage:

Now there was a man of the Pharisees named Nicodemus, a member of the Jewish ruling council. He came to Jesus at night and said, "Rabbi, we know you are a teacher who has come from God. For no one could perform the miraculous signs you are doing if God were not with him."

In reply Jesus declared, "I tell you the truth, no one can see the kingdom of God unless he is born again."

"How can a man be born when he is old?" Nicodemus asked. "Surely he cannot enter a second time into his mother's womb to be born!"

Jesus answered, "I tell you the truth, no one can enter the kingdom of God unless he is born of water and the Spirit. Flesh gives birth to flesh, but the Spirit gives birth to spirit. You should not be surprised at my saying, 'You must be born again.' The wind blows wherever it pleases. You hear its sound, but you cannot tell where it comes from or where it is going. So it is with everyone born of the Spirit."

"How can this be?" Nicodemus asked.

"You are Israel's teacher," said Jesus, "and do you not understand these things? I tell you the truth, we speak of what we know, and we testify to what we have seen, but still you people do not accept our testimony. I have spoken to you of earthly things and you do not believe; how then will you believe if I speak of heavenly things? No one has ever gone into heaven except the one who came from heaven—the Son of Man. Just as Moses lifted up the snake in the desert, so the Son of Man must be lifted up, that everyone who believes in him may have eternal life.

"For God so loved the world that he gave his one and only Son, that whoever believes in him shall not perish but have eternal life. For God did not send his Son into the world to condemn the world, but to save the world through him. Whoever believes in him is not condemned, but whoever does not believe stands condemned already because he has not believed in the name of God's one and only Son. This is the verdict: Light has come into the world, but men loved darkness instead of light because their deeds were evil. Everyone who does evil hates the light, and will not come into the light for fear that his deeds will be exposed. But whoever lives by the truth comes into the light, so that it may be seen plainly that what he has done has been done through God."

John 3:1–21, italics added

In this engaging interchange between Jesus and Nicodemus, we discover many significant insights into one of the earliest stories of Jesus' evangelistic outreach. Nicodemus, a wealthy Pharisee and ruler of the Jews who belonged to a distinguished family and knew the law better than most, came to Jesus one night in search of some answers. His questions had obviously been stirring around in his head since Jesus first came to town. He wanted a private, undisturbed conversation with Jesus. As a puzzled and perplexed man, he came to the personification of Light in the dark stillness of the night.

It's fascinating to see how the conversation emerged between Jesus and Nicodemus. John had a distinct scheme for recording such conversations with Jesus and his enquirers. We see that scheme very clearly here:

- The enquirer says something: "Rabbi, we know you are a teacher who has come from God. For no one could perform the miraculous signs you are doing if God were not with him" (v. 2).
- Jesus answers in a saying that is hard to understand: "I tell you the truth, no one can see the kingdom of God unless he is born again" (v. 3).
- Jesus' saying is misunderstood by the enquirer: "How can a man be born when he is old? . . . Surely he cannot enter a second time into his mother's womb to be born!" (v. 4).
- Jesus answers with a saying that is even more difficult to understand: "I tell you the truth, no one can enter the kingdom of God unless he is born of water and the Spirit" (v. 5).
- This is followed by a discourse and an explanation: "Flesh gives birth to flesh, but the Spirit gives birth to spirit. You should not be surprised at my saying, 'You must be born again.' The wind blows wherever it pleases. You hear its sound, but you cannot tell where it comes from or where it is going. So it is with everyone born of the Spirit" (vv. 6–8), with additional explanation in the following verses.[1]

The "born again" phrase caught Nicodemus short. He couldn't imagine such a concept! His understanding of the Greek word *anothen* had different meanings: (a) from the beginning, or completely radical; (b) again, in the sense of "for the second time"; and (c) from above, and therefore, from God. For Jesus to have used this word to mean all three connotations was perplexing for Nicodemus. "To be born anew is to undergo such a radical change that it is like a new birth; it is to have something happen to the soul which can only be described as being born all over again; and the whole process is not a human achievement, because it comes from the grace and power of God."[2] How could this devoted Pharisee give up everything he had lived for and follow such a radical thought, never mind such a radical *person*? It was preposterous—unless of course it was perceived as being "of God." Nicodemus's literalism kept him from understanding the deeper message being conveyed so lovingly by Jesus. As a result, even the continuation of the dialogue never penetrated the depths of his soul.

The Context (John 3:14–15)

In order to grasp the significance of John 3:16 (the key verse of this trait of a healthy disciple), the context of conversation between Jesus and Nicodemus must be considered. Jesus took Nicodemus back to the Old Testament story of Numbers 21:4–9 when he said, "Just as Moses lifted up the snake in the desert, so the Son of Man must be lifted up, that everyone who believes in him may have eternal life" (John 3:14–15). When the Israelites were on their journey through the wilderness, they murmured and complained and regretted that they had ever left Egypt. Barclay says,

> To punish them, God sent a plague of deadly, fiery serpents; the people repented and cried for mercy. God instructed Moses to make an image of a serpent and to hold it up in the midst of the camp; and those who looked upon the serpent were healed. That story much impressed the Israelites. They told how in later times that brazen serpent became an idol and in the days of Hezekiah had to be destroyed because people were worshipping it (2 Kings 18:4). The Jews themselves were always a little puzzled by this incident in view of the fact that they were absolutely forbidden to make graven images. The rabbis explained it this way: "It was not the serpent that gave life. So long as Moses lifted up the serpent, they believed on him who had commanded Moses to act thus. It was God who healed them." The healing power lay not in the brazen serpent; it was only a symbol to turn their thoughts to God; and when they did that they were healed.[3]

Jesus was explaining to Nicodemus that in the same way the serpent was lifted up for the people to see in order that their thoughts would return to God and they would be healed, so it was with Jesus. He must be lifted up so that when the people turn their hearts and minds to him and believe in him, they will in turn be healed and granted the gift of eternal life.

Jesus was lifted up on the cross *and* lifted up in glory. The two "liftings" are inextricably connected. The one could not happen without the other. "For Jesus the Cross was the way to glory; had he refused it, had he evaded it, had he taken steps to escape it, as he might so easily have done, there would have been no glory for him. It is the same for us. We can, if we like, choose the easy way; we can, if we like, refuse the cross that every Christian is called to bear; but if we do, we lose the glory. It is an unalterable law of life that if there is no cross, there is no crown."[4]

Therefore, by affirming the centrality of the cross of Christ, the seeker begins to grapple with two other essential principles: believing in Jesus and experiencing eternal life. Believing in Jesus is the starting point of a life of faith. It means that with all our hearts we affirm what Jesus declared: God loves and cares for us and longs to forgive us of our sins, and that Jesus is God's Son who came to earth to tell us the absolute truth about God. Three times in John 3:1–15 Jesus is quoted as saying, "I tell you the truth." Believing in Jesus is believing in his truth. As a result we can stake everything on the fact that what Jesus says is true. Belief in Jesus leads to an understanding that God is our loving Father, Jesus is his one and only Son, and as Jesus has taught us truth about God and life, we must unswervingly respond with an open heart of love and obedience.

Then, having believed in Jesus, the gift he offers is eternal life. Eternal life is the very life of God himself. To have eternal life envelops every relationship in life with peace.

- *Peace with God:* We are no longer cringing before a tyrannical king or seeking to hide from an austere judge. We are at home with our Father.
- *Peace with others:* As forgiven ones, we must be forgiving. In his peace, we see others as God sees them. This brings us into the family of God, joined in love for one another.
- *Peace with life:* God our Father is working all things together for good. Such a loving Father will not cause his child a needless tear. We may not understand life any better, but we will not resent life any longer.
- *Peace with ourselves:* In the midst of our own weaknesses, temptations, tasks, and demands of life, we know that we

face it all with God by our side. It is not we who live, but Christ who lives within us.

- *Peace with eternity:* We know that by believing in Jesus, the deepest peace we experience here on earth is only a shadow of the ultimate peace, which is to come. This is our hope and our goal for the journey we travel on earth and in heaven.

The Conclusion (John 3:16)

Fully aware of the significance of his message, Jesus jumped right into the heart of his interchange with Nicodemus by stating, as Paul Harvey would say, "the rest of the story." This singular verse, known as "everybody's text," is the essence of the gospel that needs to be shared generously with everyone we know. This favorite-of-favorite texts, the one we memorized at the start of our Christian journey, tells us specific truths of note. "For God so loved the world that he gave his one and only Son, that whoever believes in him shall not perish but have eternal life."

By jumping to the conclusion, or the goal, Jesus is saying that when we speak of salvation, the initiative lies with God.

It is with God that it all started. It was God who sent his Son, and he sent him because he loved men. At the back of everything [about the gospel] is the love of God. It shows us God acting not for his own sake, but for ours, not to satisfy his desire for power, not to bring a universe to heel, but to satisfy his love. God is the Father who cannot be happy until his wandering children have come home. He yearns over them and woos them into love. And, it tells us of the width of the love of God. It was the world that God so loved. It was not a nation; it was not the good people; it was not only the people who loved him; it was the world. The unlovable and the unlovely, the lonely who have no one else to love them, the man who loves God and the man who never thinks of him, the man who rests in the love of God and the man who spurns it—all are included in this vast inclusive love of God. As Augustine put it: "God loves each one of us as if there was only one of us to love."[5]

Jesus' invitation to Nicodemus is the same invitation he offers to us. God, who Jesus represents as a person of the Trinity, desires more than anything else to draw us into his loving arms and make us part of his family. The offer extends to all people in all corners of the earth until he comes again and ushers us into glory forever. What greater love can there be than this incredible invitation of love from God?

The Choice (John 3:17–21)

Making the choice to receive the gift of salvation in Jesus Christ reveals one of the great paradoxes of the Christian faith. In this passage we learn of the paradox of love and judgment. On the heels of hearing about the apex of love through Jesus, we are brought back to the stark reality for those who reject his love. The end result for those who choose darkness is the verdict of judgment and damnation.

We generally don't like to talk about or even hear about such a gloomy topic. Yet the choice for the seeker is made crystal clear for Nicodemus through this loving confrontation with the Savior. If a person is confronted with Jesus and responds to that wonder and beauty, he or she is certainly on the way to salvation. "But if, when he is confronted with Jesus, he sees nothing lovely, he stands condemned. His reaction has condemned him. God sent Jesus in love. He sent him for that man's salvation; but that which was sent in love has become a condemnation. It is not God who has condemned the man; God only loved him; the man has condemned himself."[6]

When people react in hostility to Jesus, they are loving the darkness instead of the light. By one's reaction to Jesus, a person stands fully revealed and one's soul is fully exposed. If we see that others regard Christ with love and affection, even if not with overwhelming flamboyance or enthusiasm, for them hope remains. If there is total disregard for Christ, however, that person has condemned himself or herself for now and all eternity.

Jesus spoke a powerful word of truth to Nicodemus, and we listen over the shoulder of history for his response. Eternity rests in the balance for this seeker, as it has for each seeker since.

What Jesus said to Nicodemus turned his internal universe of faith upside down. He was a curious inquirer and obviously a man of spiritual perception. Beyond that, we know very little about him with the exception of a few verses that reintroduce him later. (John 7:50–52 shows Nicodemus's fair-mindedness toward Jesus, even taking the risk of stating his viewpoint in front of his fellow Pharisees. John 19:38–42 displays his loving, although belated, service to Jesus as he assists Joseph in preparing him for burial.)

Regardless of the response Jesus received from each seeker he met, we know with certainty that the gospel he lived and preached ultimately transformed the world. Ever since then, disciples have been following what Jesus began as a word-of-mouth movement that won't end until he comes again. Praise God for his soon coming glory!

What Would Jesus Do?

Earlier in John's Gospel, we read about how the first disciples were selected by Jesus. In John 1:35–51, the writer gives us a glimpse into who made up this motley crew of Christ-followers. The first thing an excited Andrew did after meeting Jesus "was to find his brother Simon [Peter] and tell him, 'We have found the Messiah'" (v. 41). After Philip was found by Jesus, "Philip found Nathanael and told him, 'We have found the one Moses wrote about in the Law, and about whom the prophets also wrote—Jesus of Nazareth, the son of Joseph'" (v. 45). The twelve disciples were found by the Messiah and/or introduced to him one by one, and the group that came together as a result was destined to commence a revolution.

Twenty-first-century disciple Iain's behind-the-scenes outreach ministry includes a relationship with a longtime work associate, Graham, who has recently become a seeker. The two men meet on a weekly basis exploring God's Word and discussing many important issues surrounding Graham's family life, his professional career, and most importantly, his understanding of the love of Christ in a personal, intimate manner.

Kevin and Leila have seen a long-established relationship with a workplace colleague and spouse grow to the place where Barnaby and Joanne are ready to receive specific spiritual counsel. They are beginning to ask life's most basic questions about faith and have turned to the only genuine Christians they have known over the years, Kevin and Leila. The conversations have been fascinating, in fact almost mind-boggling, and the rapid approach of Barnaby and Joanne to the entrance of the kingdom of God is exhilarating to the ones who are bearing witness of Christ. As blossoming, un-suspecting evangelists, Kevin and Leila are discovering firsthand the joy of serving Christ through open conversations about the Christian walk with those they have known for many years.

Paul's swimming buddies at the town pool have provided a seedbed of opportunity to share the love of Christ. Paul has been swimming with the same group of men for several years, and the level of inquiry about faith issues has grown considerably. Although none have crossed the line from unbelief into the Chris-tian faith, the relationship vitality among these men is staggering. Paul has a great sense of humor, a deep love for God, and a heart for the lost worldwide, and the impact of his witness is strong in some of the most unlikely places—yes, even at the town pool.

Bob and Betty Jacks would call these "divine appointments" (consider reading their two books on this subject, *Your Home A Lighthouse* and *Divine Appointments*).[7] Divine appointments are those connections with people with whom we have ongoing con-tact, in the natural places where we intersect with others—the fam-ily, neighborhood, community, workplace, school, and a myriad other crossroads of life. It is in these settings where we are given the rich privilege of allowing the love of Christ to flow out of our hearts and into the lives of those we meet every day.

The ongoing work of evangelism is a daily discipline similar in nature to our personal spiritual disciplines of Scripture study, prayer, and reflection (which embody the priorities of trait 3, the practice of the spiritual disciplines). Annie, a friend in rural Maine, innocently asks God each day for someone to cross her path that day to whom she can minister in the name of Christ. At a recent evangelism seminar, when the leader asked the group for answers to the question "How can we pay attention to divine appointments in our lives?" Annie answered very simply, "Well, I guess God gives us what we ask for. Aren't we supposed to ask him to send us people to serve each day?" The seminar leader answered with glee, "Yes, Annie, you have hit the nail on the head!"

Annie is right—healthy disciples who desire to share the love of Christ generously make it a point each day to ask God for the opportunity to do so. As a result, the eyes of our hearts are opened to see the needs of others all around us. It's really that simple—and yet for many of us, it's really that hard.

For decades people have tried to simplify how to share the message.

- Consider the bridge illustration: We are on one side of the road, and God is on the other. There is a chasm of sin between us that separates us forever unless we accept the love of Christ for ourselves. It's the cross of Christ that leads us safely from our side of the road to God's for all eternity. Based on Romans 6:23, "For the wages of sin is death, but the gift of God is eternal life in Christ Jesus our Lord," the bridge is easy to illustrate (wages/sin/death on one side; gift/goal/eternal life on the other; Christ Jesus our Lord is the cross/bridge from one side to the other).
- Consider the four spiritual laws: (1) God loves you and offers a wonderful plan for your life (John 3:16; 10:10). (2) Man is sinful and separated from God (Rom. 3:23). (3) Jesus Christ is God's only provision for man's sin (Rom. 5:8). (4) We must individually receive Jesus Christ as Savior and Lord; then we can know and experience God's love and plan for our lives (John 1:12; Eph. 2:8–9).
- We've also encouraged people to learn how to write out and share their testimony. Consider the following testimony outline: (1) Start with the particulars of your previous life of sin. (2) Share about the people or incidents that opened your eyes to your need for God. (3) Support your story with

Scripture. (4) Select ways your life has changed as a result.
(5) Then practice telling one another so that you're fully
prepared to do so with a seeker.

All the while, we haven't seen a marked increase in interest and
involvement in evangelism. How much simpler can we summa-
rize the gospel, our testimony, and the need to be involved *daily*
in the work of evangelism? How many more books, seminars,
tape series, lectures, and radio shows do we need before we finally get it? Don't misunderstand me here; I love simplifying the
gospel story and my life testimony so that I can remember the
main parts. I've taught semester-long evangelism courses, one-
day seminars, and hour-long workshops on evangelism. I've read
countless books on the subject and had lengthy conversations with
leaders on the topic. I've even led a ministry for fourteen years
that specializes in evangelism. I care deeply that this generation
gets a grip on our responsibility to share the love of Christ with
the next generation.

Yet I'm perplexed as to how much more effort can be expended
beyond what church and parachurch leaders are already saying
and doing about evangelism. What will it take for the majority of
Christians to embrace this priority? What will it take for *me* to be
motivated to be more active in daily evangelism? I'm afraid the
answer is as simple as saying that *it's a matter of the heart.* Unless our hearts are attuned to God's priorities in this area, unless
our hearts become broken because of the desperate needs of lost
people, and unless our hearts begin to inform and redirect our
minds, our missions, and our ministries, we will have wasted our
lives in self-satisfying endeavors.

Eventually we have to ask ourselves, "Where are my priorities?"
We live in an age of narcissistic marketing, advertising, sales,
fund-raising, and every possible way of getting the message across
without regard for the specific needs of the real people all around
us. We see our neighbor as having "generic" needs, just like every
other person down the street. However, savvy Christian disciples,
concerned about the message of the gospel and the need to be
effective evangelists, understand completely that each person has
a *unique* set of needs. They recognize the necessity of getting to

know what those needs are so we can in turn speak directly into those areas of concern with the hope-filled gospel of Christ.

The message of the gospel is not worn out; it's as alive today as it was when Jesus talked with Nicodemus and built his band of disciples. Why? Because Jesus is as alive today as he was since the dawn of time and when he walked the face of this earth. We are his ambassadors, his representatives to a lost and needy world. Wow, what an awesome privilege!

For Iain, Kevin and Leila, Paul, Annie, and literally thousands of other Christ-followers, the initial thought of reaching out evangelistically to a friend caused fear and incredible discomfort. Yet ask these same people today how they feel about the privilege and joyful excitement of seeing God work through them in their friends' lives and a bright smile will emerge. For unsuspecting evangelists who didn't think they had it in them to reach out evangelistically, it is a shock to discover how incredibly joy-producing it becomes. That's the way it is meant to be. Why else would God allow us the privilege of participating in his redemptive work here on earth? For our joy . . . and for his glory!

Not out of Fear or Intimidation!

A very small percentage of us have the gift of the evangelist (many studies state that it's 5 percent, and none say higher than 10 percent). So for the average disciple (the remaining 90 percent or more of us), the fear of evangelism is often exacerbated by the success stories of others (which we fear we could never duplicate) and/or tragic stories (which we are certain we will duplicate). What is it that keeps you from the work of evangelism?

- Is it fear that you will be rejected?
- Is it fear that you won't have an answer to a difficult question?
- Is it fear that you won't have the time to care and follow up?

- Is it fear that you will disappoint, disillusion, or disassociate with the person you are reaching as a result of your sharing?
- Is it fear that comes from your own insecurities in the faith?
- Is it fear that you aren't holy enough, smart enough, or bold enough?

No matter what you answered above, God does not want his children to fear representing him in this world. God delights in showering us with his love, for it overflows as we share that love with those around us. Are you living in the overflow of God's grace, or are you in a state of depletion? If you're depleted, then spend time being refilled. Otherwise, let his light shine; let his joy overflow; let his love be shared generously, faithfully, and obediently. The faith this will impart within and around you will be marvelous to behold.

I cringe at the evangelistic elitism that emerges from the ranks of the evangelism zealots among our Christian tribe. I don't see how it can be helpful or instructive to be intimidated into an action that should instead be a joyful privilege. As much as I appreciate those who are always challenging others to speak up for their faith, I share a deeper concern for those within the faith community who hear and are intimidated by a challenging rebuke.

Isn't it far more effective to excite than it is to disparage; to encourage than it is to discourage; to empower than it is to denigrate? I don't think the passionate evangelists in our midst realize how often they discourage other believers who want to be more involved but don't feel they measure up to the success ratio of the "zealots." This is merely a caution to those who think evangelism is the beginning, middle, and end of every breath we breathe and every step we take. Is it important? Absolutely. Is it God's intentional priority? Without a doubt. Does it materialize in various forms, means, and styles by myriad types of people? Yes, praise the Lord! Do we need to encourage one another to allow the love of Christ to flow out of our hearts, minds, lifestyles, and words in ways that reflect our true personality as believers? Most certainly.

It's time to celebrate the joy of sharing the love of Christ and join in the chorus with all God's people in delighting in how he chooses to use us for his eternal purposes. We won't all approach this in the same exact manner; in fact, we shouldn't. Instead, we need to seek the Lord daily in determining how, when, and where to share the gospel with the lost and the seeking who reside with us on this planet.

The emphasis in this chapter is on the evangelistic mandate for the healthy disciple, and that was selected purposefully. Why? Because we often try to avoid this aspect of our outward focus and leapfrog over evangelism prematurely into other less direct, although increasingly more challenging, areas of service. If we cannot find ways to sensitively and consistently share the love of Christ in our center circles of influence, we teeter on living a life of contradiction and hypocrisy. Our effectiveness in living out the evangelistic mandate leads us naturally into ministries of compassion within our neediest rural and urban settings and then into the international ministry arena. A healthy disciple keeps all three areas (evangelism, social action, and international missions/care for the poor) in balance while maintaining an ongoing, active, and sincere service to those within our reach.

Principle 7.1 Evangelism

Paul Revere's ride from Boston to Lexington and Concord is perhaps the most famous example from U.S. history of what happens when news travels effectively by word of mouth. When a piece of extraordinary news travels a long distance in a short period of time and mobilizes an army of the committed to come to arms, you know you're onto something big. People pass on all kinds of information to one another all the time—consider the impact of the Internet and the advertising industry upon our lives. It's rare, however, when information alone ignites a movement of epic proportions.

When John the Baptist gave testimony to the one in whom he believed, he said, "A man can receive only what is given him from heaven. You yourselves can testify that I said, 'I am not the Christ but am sent ahead of him.' The bride belongs to the bridegroom. The friend who attends the bridegroom waits and listens for him, and is full of joy when he hears the bridegroom's voice. That joy is mine, and it is now complete. He must become greater; I must become less" (John 3:27–30). John the Baptist's heart was opened up and filled by the love of Christ, and he couldn't help but share his life with others. In many respects the process of effective evangelism is seen in the lives of John the Baptist and the twelve disciples. Their lives exemplified the key ingredients of sharing the love of Christ with those within our spheres of influence:

Persons	God uses people just like you and me who claim the name of Jesus,
Power	who are empowered by the Spirit of God to live and serve in his name,
Prayer	knowing that our complete dependence is upon God to live and speak through us,
Presence	recognizing that offering a cup of cold water in his name is often the place to begin,
Proclama-tion	verbalizing the gospel account in stories from the Scriptures and our personal lives,
Persuasion	urging and encouraging others to receive the gift of God represented in the life, death, and resurrection of his Son, our Savior, Jesus,
Praise	knowing that as people of the Christian faith we will share eternal life in the presence of God!

As disciples in pursuit of spiritual health and ministry vitality, what will our response be to the mandate, message, and ministry before us? Will we choose to share the love of Christ generously so the whole world will know of the unending, unconditional, extravagant love of God the Father, Son, and Holy Spirit? Or, will we neglect the mandate we all share as Great Commission disciples?

Evangelism is a word-of-mouth epidemic that has altered planet earth since the dawn of time. In every generation, faithful men and women of Christ have been sharing his love with boldness, sensitivity, and singleness of heart. It's time we join the movement and step up to the plate unapologetically and enthusiastically. There is joy in this journey—guaranteed!

Principle 7.2 Social Concern

The Root Cellar is a compassion-based ministry in Portland, Maine, in one of the poorest white neighborhoods in the United States. They have successfully rallied local churches and their members to partner with them in reaching out to children and families surrounding their ministry headquarters, which is located in the hub of their mission field. The Root Cellar hosts after-school programs for children, daytime training classes for single parents, a free medical clinic, summertime ministry with families, and numerous additional services for their urban clientele.

If it weren't for committed believers from several churches who fully support this ministry with time, talent, and treasure, there would be no Root Cellar. This fabulous success story needs to be replicated in cities across America. It's a model for effective ministry within a needy urban neighborhood. Why? Because for several years the founding leaders spent time identifying the tangible and spiritual needs of the community and chose strategic ways to meet those needs. This opened the door for the proclamation of the gospel, and as a result of God's blessing, many individual lives and families have been reached with the love of Christ.

Where are you extending kingdom influence in the neediest rural and urban settings within your reach? It may be through a soup kitchen, a rescue mission, a tutoring program, a moral alternative to a political action, a summer internship, or myriad other opportunities. It may not occupy your central outreach initiative, but even when participating on an occasional basis, you become better informed of the desperate needs that exist in settings in which we don't normally find ourselves.

When Jesus reached out to the Samaritan woman in John 4:1–26, he was modeling for his disciples the need to be indiscriminate in our outreach. "To a Jew this was an amazing story. Here was the Son of God, tired and weary and thirsty. Here was the holiest of men, listening with understanding to a sorry story. Here was Jesus breaking through the barriers of nationality and orthodox Jewish custom. Here is the beginning of the universality of the gospel; here is God so loving the world, not in theory, but in action."[8]

When our service is done in his name, the barriers that usually keep us apart are penetrated by his love, grace, and mercy. Our lives are enriched as we get to know people of different ethnicity, socioeconomic status, lifestyle, and family of origin. Those who serve at the Root Cellar, and a host of similar ministries across the country, have found their commitment to the cause of Christ deepened through their experiences in ministries of compassion and social concern. It's the love of Christ that leads us into these settings and empowers us for faithful service.

Principle 7.3 International Missions

Jesus reminds us in John 4:35, "I tell you, open your eyes and look at the fields! They are ripe for harvest." One prepares the ground, another plants the seed, still another waters, another weeds, and another brings in the harvest (see John 4:34–38).

There is tremendous need for Spirit-filled servants of Jesus Christ to consider the fields that are ripe for harvest and make an investment to ensure there are adequate workers around the world "to do the will of him who sent me and to finish [the] work" Jesus came to do (John 4:34). International missions, as well as relief and development work, should be a growing concern for the healthy disciple. What do we know about our world? How aware are we of the intricacies of worldwide concerns? Where is the Christian community most active in spreading the Good News? What can we do together to impact the growth of the movement of God on every continent of our world?

These are just a few of the penetrating questions before us in the area of international missions and relief ministries. This book can't come close to touching the complexity and enormity of the subject. Yet it can raise high the banner of missions and highlight the gaping holes that exist in our personal efforts to share the love of Christ generously throughout the world. It's obviously God's intention to have the entirety of the gospel shared with every person in every generation in every corner of the world. The relevant question for our discussion about discipleship health is: Where is

God leading our church, our families, and us in contributing to the overwhelming needs of the international community?

Although it is impossible for us as individuals to meet the needs of the whole world, we still have an important role to play. We must be realistic in what we can accomplish as a church, as families, and as individuals and consider creative ways to fit this into an already filled-to-the-brim lifestyle.

In the beginning of this chapter, I introduced three children our family supports on a monthly basis. It's not the sum and total of our international missions and relief efforts, but it's a significant part of our commitment. For some, this may be all they can handle. For us, it is just the beginning. What about for you? Consider ways to introduce an international flavor into your journey of faith. Pray for a specific country or people group, begin reading intently in this regard, attend a missions festival in your local church, volunteer to serve on a summer missions trip, or begin supporting a child through World Vision or Compassion. It may be a small step at first, but it's the best way to start to cultivate your heart for the lost, hurting, imprisoned, malnourished, sick, and dying throughout this world whom God created and loves with an infinite and matchless love.

Principle 7.4 Diversity of Friendships

When our son, Nathan, first spoke about his new friend Lee, we had no idea Lee had cerebral palsy and was wheelchair bound. Nathan was in the third grade when he was invited over to Lee's house for a play date. When Ruth drove Nathan to Lee's house, she noticed a wheelchair ramp encircling the back side of the house. When she innocently remarked that someone must need a wheelchair in the family, Nathan blurted out, "It's for Lee, Mommy."

Nathan knew Lee as a friend. It never occurred to this innocent child that he had to tell us Lee had severe disabilities. It didn't matter to Nathan, and it became a very natural part of life for our family. In fact, the ways in which Lee's family dealt with his disability prepared us for how we would handle Nathan's disability. Nathan has had twelve surgeries on his right leg over the past seventeen years. He too has been wheelchair bound at times and on crutches for several years, and he has learned the hard way what the word *perseverance* means. Thankfully, as a child he had a role model in Lee, and this friendship has been special ever since.

What do your eyes tell your heart and mind about people who are different from you? Have rose-colored glasses affected the eyesight of your heart? When you look around, who do you see? Do you see men and women, boys and girls with external looks and descriptive titles, or are you able to see beneath the surface and listen for the condition of their hearts? It may take a child to teach you this lesson, for generally children don't focus on the externals and are able to see and feel what's going on inside. Isn't that what really matters most?

When Jesus found himself near the pool at Bethesda (John 5:1–15), where the blind, the lame, and the paralyzed gathered in the hope of being healed, he looked beneath their physical limitations. He focused on their hearts. When the invalid was healed by Jesus after waiting by the pool for thirty-eight years, he was overjoyed in his ability to walk. Jesus warned him not to focus on his ability to walk but instead to remain mindful of his sin: "See, you are well again. Stop sinning or something worse may happen to you" (John 5:14). It wasn't the physical healing that was Jesus' priority, it was the healing of his heart. So it should be with us.

Jesus calls us to reach out to others who have different life situations, ethnicities, abilities, or disabilities than we have and to learn what it's like to have friends who are different from us. Having such diversity in friendships will prepare us for reaching out to all whom Jesus loves and for whom he died.

Principle 7.5 Dispenser of Grace

After experiencing the feeding of the five thousand along the shore of the Sea of Galilee, Jesus was followed across the lake by the crowds who had witnessed this miracle firsthand (John

6:1–15). When they found him, Jesus confronted them about what they were seeking: "I tell you the truth, you are looking for me, not because you saw miraculous signs but because you ate the loaves and had your fill. Do not work for food that spoils, but for food that endures to eternal life, which the Son of Man will give you. On him God the Father has placed his seal of approval" (John 6:26–27). Then he continued, "The work of God is this: to believe in the one he has sent" (v. 29).

Everywhere Jesus traveled he dispensed tangible gifts to his followers (healings, miraculous signs, even food), but those were merely a foretaste of what he wanted most to offer. Jesus was a dispenser of grace, and everyone who received it was transformed from the inside out. As his disciples, sharing his love generously throughout the world, we are also to be dispensers of God's grace.

As is often the case, we are generally more inclined to be consumers of God's grace than dispensers. Each of the ten traits we are exploring in this text are to be dispensed with generosity. None of them, however, is as explicit as this one. As recipients of God's boundless grace, our response is to be one of dispensing with gratitude and generosity that same grace toward others.

Becoming dispensers of God's grace will require that we reevaluate our commitment to the centrality of the gospel. It will mean making changes that will afford us the necessary time to invest in the lives of lost people within our grasp, throughout our cities, and around the world. It will demand more of us than we ever imagined because it will require that we take risks and respond to daunting needs in dramatic ways. However, the health of our generation of Christ-followers will be measured almost exclusively by how we respond to this very issue. Are we willing to put our faith into action evangelistically, addressing the societal ills of our day, and reaching out to every culture, every people group, every nation, every malnourished child, and every sick and impoverished person in the name of Jesus Christ? How we answer that question intellectually, practically, and spiritually will mark our lives forever.

A DISCIPLE'S PRAYER

Lord, I know that as I gaze upon your holiness I see in you a heart that pounds for the desperate needs of people worldwide. I want to feel that same pounding within my soul. Grant me, Lord, in this season of my life, a renewed heart for the lost, the needy, the lonely, the imprisoned, the destitute, the hungry, the dying, and the spiritually confused. I want to do my part in fulfilling your redemptive plan here on earth.

So, dear Lord, make me an instrument of your peace. Live within me in such a dynamic way that my life will be a reflection of your heart for this world. Help me to address priorities in my life that need some readjustment. Help me to see the world through your eyes. Help me to feel the pain of the impoverished, and lead me into action on their behalf. I know that you weep over lost lives, hurting families, broken relationships, fractured communities, suffering and spiritually starved children. Give me a portion of your heart that will lead me into relationships with others that will allow me the joyful privilege of dispensing your grace. Oh, for the joy of sharing your love generously. I ask all these things in your precious and holy name, Lord Jesus. Amen.

For Reflection and Renewal

The healthy disciple maximizes every opportunity to share the love of Christ, in word and deed, with those outside the faith.

1. In what ways do you resonate with Nicodemus as a seeker, a law-focused enquirer, who was sensitized to the work of Jesus and was even tenderly and compassionately moved by the death of Jesus but had a hard time fully believing in him and accepting his love and leadership over his life?
2. Which of the three main areas of outreach (evangelism, social action, and international missions/relief and development) are your strongest? Which area needs some work, and what can you do about making alterations in your lifestyle to accommodate the necessary changes?

3. How would you describe your circle of friendships today? With whom are you spending time that is stretching you to think about life and service to others in new and different ways? Are there people within your reach who are of different color, ethnicity, ability, or socioeconomic background with whom you can begin to spend time in order to broaden your perspectives on the issues and needs of our world today?

4. In what practical ways can you be a dispenser of God's grace toward a family member, work associate, neighbor, or friend in this coming week without needing to receive anything in return? Try it and see how it changes your heart toward that person.

5. Can you articulate the essence of the gospel to a seeker? Are you able to succinctly share the main points of your personal testimony in two to three minutes? If not, please be sure to work on these and add them to your arsenal of tools that are ready for use at a moment's notice. You too are a part of the word-of-mouth revolution!

8

Manages Life Wisely
and Accountably

The healthy disciple develops personal life management skills and lives within a web of accountable relationships.

As long as it is day, we must do the work of him who sent me.

John 9:4

Ever get lost? I mean really lost. So lost that you thought you'd never find your way home?

I've had a variety of "getting lost" experiences. Everything from refusing to map out a trip into the city (almost any city, actually—it happens more times than not for yours truly) and needing last-second directions from anyone available on the street corner, to "winging it" out of an airport in a new state I'd never visited before—only to discover I had driven nearly forty miles in the wrong direction, to walking in the woods and discovering later that all we had done was make one big circle instead of moving toward our destination. It occurs more often than I care to admit.

By far the most dramatic experience of getting lost in my life occurred when I had flown into St. John's, Newfoundland, Canada, and thought I had landed in my city of destination, which was St. John, New Brunswick, Canada. It was 9:00 P.M. on a Friday in September. I was scheduled to teach an evangelism seminar at a local church (in New Brunswick) at 9:00 the following morning.

I had left Boston on time, on the correct flight indicated on my ticket. We had a stopover in Halifax, Nova Scotia, which required all passengers to go through customs before heading to our next flight. Thinking nothing of the whole experience, I went through customs and headed to the gate for the flight to St. John. After we took off, I made myself comfortable and continued to read my book, enjoying what I thought was an uneventful flight.

Uneventful, that is, until I landed in Newfoundland, gathered my belongings, and began to search for the Howard Johnson sign on the perimeter wall of the baggage claim area. I was told there would be a courtesy phone available for me to call for a ride to the hotel. After an arduous search process (obviously, *I* wasn't going to ask for help or directions), I realized that the bright orange and teal sign was nowhere to be found. It wasn't until that moment that I came to the humiliating realization—after finally asking for help—that I was in the wrong city. If you know your Canadian map, you realize as well that I was in the wrong province. In fact, I was in the wrong time zone! I was about five hundred miles away from where I was supposed to be.

In order to get to my intended destination on time the following morning, I had to get up at the crack of dawn. (You see, I also had no hotel room waiting for my arrival in this wrong city and landed instead in a truck stop about thirty miles out of the city—yep, it was me and the truckers.) Then I had to retrace my steps, head back in the same direction I had flown the night before, and find my way once again in yet another new city. From oblivious to lost to forlorn and forgotten to lost again and then found. Thankfully, my hosts for the seminar were very gracious. They weren't upset that I was thirty minutes late for the seminar and thoroughly enjoyed razzing me all day long about my foolish error.

One of the ironies of this experience was the book I was engrossed in reading throughout my flights. It was the new best-seller (at that time), *The Seven Habits of Highly Effective People* by Stephen Covey.[1] *Effective* was the last word to describe me that weekend. That experience was a wake-up call of epic proportions.

As a result of this life-defining experience, I realized that I was living my life in the same manner as this stranger-than-fiction-I-hate-to-admit-it's-true story. I was the embodiment of a life without purpose or mission. I was merely living life with a desire to fill every waking moment with activity. It almost didn't matter what the activity was, as long as I could brag about my travel schedule and the multiple demands being placed upon me. There was no discrimination regarding whether the activity in which I was engaged was an appropriate use of time. I was on an unintentional mission of being busy. If I had the time, I said *yes*. It was almost as though I was hopping on one wrong airplane after another, landing in one wrong destination after another.

Little did I realize how lost I really had become. The treadmill of activity had landed me back at my original starting point. The circle I had traveled wasn't getting me to my destination. It took months to reorient my life around an earnest desire to begin managing my life with wisdom and accountability, and for that season of reconfiguration I am eternally grateful. The lost had been found, and I discovered a renewed sense of direction. Since that humbling experience my life has never been the same.

Ever get lost? I mean really lost. So lost you thought you'd never find your way home? Thankfully there are principles to follow that will keep you from making the same mistakes I have made walking in circles or landing in the wrong destination. It will be turbulent at times, but from this vantage point there's no turning back.

A Work of God on Display

Jesus found himself heading in the right direction throughout his years on this earth. The Gospel of John (as well as the other three Gospels of Matthew, Mark, and Luke) repeatedly tells us incidents in which the lost are found, the hurting are healed, and the hopeless are redirected by the living Christ. In John 9 the focus is on the blind receiving sight. In the first few verses

(vv. 1–12) we learn about a man who was born blind and received the miraculous gift of his sight from Jesus. In the center of the chapter (vv. 13–34) we discover once more how blind the eyes of the Pharisees' hearts really were to a genuine work of God.

At the end of the chapter (vv. 35–41) we see Jesus conversing once more with the man who had been healed of his blindness. This man's belief in Jesus was confirmed through his heart of genuine faith and worship. Jesus reminded the man, "For judgment I have come into this world, so that the blind will see and those who see will become blind" (John 9:39). His reference to "those who see will become blind" was about the Pharisees, who in observing all that had taken place had hardened their hearts to what Jesus was saying and doing in their midst.

In commenting about the man's blindness, Jesus said that it had not occurred because of the sin of his parents, "but this happened so that the work of God might be displayed in his life. As long as it is day, we must do the work of him who sent me. Night is coming, when no one can work. While I am in the world, I am the light of the world" (John 9:3–4).

Displaying the work of God was Jesus' intentional mission. He managed this with integrity, wisdom, and sincerity. He also called those around him to this same goal: In everything *display the work of God. As long as it is day, we must do the work of him who sent me.* Displaying the work of God was integral to all that Jesus did for those he had been called to serve. Why? So he could display the glory and power of God, so he could demonstrate his compassion, and so God's grace could be revealed to all who suffer from affliction, sorrow, pain, or disappointment. The wisdom and discernment of Jesus was shown over and over again in the healing work he performed, but more importantly it was shown in the redemptive work he was called to fulfill in the hearts and lives of others.

Jesus is concerned that all of his followers do God's work while there is time to do it.

God gave men [and women] the day for work and the night for rest; the day comes to an end and the time for work is also ended. For Jesus it was true that he had to press on with God's work in the day for the night of the Cross lay close ahead. But it is true for every person. We are given only so much time. Whatever we are to do must be done within it. Take thought of time before time is ended. We should never put things off until another time, for another time may never come. The Christian's duty is to fill the time he has—and no person knows how much that will be—with the service of God and of his fellow humanity. There is no more poignant sorrow than the tragic discovery that it is too late to do something which we might have done.[2]

Jesus continues, "While I am in the world, I am the light of the world" (John 9:5). Our intention, as his disciples, is to reflect that light in all that we say and do for him. While *we* are in the world, *we* are to be light in the world. The light of Christ's love shines through the disciple who lives in hot pursuit of spiritual health and vitality. The work we do, the decisions we make, and the directions we head all must reflect his light and glory—while it is still day.

The display of God's work through us is embodied in this trait, "managing life wisely and accountably." It begins with a fervent study of how Jesus fulfilled this quality in his own life. Wisdom was evident throughout his daily decisions, and his accountability came out in his embodiment of Trinitarian interdependence—a perfect rendition of Father, Son, and Holy Spirit embodied in the person of Christ. There is no contradiction within the godhead. Therefore, what Jesus came to do was in direct alignment to the fullness of our Triune God. That alone is worthy of our praise and adoration!

Jesus held his disciples accountable to the completion of their work. He made it clear that if they were to reflect his glory and fulfill their call, their lives were to be consistent with the commitments they had made to follow him. To fall short of that level of maturity meant that the fruit of their labor would inevitably be compromised.

Earlier in the Gospel (John 2:12–25), Jesus held the Jews accountable for their treatment of the temple in Jerusalem. "In the temple courts he found men selling cattle, sheep and doves, and others sitting at tables exchanging money. So he made a whip out of cords, and drove all from the temple area, both sheep and cattle; he scattered the coins of the money changers and overturned their tables. To those who sold doves he said, 'Get these out of here! How dare you turn my Father's house into a market!'" (John 2:14–16). Angry at the mistreatment of the temple, he swept the place clean with his indignation over this atrocity. How had it come to this for the people of God? Had no one else held them accountable for their actions? Had no one else thought about the implications of a temple court filled with activity juxtaposed to the primary purposes of God for that holy space?

None of us necessarily *likes* to be held accountable for our actions. Yet if our goal is to manage our lives with wisdom from on high, the cost of accountability is significant. Jesus was serious about how well his disciples were reflecting his priorities for them, and he held them accountable. Even if it means turning the courtyard tables of our lives upside down, we should welcome the rebuke and learn from the error of our ways. That's the fruit of a life of discipline in discipleship.

> Watch our thoughts; they become words.
> Watch our words; they become actions.
> Watch our actions; they become habits.
> Watch our habits; they become character.
> Watch our character; it becomes our destiny.
>
> Author Unknown

Thank God for the example of Jesus, who was sold out and committed (yes, even unto death on the cross) to embodying a life of wisdom and accountability. May his example of faithfulness be evidenced in our lives as well. All for the display of his glory!

Internal Motivation

Stephen Covey, at a leadership training event in Boston, caught my attention when he said, "Successful people daily weave habits of effectiveness into their lives in order to achieve desired results.

They are internally motivated by a strong sense of mission." For Willie and Cindy Batson, successful leaders within their family and community, that strong sense of mission is articulated in their family mission document, which addresses four key questions:

1. *Core family values:* What are the principles and truths that guide our marriage and family life?
2. *Family mission statement:* What is God calling us to do/be as a couple and family?
3. *Family Scripture:* What is a Bible verse that supports our mission?
4. *Family objectives:* How will we fulfill our mission?

In speaking about this document, Willie communicated the passion of each statement. He and Cindy had worked long and hard to complete this paper of guiding principles for their daily lives as a family. Being held accountable to write it within their couples' small group, they now are committed not only to embody what's written but also to encourage others to do the same. They believe wholeheartedly that managing life wisely and accountably begins with their household. It is within the walls of family life that they learn how to love and serve in Jesus' name. It is within the family system that children discover the appropriate ways to live peaceably in this world. Then, it is out of the quality of family life that others are taught to live in a manner befitting Christ and his purposes here on earth.

Taking the time to produce such a paper was just the beginning. Willie and Cindy are serious about living it out in intentionally focused ways. See for yourself how each statement is carefully crafted. For example, in their core family values:

- We build our marriage and family on a strong spiritual foundation with a sense of purpose: to love God without reservation and to practice his Word as a means of witnessing for Jesus Christ to our neighbors and friends.
- Authentic, unconditional love is the basis of our relationships.

- We are intentional in creating a schedule that helps us to celebrate our life together.
- Our home is a place of refuge and safety.
- Healthy communication and conflict resolution skills are essential for the unity of our home.
- Loving, firm discipline is necessary for raising children to become healthy adults.
- Wise stewardship of our resources helps us promote the gospel of Jesus Christ.

Taking the time to articulate their mission has brought vitality to Willie and Cindy's marriage and depth of wisdom to their parenting. Instead of focusing on the purely practical implications of what it means to live wisely and accountably, they are living that way from the inside out. The growth in Christ that will emerge in the days ahead will benefit their children and grandchildren. What better reason to do so than for the sake of the children? Willie and Cindy, and scores of others like them, are discovering firsthand what a difference it makes when you press the pause button of life, hop off the treadmill of activity, and focus afresh on God's unique call, mission, and/or purpose.

Principle 8.1 Mission, Roles, and Goals

For the disciple who is carefully pursuing a life that is managed wisely and accountably, there is an earnest desire to serve the purposes of the kingdom of God. Yet what are those purposes, and how do we discern them? To comprehend the overarching purposes of the kingdom, it's imperative that we understand the mission of the King. On several occasions Jesus specifically stated his mission by sharing why he had come:

- "For I have come down from heaven not to do my will but to do the will of him who sent me" (John 6:38). Jesus lived a life of submission to the will of the Father and showed the greatest integrity in living it out in love.

- "I have come that they may have life, and have it to the full" (John 10:10). Jesus came to encourage his disciples to live with an abundance mentality and an expansive view of cultivating their greatest capacities for kingdom priorities to be fulfilled in them.

- "For this reason I was born, and for this I came into the world, to testify to the truth. Everyone on the side of truth listens to me" (John 18:37). Jesus embodied truth in his words, thoughts, and actions.

- "For even the Son of Man did not come to be served, but to serve, and to give his life as a ransom for many" (Mark 10:45). Jesus came to serve sacrificially for the sake of empowering others to be a part of building his kingdom.

- "For the Son of Man came to seek and to save what was lost" (Luke 19:10). Jesus' primary goal was to invite lost people into a reconciled relationship with God.

Jesus clearly articulated his mission and embraced it in every aspect of his life. We see this over and over again in his obedience to the Father, his abundant gift of life, his embodiment of truth, his servant leadership, and his redemptive seeking of lost people. Everywhere he went, his life mission was apparent. It emerged in his loving confrontations, his divine healings, his intimate relationships, and his ministry of reconciliation. His was a mission-focused life, and ours is to be the same. Taking the time to discover and enrich that mission is a lifelong journey, filled with ups and downs, successes and failures, but it is always enriching and fulfilling.

For the prophet Jeremiah, the purposes of God are to prosper the people of God as they pursue his plans for their lives. "'For I know the plans I have for you,' declares the LORD, 'plans to prosper you and not to harm you, plans to give you hope and a future'" (Jer. 29:11). Discovering the plan of God for your life is an exhilarating process. It is in this discovery process that we begin to specify the mission and purposes for which we exist.

In a generalized sense, his plan for us is simply:

- to foster a daily love relationship with God,
- to participate daily in his work of redemption in this world,
- to share in fellowship with him for all eternity.

Out of that overarching plan, we as disciples of the living Christ need to come to understand and align our lives around a specific, very personal sense of mission and purpose. Once discovered, we begin to realize how life-changing it can be. As Willie and Cindy came to grips with the missional realities of their marriage and family life, they were able to articulate the general principles of the Word of God in distinct and personal language that fit their family most appropriately. In turn, their family mission is being realized, and the focus of their life together is greatly enhanced.

When the apostles were confronted by myriad needs in the early church, their mission defined the strength and significance of their ministry. Acts 6:1–7 relates that when the widows were being overlooked in the daily distribution of food, this need was brought to the attention of the apostles. Instead of dropping what they were doing in serving the early church, they called together all the disciples and addressed the issue. "It would not be right for us to neglect the ministry of the word of God in order to wait on tables. Brothers, choose seven men from among you who are known to be full of the Spirit and wisdom. We will turn this responsibility over to them and will give our attention to prayer and the ministry of the word" (Acts 6:2–4).

By maintaining a posture of remaining mission-focused, the apostles were able to say no to the meeting of one particular need and instead were able to include others in responding to that ministry need. They were able to focus on their priorities. In the same way, for those who remain mission-focused as disciples of Jesus Christ today, there is great satisfaction knowing that the meeting of one need does not have to mean the neglect of another. In fact, when handled properly, all members of the body benefit from the focused intentionality of the mission-minded disciple. In turn, the mission-minded disciple can help the unfocused disciple begin to get a grip on the need to define one's mission in light of several key factors.

How then will we get to a deeper understanding of our personal mission as determined by the heavenly Father? Just like the apostles in the early church, we can discover the richness of our dream to become all that God intends for us, living out his image in a manner that's clearly defined by the Holy Spirit—if we'll only take the time to listen! I have adapted the following suggestions for Christian disciples from the work of Stephen Covey and his associates, who helped to formulate a basic set of mission development exercises that complement the book *Seven Habits of Highly Effective People*.[3]

Listening prayerfully and reflectively to the work of God in us, through us, and around us is the place to begin. Paying active attention to the presence and power of the Holy Spirit in our lives is essential to this process. Prayerful reflection, journaling, and listening to the still small voice of God are the starting points of this exercise of faith. It is in the prayer closets of our daily lives that we hear from God and dialogue with him in open, honest prayer. Listening for the fresh wind of his Spirit to swirl around and within us comes out of our silence, solitude, and the basic spiritual disciplines we covered earlier in this book. Want to know your mission? Listen attentively to the Spirit of God. He's waiting for you to stop doing and begin being. It's out of a context of prayerfulness that we discover our mission.

Recounting the experiences and people who have influenced your life positively since childhood is the second step in the process. Here one begins to write down names, places, and events that occurred in the past as significant markers in life. It may be a parent or family member who jumps to mind first or a special friend, teacher, pastor, mentor, or neighbor. Or it may be moving to a new city, receiving a special honor, learning a new trade, or discovering a hidden area of giftedness. Without my suggesting any more options to influence the list, write down even in the margin of this book a few thoughts that jump quickly to mind. Pay attention to how the list develops and what people or experiences end up at the top of the list of significant markers of your past that have shaped and influenced your present.

Listing the character traits of the most influential people in your life is the next step. What are those qualities you are seeking to emulate in your life as a result of observing them in others? Be as specific as possible in describing how those around you have directly or indirectly shaped the way you look at life, live your life, and share your life with others. We need to recognize that we are relational beings, and the people who have surrounded us in life have made a difference in who we've become today. It may be the shaping of our attitudes about marriage and family, the defining of our ethics in the workplace, treatment of others who are different from us in ethnicity, or ways in which we use our free time. Again, allow your pen to meet the paper as your heart and mind flip through the catalog of experiences with significant people of your past and present. Taking the time to do this part of the exercise will enhance one's self-understanding in surprisingly wonderful ways.

What about the negative people and hurtful experiences of our lives? These are important to recognize and identify, for they too have influenced the kind of people we have become. However, for this exercise flip the negatives upside down and focus instead on what you have learned about how *not* to repeat the harmful qualities of others and how to learn from the painful times while discovering the meaning and purpose of such experiences. For many of us, the pain of our past is more predominant in our thoughts than the positive. We don't want to gloss over the pain, but rather learn from it and ultimately redeem it. As we look forward in fulfilling dreams, mission, and goals, the roles we identify become all the more critical to understand because it is in these roles that we embody our priorities as we intersect with others. We need to break the chain of destructive behavior so the influence we have on others' lives will be constructive and productive for generations to come. This is a daunting subject and would require another book to fully and more appropriately handle. It's mentioned here to highlight the importance of recognizing this reality within the sequence of steps needed for defining mission, roles, and goals.

Summarizing the prayers, people, and places of the past that have shaped your present experiences is the next step to take.

From what you've written already, are there themes that emerge that are noteworthy? Are there characteristics of your personality that have been identified as coming from a particularly dominant source? Hopefully this will be an affirming experience of sorting through the key stepping-stones of your lifelong journey. Putting down on paper some identifiable highlights of your life helps you see where you've come from and who or what has most influenced the person you are today. Repeating the above steps a few days later enhances the listing even further as God brings to mind other people or incidents that you didn't initially recall when starting the exercise.

Defining some of the goals you have for the future is the next step to take. Here it's important to begin to list some of the ways you have been dreaming about where to head in the upcoming days of life and service to others. It is permissible to list virtually anything that lands in the category of "the desires of your heart." In this step the areas to consider are summarized in three questions: What do you hope to attain? What do you hope to experience? What kind of person do you hope to become?

What you hope to attain may be an educational degree, a deeper understanding of the Bible, marital joy, parental fulfillment, new friends, or even something as tangible as a new possession (although if this is first on the list, it most certainly needs to be reevaluated!). What you hope to experience may include a short-term missions trip, travel to other parts of the world, white-water rafting, living in a different city, or a new vocation. What you hope to become is the list of character qualities you want to work on or acquire that are not currently at a status that pleases you. In this section the focus begins to shift forward to the next stage of one's personal development.

Determining the roles we must embody in order for some of the above definition to be realized is the next step to take. If some of our dreams are to become reality, what roles in life need to be readjusted in order to make room for the mission-focused person to emerge? There will be some roles that are given, such as marriage and family roles, personal discipleship, friendship, and workplace roles. Yet within the major categories of your interface with others, there may need to be some refinement of those roles.

This becomes most evident in the workplace or vocational aspirations of the disciple. Since this occupies such a major part of our daily routines, it most likely is the paramount role(s) that needs readjustment along the way. However, within the more defined areas of life that all of us share in common (family, friend, disciple of Christ), determining how these roles can be enhanced is also a good exercise to embrace.

Drafting a statement of mission comes out of the reflective work noted above. As we prayerfully flesh out the character traits and experiences that have shaped the way in which we have lived our lives, it's time to begin articulating a personal mission statement that encompasses our giftedness and the dreams we have for the future. Identifying how that future is to be realized shapes the wording of the mission statement, showing how the lifestyle of the disciple will prepare for that preferred future. For example, if the future desire includes a vocational priority, the mission statement will reflect that outcome: "My mission is to reflect the love of Christ to my family, friends, and work associates in the _____ industry, while pursuing my dream of _____." If the future encompasses a ministry priority, the mission statement will reflect that outcome: "My mission is to follow after the heart of God in all of my key relationships with family and friends, while pursuing my dream of _____." Sharing early drafts with key individuals will help you to refine the statement until it truly represents your mission as a disciple of Christ.

Regularly reviewing and revising the mission statement, making sure to align roles and goals to support the fulfillment of the mission, is the ongoing step in this process. It's important all along the way to consider the following questions: Is this the mission I am continuing to sense coming from the Lord? Does this mission motivate me? Are my defined roles in their proper priority order? Are the goals I have articulated still in line with the direction I am heading?

The healthy disciple realizes that the world continues to rapidly change all around us. Therefore, keeping these statements freshly updated is the key to wisely managing the life God has so richly and generously bestowed upon us. If the articulated mission is from the Lord and has been affirmed by trusted members of the community of faith that surround you, then it's incumbent upon the disciple to move forward in fulfillment of that mission.

In summary, the process of developing our mission, roles, and goals is as follows:

- *Listening prayerfully and reflectively* to the work of God in us, through us, and around us.
- *Recounting the experiences and people* who have influenced our life positively since childhood.
- *Listing the character traits* of the most influential people in our lives and how these are being emulated in us.
- *Summarizing the prayers, people, and places* of the past that have shaped our present experiences.
- *Defining some of the goals* we have for the future.
- *Determining the roles* we must embody in order for some of the above definition to be realized.
- *Drafting a statement of mission* in light of our experiences, relationships, giftedness, and passion.
- *Regularly reviewing and revising* the mission statement, making sure to align roles and goals to support the fulfillment of the mission.

While this isn't a comprehensive or conclusive listing of the areas to cover in this process, it certainly is a great place to begin. Go for it!

Principle 8.2 Balanced Lifestyle

Maintaining balance while pursuing a missional direction for daily life and service is by far one of our greatest challenges. Who among us is living a well-balanced life? It seems that the only ones achieving success in this area are the very young and the very old. Any age in between is having a hard time.

Consider our children—the competition for nursery school entry is the dominant concern of many parents of preschoolers today. Waiting lists are growing in the more prestigious schools, and with programs available sunup to sundown, there is a mindset emerging that is frightening: "Will my child's attendance in a certain nursery school determine his or her Ivy League status?" Sound preposterous? It's a reality in many of the more affluent communities of our country. Or look at the stress of schoolwork on elementary age children. It's become one of the main burdens of growing families. Who really has the time to help children with two hours of homework each night as well as balance all the projects, extracurricular activities, and latenight stresses of family life?

Need we say anything about life with a teenager? That stage of life is stress inducing enough without adding to it the myriad relational, educational, emotional, and spiritual intricacies of learning how to balance life as an adolescent. Young adulthood is not everything it's cracked up to be either! Getting into college is more competitive, and getting a job after college in one's area of expertise is difficult, particularly in a challenging economy.

Then there's the young family stage, followed by midlife, and into the retirement years. Each stage of life has its stresses and challenges, which in turn leads to an imbalance in most of our lives. The answer? There isn't an easy one, to be sure.

Finding balance begins with understanding one's mission, roles, and goals for life and service. Yet in the fulfillment of our mission, roles, and goals, there are daily choices that impact how balanced we will become. Our reality needs to be considered in light of God's priorities for us. "Jesus grew in wisdom and stature, and in favor with God and men" (Luke 2:52). Now that's balance! In another place Jesus reminds his listeners of the priority commandment, "The most important one . . . is this: 'Hear, O Israel, the Lord our God, the Lord is one. Love the Lord your God with all your heart and with all your soul and with all your mind and with all your strength.' The second is this: 'Love your neighbor as yourself.' There is no commandment greater than these" (Mark 12:29–31).

If we take the teachings of Jesus as the pattern for finding balance in our lives, then his Word is of primary importance. Jesus found his balance in wisdom (intellectual), stature (physical), favor with God (spiritual), favor with mankind (emotional/relational), and he discovered ways to maintain that balance each day he walked this earth. What are we doing to cultivate each of these aspects ourselves?

- *Regarding wisdom:* What are we filling our minds with as Christ-followers? How much comes from quality reading, listening to others, participating in dialogue about issues of our day, and learning what it means to think about whatever is true, noble, right, pure, lovely, admirable, excellent, and praiseworthy (Phil. 4:8)?

- *Regarding stature:* How well are we caring for our bodies as the temple of the Holy Spirit (1 Cor. 6:19–20)? Are we honoring God with our respect for the need of rest, relaxation, and Sabbath? Are we exercising, watching our diet, nutrition, health, and hygiene? Does our schedule reflect our missional priorities so that our time can be maximized for kingdom purposes?

- *Regarding favor with God:* Are we seeking to reflect his love, grace, and mercy in the fulfillment of our mission and calling? Have we recognized that our giftedness comes from the hand of a loving and generous God? Are we pursuing daily intimacy with the Savior in our centers of quiet, prayer, Scripture meditation, and reflective disciplines (Pss. 42:1–2; 63:1)?

- *Regarding favor with others:* Are we following the command in Colossians 3:12–14 ("As God's chosen people, holy and dearly loved, clothe yourselves with compassion, kindness, humility, gentleness and patience. Bear with each other and forgive whatever grievances you may have against one another. . . . And over all these virtues putting on love, which binds them all together in perfect unity")? If so, then our relational wholeness will evidence itself in honesty, openness, empathy, laughter and joy, tears and sorrow, interdependence, and service to one another.

Wisdom, stature, favor with God, favor with men, and loving God with heart, soul, mind, and strength. These are the priorities that keep the disciple balanced, fully able to handle the stresses and strains of life. It's not easy, but pursuing them will bring great joy for the journey.

Principle 8.3 Stress Reduction and Management

Getting to the place of balance requires a dogged determination to reduce and manage the stress points of our lives. There will be times in life, however, when nothing we do will help to reverse the circumstances swirling around us. Habakkuk understood this when he wrote, "Though the fig tree does not bud and there are no grapes on the vines, though the olive crop fails and the fields produce no food, though there are no sheep in the pen and no cattle in the stalls, yet I will rejoice in the LORD, I will be joyful in God my Savior. The Sovereign LORD is my strength; he makes my feet like the feet of a deer, he enables me to go on the heights" (Hab. 3:17–19).

I recall distinctly the season of my life when my father died, our son was facing another major surgery, and a huge disappointment in ministry was adding untold stress that was totally out of my control. The only choice we have during such times is to let go, trust unswervingly, and hang on to the hope of our faith, believing in the depths of our being that God has our very best interests in mind despite the circumstances that surround and sometimes engulf us. There is no other place to reside during such times, and there is no *better* place to rest. It is in that place where there is joy in the Lord, for he alone is the Provider and Sustainer of life.

What are those factors—times, seasons, issues, schedules, and circumstances—that contribute most to the stress points of our lives? Consider the following:

- Change—we shouldn't underestimate its power
- Mobility—we need to learn how to adapt to the new while severing the old

- Expectations—we must realize that too many of them equal disappointment
- Time pressures—the clock is dominant today, but it doesn't have to rule our lives
- Work—especially if we're outpacing our abilities, outrunning our hearts, or not working at all
- Control—people around us vying for domination
- Fear—at the root of many of our stresses and contributes to our worry and anxiety
- Relationships—the healthy ones being dissipated and dismantled
- Competition—often we are in a win-lose situation that is destructive
- Overload—we try to do too much and are continuously weary
- Illness, death, divorce, aging, family dysfunction, etc.—the list goes on and on!

Which ones contribute most to your own life spinning out of control? How can we begin to deal with these stress points in ways that are constructive and productive for the future?

Experts in the field tell us the best way to handle stress is to either reduce it or manage it. Reducing stress means that we decrease our stress load by courageously changing and re-arranging our lifestyle so that we are not contributing to our own stress via the daily choices we make. Managing stress means we discover we do indeed have some control over monitoring and proactively managing our lives. We must remain in the driver's seat, on the lap of God, making choices that will lead to healthier, more balanced living.

Take your own pulse. How has your stress level been this past week? What are the main contributors to your stress level today? What could you have done differently this past week to avoid or manage it better? What choices can you make that will eliminate, lessen, or manage stress in the week ahead?

Principle 8.4 Accountable Relationships

It has been said among men's ministry circles that all of us need at minimum a "Paul" (as in the apostle Paul) to lead us, a "Timothy" in whom we can invest, and a "Barnabas" to encourage and bless us. The same would be true for women, as attested in Titus 2:3–5, "Teach the older women to be reverent in the way they live, not to be slanderers or addicted to much wine, but to teach what is good. Then they can train the younger women to love their husbands and children, to be self-controlled and pure."

Subjecting ourselves to accountable relationships enhances our ability to walk the high road in managing our lives with wisdom and discernment. "Going it alone" in life is not at all healthy. We have been created to live in community, and within the faith community we are to submit out of love and highest regard for one another. With whom are you accountable today?

In order for God-honoring accountability relationships to be established within the body of Christ, there must be recognition of the need. Until we get to that point, we won't be in search of others to speak into our lives at the deepest levels. As far as this author is concerned, we never outgrow the need for accountability. At times it's in a formal relationship, and at other times it's very informal. Regardless of the structure, the need for such relationships is essential if we are to move ahead regarding the wise management of our lives.

In many respects, life management is defined by one's abilities (or lack thereof) in self-management. Some of us do better than others in this arena, but for the majority of the population, this is not one of our greatest strengths. Therefore, the need for accountability continues to grow. Accountability is more than friendship, for a friend will often "cut us some slack," which allows for slippage in character issues. For example, a friend may find it difficult to confront us on a bad attitude, a harsh word, or even a lifestyle choice that's unbecoming. Yet in accountability, loving confrontation and truth telling is an essential ingredient to the relationship.

Who in your life is speaking truth in love? It may be time to seek out that "Paul" who will mentor and lead you into a deeper quality of righteousness. To those who have been blessed with such a relationship, it's astounding to see how significantly a life is transformed.

Principle 8.5 Nine No's for Every One Yes

A mentor of mine once reminded me to reconsider a decision I had made about yet another night out away from my family. Since I was open to his accountability, I asked him for advice about how to avoid such temptations in the future. He said very simply, "Generally, the principle needs to be nine no's for every one yes. Others can handle most opportunities afforded to us. We don't need to be involved in everything. If we are saying nine yes's before saying a single no, then we are demonstrating to others and ourselves that we lack the discernment to know the difference between a good option and the best option." I have clung to those words ever since, but I still have a hard time bringing it to fruition. Saying no isn't always easy!

The principle has much validity, particularly for those of us who have more activities and responsibilities than we can possibly ever handle effectively. In accountable relationships, we should consider often whether we are saying nine preceding no's before saying one yes.

Jesus had a healthy understanding of this principle. Why? Because his mission was clear, his life was in balance, he eliminated or managed his stress level, he was accountable to the Father and Holy Spirit, *and* he knew when to say yes and when to say no. In Mark 1, on the heels of a busy day of ministry, we find Jesus in a solitary place in prayer (v. 35). When Simon and his companions found him, "they exclaimed, 'Everyone is looking for you!' Jesus replied, 'Let us go somewhere else—to the nearby villages—so I can preach there also. That is why I have come.' So he traveled throughout Galilee, preaching in their synagogues and driving out demons" (vv. 36–39).

Instead of saying yes to the demands of Simon and the others, Jesus said no because he knew he needed to move on. He said, "Let us go somewhere else," and with that no, he turned on his heels and headed to the nearby villages. Why? Being intentionally mission-minded, he knew with certainty the direction he was to go. Admirable indeed, and with that he moved on to fulfill that which was his calling. He lived out this simple principle with ease. It's not always like that for us.

Heart Alignment

When all is said and done, managing life wisely and account-ably comes back to our hearts remaining in alignment with God's heart for us. This essential trait of disciple health begins with our love for the Lord. Everything else emanates outward from that point. Therefore, the issues that must be addressed early on revolve around the following:

- The cultivation of our first love relationship—is God really number one? If so, how is this evidenced in our daily life mission?
- The consecration of our daily life—remaining in full accord with his mission and in submission to his will.
- Restoration of the joy of relationship with the God of the universe—for he loves us with an infinite, matchless love and desires a life of balance for his beloved children.

When we are living with our priorities in order, then the manage-ment of life with wisdom and accountability will more readily occur. As that process emerges within us, the joy for the journey grows beyond measure.

Ever get lost? I mean really lost. So lost you thought you'd never find your way home? No need to be discouraged; help is on the way!

A Disciple's Prayer

Lord Jesus, managing life in my sea of distractions is getting harder and harder. I know the general direction in which I'm to head, but along the way I discover that the waves and wind are keeping me from moving forward. I trust that in the midst of the storm of uncertainty and instability you will be there to reach out your guiding hand. In that moment, I long to hear your voice, see your face, and feel your gentle touch of grace.

If I'm to manage my life wisely and accountably, I not only need your help, but I also long for others to join me in this often very lonely journey. The community of faith is crucial to my growth and development, in understanding my mission, and in fulfilling my call. Lead me to those individuals and groups who will draw out the very best in me and will assist me in developing my priorities for faithful love and service.

I am devoted to participating in your redemptive work here on earth, so please be delighted to give me a role that reflects my gifts and passions, my abilities, and my greatest joy. Help me reduce and manage my stress level so I will live a more balanced life before you. Guide me in your truth, lead me in your way, and give me hope for the journey ahead. In the precious name of Jesus, my guiding Light. Amen.

For Reflection and Renewal

The healthy disciple develops personal life management skills and lives within a web of accountable relationships.

1. This chapter included several exercises for your consideration. For example:
   a. Write a mission statement (eight steps recommended in the text).
   b. Outline personal roles and goals.
   c. Identify areas of stress and ways to manage/eliminate stress—beginning today!
   Complete as many of these as possible, and share them with a friend or with members of a small group.
2. Read John 9. What is the gift the blind man received from Jesus in verses 1–12? What is the reaction of the Pharisees in verses 13–34? What conclusions can you glean from the

final paragraph in verses 35–41 about spiritual blindness and the need for God's gift of spiritual eyesight?

3. How can you help a fellow disciple in the pursuit of his or her personal mission as "a work of God on display" in the coming week?

4. Review the mission statements of Jesus (John 6:38; John 10:10; John 18:37; Mark 10:45; Luke 19:10). How do these statements inspire the management of your life with wisdom and accountability, and how do they affect the development of your own mission statement?

5. Write out a prayer asking God to help you balance the multiple demands upon you during this season of life and service.

9

Networks with the Body
of Christ

The healthy disciple actively reaches out to others within the
Christian community for relationships, worship, prayer, fellow-
ship, and ministry.

May they be brought to complete unity to let the world know that
you sent me and have loved them even as you have loved me.

John 17:23

For more than forty years, Christians in New England have been
gathering each winter at Congress, an annual event hosted by
Vision New England (my former ministry leadership assignment
for more than fourteen years). More than ten thousand believers
assemble under the same roof for three spectacular days of worship, networking, prayer, fellowship, and instruction. Dominated
primarily by committed Christian laypeople, as well as several
hundred pastors, this meeting has been a significant catalyst for
spiritual renewal throughout the region.

The beauty of the event is evidenced in the variety of people who
come together for this purpose. Although mostly New Englanders,
there are those who attend from nearly thirty other states across

194

the country as well as the eastern provinces of Canada. There are men and women of all ages, including a few thousand youth, in attendance. They come from urban, rural, and suburban communities, represent a cross section of socioeconomic backgrounds, a few dozen denominations, several hundred churches, and a variety of ethnicities. In addition to the mostly evangelical Protestants who are present, Catholic, Anglican, Pentecostal, charismatic, and a variety of independent religious persuasions are also represented at this unique weekend event.

Over the years, the most often repeated comment about the significance of the event dovetails with the focus of this chapter—unity in the body of Christ. Where else do we come together in such a mixed crowd to proclaim the richness of our Christian faith? In what other venues do we find ourselves worshiping with several thousand believers who represent such a healthy cross section of the church of Jesus Christ? Where else is there opportunity to rub shoulders with believers from a host of religious and community backgrounds in such a concentrated time frame? How can this experience, a "foretaste of heaven," be replicated in our daily lives? What kind of mutual service can emanate out from such a fabulous worship experience, brought together under the love and lordship of Jesus Christ?

These are the questions that surface on the heels of such an event. Networking with the body of Christ isn't something that's just for one weekend a year. Yet for many believers it's about the only opportunity to do so!

For those who live in rural America, where great diversity often doesn't exist, it requires a much more proactive approach for the believing community. Take, for example, those who live in small, remote towns where the majority of residents are very similar in ethnicity and socioeconomic situation. In many such communities there may be only one or two Christ-following congregations. How do these believers experience networking within the body of Christ? At minimum, they need to be communicating and cooperating with one another in their community toward similar kingdom-building goals. Ideally, they could consider creative ideas, such as adopting congregations from other parts of the country or world, that will enhance their understanding of the richness of the body of Christ. Merely raising the issue and the need for developing relationships with others who represent the diversity of the body of Christ is a great starting place. From there, it's amazing how creative the people of God can become.

Or what about those of us who live in urban settings, where the ethnic diversity of the body of Christ is tremendous but the coming together of various people groups simply does not occur? Boston is one of the few urban areas in the country in which the body is genuinely coming together. For several decades, key leaders throughout the city have covenanted with one another to maintain strong personal ties, which in turn has created effective synergy in ministry. Consider the fabulous work of the Emmanuel Gospel Center (EGC), where for more than thirty years Doug and Judy Hall have led a growing team of pastors and lay leaders in developing a unique cross-denominational, multiethnic ministry. Their ministry builds unity in the body of Christ and develops significant resources that empower a large number of churches and individuals for cooperative service. Out of the quality of very diverse relationships, EGC has been used of the Lord to strengthen the church like few other urban initiatives. There is still much to be done to bring the body together, and it's in places such as this that hope for unity through networking is offered in abundance.

What about those of us within churches where the denominational ties outweigh connecting with other churches and believers who approach faith and ministry in slightly different ways than we do? For our brothers and sisters in Christ who come from this persuasion, there are a plethora of ideas to consider. How about joining with others in the community who major on the same majors as we do (e.g., the centrality of Christ, the truth of God's Word, the ministry of the Holy Spirit, the significance of missions, evangelism, and outreach)? Consider attending one another's churches, sharing one another's pastors for occasional pulpit supply, praying for the success of one another's ministries, attending one another's programs, inviting one another into your homes, brainstorming how to do outreach services together, planning community worship events, praying together, playing together, strategizing together, and serving side by side for the sake of the gospel.

Unfortunately, our natural instincts don't usually make us open to diversity. We are generally separate from one another because we have chosen to be distinct. We don't worship *that* way, or we don't do *those* programs, or we're not like *those* people, and as a result we have contributed to creating the barriers that have kept us apart for so long. In fact, the reason we have so many denominations within the Protestant church is because we historically started these enclaves of churches out of protest with one another.

Over the years, new denominations have sprung up because people wanted to separate from their previous denomination due to a variety of reasons, such as the leadership of a strong personality, a deeply held theological conviction, or a specific practice in worship or witness. By separating, they were seeking to establish their distinctive form of Christianity. Initially there may have been positive energy exerted toward the creation of this new work, but over time the lines in the sand became darker and more established. As a result, our Protestant subculture is represented in well over one hundred denominations and on top of that a growing number of independent churches and movements. We are now all over the map in our diversity; thus the growing need for unity within the church of Jesus Christ today and into the future.

The question of focus for us becomes, "What can I do, as a disciple in pursuit of spiritual health and vitality, to network with the body of Christ and help build unity within the church?" The best place to begin to wrestle with this question is in expanding our understanding of Christ's priority for this particular area of discipleship.

Prayer for Unity

In John 17 we discover, through a fabulous prayer of Jesus, the essence of God's heart for the unity of his disciples worldwide and throughout all generations.

I am coming to you now, but I say these things while I am still in the world, so that they may have the full measure of my joy within them. I have given them your word and the world has hated them, for they are not of the world any more than I am of the world. My prayer is not that you take them out of the world but that you protect them from the evil one. They are not of the world, even as I am not of it. Sanctify them by the truth; your word is truth. As you sent me into the world, I have sent them into the world. For them I sanctify myself, that they too may be truly sanctified.

My prayer is not for them alone, I pray also for those who will believe in me through their message, that all of them may be one, Father, just as you are in me and I am in you. May they also be in us so that the world may believe that you have sent me. I have given them the glory that you gave me, that they may be one as we are one: I in them and you in me. *May they be brought to complete unity to let the world know that you sent me and have loved them even as you have loved me.*

Father, I want those you have given me to be with me where I am, and to see my glory, the glory you have given me because you loved me before the creation of the world.

Righteous Father, though the world does not know you, I know you, and they know that you have sent me. I have made you known to them, and will continue to make you known in order that the love you have for me may be in them and that I myself may be in them.

John 17:13–26, italics added

On the heels of praying for himself (John 17:1–5), Jesus went on to pray to the Father for the disciples who had followed him during his earthly ministry (vv. 6–19) and then for all believers for generations to come (vv. 20–26). In the center of this prayer, we discover again Jesus' meaning of discipleship. First of all, discipleship

is based on the realization that Jesus came forth from God. The disciple is essentially a person who has realized that Jesus is God's ambassador, and that in his words we hear God's voice, and in his deeds we see God's action. The disciple is one who sees God in Jesus and is aware that no one in the entire universe is one with God as Jesus is.

In addition, discipleship issues in obedience. The disciple is one who keeps God's word as he hears it in Jesus. The disciple is one who has accepted the mastery of Jesus. So long as we wish to do what we like, we cannot be disciples; discipleship involves submission. Also, discipleship is something which is destined. Jesus' men were given to him by God. In God's plan they were destined for discipleship.[1]

Jesus believed in small beginnings, and out of his love for his small band of very ordinary men, he knew that the world would change. It was out of his love for them that he was "always dreaming of their future and planning for their greatness."[2]

Pause and reflect for a moment on the thought, if we love someone we are "always dreaming of their future and planning for their greatness." Does that concept resonate with your spirit? Are you that kind of lover of others within the body of Christ—in your family, in your circle of friends, among colleagues, and with fellow believers in your local church and the extended Christian community? Disciples of Jesus Christ become lovers of others within the faith community as a direct reflection of how Jesus has loved us as his disciples. It may feel rather circular in thought and design, and in fact it is. The prayer in John 17 ascribed to Jesus himself is very much that way—he prayed for himself; he prayed for his disciples; he prayed that the love he had from the Father would remain in him and be given away to his disciples, who in turn would share it with one another so the world would know about the love of the Father through his Son and fulfilled in the unity of disciples everywhere and for all generations! Dizzy yet? It may feel as though it keeps going round and round, but in actuality it's drilling the truth deeper and deeper into the inner recesses of the disciples' hearts.

As disciples of Jesus Christ, the Spirit of God moves our hearts to respond to the strong appeal of Jesus in this tremendous prayer. His appeal was that the glory of the Father would be made manifest in the hearts and souls of his beloved disciples and would be shared with the world for whom he came to die. Through the life of a faithful disciple of Jesus Christ, glory comes to him. "The patient whom he has cured brings honor to a doctor; the scholar whom he has taught brings honor to the teacher; the athlete whom he has trained brings honor to the trainer; the person whom Jesus has redeemed brings honor to him. The bad man made good is the honor of Jesus."[3] Then, as we bring honor and glory to Jesus, we are commissioned to fulfill a task, and that task is only truly fulfilled if done so within the unity of the faith community. Then the world will finally see the glory of God. That is the essence of this prayer.

What then did Jesus pray for his disciples? In this passage, which is jam-packed with truths so great we can only grasp fragments of them, we see the major themes of victory, unity, protection, truth, and glory unfold in this powerful prayer of our Savior.

Theme One: Victory

A central theme in this great prayer of the Lord's is *victory*. In essence, Jesus was praying for the victorious outcome of glory here on earth. His heart was for victory over death through the gift of eternal life. He prayed for victory over the powers of this world that rage all around us and that envelop our heart's affections. His prayer was for victory over the disunity of the body, fully aware of how human nature can seek to conquer the Spirit's desire for complete unity and settle instead for the enemy's agenda to keep us apart.

Our victory is secure in Jesus Christ. We will reign victorious because *he* reigns victorious. It's not that we resolve for this to happen, because he has already won the victory. This prayer underscores what has already been completed on our behalf through the victorious reign of Jesus Christ over this entire world. Jesus prayed here that his disciples would claim that victory and live in a united fashion as the people of God.

Jesus did not pray that his disciples should be taken out of this world. He never prayed that they would escape. He prayed instead that they might find victory. He insisted that it was in the rough and tumble of life that a disciple must live out the Christian faith. It is in this world that we will find minivictories of Spirit over flesh, but the major victory over death itself is the victory we have in Jesus Christ for all eternity. That's a victory worth going to battle for in order to claim it as our very own.

Theme Two: Unity #1

The second theme, dealt with here in two parts, is *unity*. In the early verses of this deep prayer of Jesus, he prayed for unity among his first group of disciples. Those who walked with him while he was here on earth had experienced great unity together. However, we see glimpses into their disunity when a few were vying for the closest proximity to the Savior, or when Judas betrayed the Lord. Overall, we see a band of brothers willing to sacrifice along the way for the sake of the cause and the journey on which Jesus was leading them. At this stage, they didn't really understand what was coming next, but they were generally united in mission and ministry.

Jesus prayed for his disciples' unity, "that they may be one as we are one" (John 17:11) so they may have "the full measure of my joy" (v. 13). He was very aware of their need for joyful unity because Jesus was fully aware of what was forthcoming. He knew they could not face his death on the cross unless they remained one in spirit and purpose. If division were to dominate their experiences together, then the cause for which Jesus came to this earth could potentially be thwarted.

Jesus knew well in advance of the cross, and in preparation for generations to come, that "where there are divisions, where there is exclusiveness, where there is competition between the churches, the cause of Christianity is harmed and the prayer of Jesus frustrated. The gospel cannot truly be preached in any congregation which is not one united band of brothers. The world cannot be evangelized by competing churches. Jesus prayed that his disciples might be as fully one as he and the Father are one."[4]

Theme Three: Protection

One of the most often repeated words in this prayer is *world*. Jesus prayed that his disciples, although living in the world, would not be overcome by the world's overwhelmingly evil influence and demands. Jesus prayed that God the Father would protect his disciples from the attacks of the evil one, who seeks to occupy the hearts of those who dwell on planet earth. The Bible reminds us of the powers of evil that exist in direct opposition to the power of God.

Reminded of our ultimate victory over death, we are to read this prayer as the sentiments of our Savior who empathizes with what we face as fully redeemed members of the eternal society of heaven *and* full participants of life here on earth. Thank God that we have such a Savior who focuses his prayers in our behalf on the Father's loving protection of his children. "It is uplifting to feel that God is the sentinel who stands over our lives to guard us from the assaults of evil. The fact that we fall so often is due to the fact that we try to meet life in our own strength and forget to seek the help and to remember the presence of our protecting God."[5]

Protection from the evil one was a priority for Jesus. How much is it a priority for today's disciples? "Holy Father, protect them by the power of your name. . . . [Protect] them and [keep] them safe by that name. . . . Protect them from the evil one" (John 17:11–12, 15). Whisper that same prayer on behalf of fellow disciples you bring by name to the throne of God's grace and protection. Let's add that one to our daily prayer list.

Theme Four: Truth

The fourth theme to note in Jesus' prayer is the sanctifying of himself and his disciples by the truth of God's Word and the truth of God's call. Disciples are called for a special task—to be sanctified, consecrated, or set apart to fulfill his Word and his way. This is not a new theme introduced by Jesus. When God called Jeremiah, he said to him, "Before I formed you in the womb I knew you, before you were born I set you apart; I appointed you as a prophet to the nations" (Jer. 1:5). When God instituted the priesthood in Israel, he told Moses to ordain the sons of Aaron and to consecrate them to serve him as priests (Exod. 28:41).

Not only does God sanctify us for a special purpose or mission, but he also equips us by his Spirit to fulfill that task. In the meaning of the term *sanctify* there is a powerful truth of God equipping his disciples with the qualities of mind, heart, and character that the task requires. God doesn't merely call us and set us apart by the truth of his Word and his way, but he fully equips us for the days ahead and gives us the gift of his Spirit to empower us with all that's needed.

It's one thing to believe in the truth of God; it's another thing altogether to be sanctified and consecrated to live out that same truth. If we are to serve God, we must acknowledge that we cannot do so without having some of God's goodness, holiness, and wisdom. "He who would serve the holy God must himself be holy too. We must always remember that God has chosen us out and dedicated us for his special service. That special service is that we should love and obey him and should bring others to do the same. And God has not left us to carry out that great task in our own strength, but out of his grace he fits us for our task, if we place our lives in his hands."[6] Living out God's truth is the central, all-consuming passion of the disciple in pursuit of health and vitality in worship, witness, and relationship with others. It's God's truth and his alone in which we abide, and it's the truth of his call and commission that we strive to fulfill throughout all of our days here on earth. This is our holy passion and our holy commission.

Theme Five: Unity #2

As we progress our way through this great prayer, we see the theme of unity reemerge when Jesus placed his prayerful focus on the disciples of generations to come (starting at verse 20). "That all of them may be one . . . that they may be one as we are one. . . . May they be brought to complete unity to let the world know that you sent me and have loved them even as you have loved me"

(John 17:21–23). "Now his prayers take a sweep into the distant future, and he prays for those who in distant lands and far-off ages will also enter the Christian faith."[7]

What was that unity for which Jesus prayed? It wasn't for organizational, ecclesiastical, or even political or administrative unity. It was for the unity of personal relationships among his people. As evidenced in the loving, obedient relationship between Jesus and the Father, this unity among God's people is to be a unity of love and obedience. It's a unity whereby the people of God live obedient lives before the Father and develop loving relationships with each other. Then and only then will the world learn the truth of God's love.

> Christians will never organize their churches all in the same way. They will never worship God all in the same way. They will never even all believe precisely the same things. But Christian unity transcends all these differences and joins men [and women] together in love. The cause of Christian unity at the present time, and indeed all through history, has been injured and hindered, because men loved their own ecclesiastical organizations, their own creeds, their own ritual, more than they loved each other. If we really loved each other and really loved Christ, no church would exclude any person who was Christ's disciple. Only love implanted in people's hearts by God can tear down the barriers which they have erected between each other and between their churches.[8]

It's love, based in healthy relationships among God's people, that binds us together in perfect unity.

As we express genuine love for one another and live out the unity Jesus prayed for on our behalf, we will convince the world of the truth of Christianity and the central place of Jesus Christ as Lord. Since it is far more natural (and of the flesh) that we be divided than united, the challenge of unity is forever before us. Real unity is a supernatural expression of God's people, which comes about only as we are dependent upon God's Spirit to unite us as the church. When that supernatural expression is evidenced, then there is only a supernatural explanation. It's up to the rank and file of the church (each individual disciple) to demonstrate unity of love with our fellow disciples that will express the answer to Christ's prayer.

Our responsibility? Pray for unity among God's people, depend on the Spirit of God to build that unity, and purpose daily to express that unity in heart, mind, voice, and service toward brothers and sisters in Christ. Then and only then will the world fully come to grips and *know* the love of Christ.

Theme Six: Glory

Another prominent word in John 17 is *glory*, our final major theme of Jesus' prayer. "Glorify your Son, that your Son may glorify you. . . . I have brought you glory on earth. . . . Glorify me in your presence with the glory I had with you before the world began. . . . Glory has come to me through them. . . . I have given them the glory that you gave me. . . . To see my glory, the glory you have given me because you loved me before the creation of the world" (John 17:1, 4–5, 10, 22, 24).

What is the glory of Jesus? He talked of his glory through the cross. It wasn't only that he was to be crucified, but of greater importance was that he was to be glorified. For his disciples, first and foremost is the cross that we must bear in life. We are to see this as a badge of honor, for to suffer for Jesus Christ is to be "knighted" in our role as ambassadors of Christ here on earth. It is required that we endure some suffering this side of heaven, and there is no getting around it. Our suffering will differ from person to person, but the cross we bear is to be seen as part and parcel with the glory that is given to us by God.

Consider the incredible suffering of our brothers and sisters who live in far greater hardship in places such as Colombia, South America, the impoverished land of Haiti, or throughout the continent of Africa. Think of those throughout the globe who suffer daily in desperate, diseased, dictatorial, or drought-ridden lands. Our suffering is mild in comparison to the crosses they bear daily. When we in the North American church consider the crosses we carry, there are really very few justifications for our lack of unity. Yet the reasons for our disunity can be directly linked to our lack of material or physical suffering that is experienced elsewhere in the world.

For example, the Colombian church is united around the crosses they bear each day. When the leaders of the Colombian church gather together as brothers and sisters in Christ, they share in one another's suffering and heartache (most directly evidenced in their country through abject poverty, cocaine trafficking, corrupt leadership, and political unrest), and as a result, the church is strengthened, renewed, and alive in the Spirit. Having served with our Colombian brothers and sisters on two separate occasions, I have seen firsthand how the unity of the body of Christ is to be experienced in worship, instruction, relationships, and mission. It seems the greater the heartache, the greater the potential for unity, for it's the sharing of one another's pain—at very tangible, practical levels—that builds genuine unity among the brethren.

As North American believers, we need to come together around the crosses we carry so the unity of the body of Christ will be enhanced and enriched. These crosses are not as often material as they are spiritual, emotional, intellectual, and relational. If our suffering is loneliness, we need the love of the brethren to bring about healing. If our suffering is hatred, we need the love of the brethren to bring about forgiveness. If our suffering is competition, we need the love of the brethren to bring about interdependence and cooperation. If our suffering is materialism and greed, we need the love of the brethren to bring about generosity and stewardship. You see, so many of our sufferings go deeper than the visibly tangible, and once they are discovered and named, the next step is to embrace them as our crosses and find Jesus' glory in caring for each one at his or her particular point of need.

Jesus' glory was found in the cross, but it was evidenced in his relationship with the Father and his obedience to the Father's will. "We find our glory, not in doing as we like, but in doing as God wills. When we try to do as we like—as many of us have done—we find nothing but sorrow and disaster both for ourselves and for others. We find the real glory of life in doing God's will; the greater the obedience, the greater the glory."[9] Jesus lived this out in all its fullness, for after praying this prayer he went straight ahead into the betrayal, the trial, and the cross. It's a precious thought indeed to realize before our Savior entered these terrible hours, his last words were not of despair but of glory.

Therefore, as Christian disciples in pursuit of spiritual health and wholeness, the prayer of Jesus in John 17 becomes a guide for our own prayers for networking within the body of Christ—praying with Jesus for victory, unity, protection, truth, and glory. May it become so in our generation.

Together in Unity

A few years ago I had the wonderful privilege of speaking at a dedication service for a facility that was being consecrated for use by four congregations who would be sharing this space with one another. The group consisted of Baptists, Mennonites, Messianic Jews, and Assemblies of God. The pastors of each of the congregations had offices in the same building, and their congregations would worship on Saturday and Sunday at different times. Their programs were designed to comingle as much as possible, and occasionally they would all meet together to worship as one.

On this particular Sunday afternoon we gathered to dedicate their new building. The theme was "Together in unity to reach our community." The four congregations were making a pledge to one another and to the townspeople that they would serve together as a seamlessly woven faith community. Their posture would be to love one another together in order to make Christ's love known to the town and the region.

It reminded me of Gerry Sittser's book, *Loving Across Our Differences,* in which he shared the following story about unity:

Lynda and I used to watch old movies on public television. It gave us a chance to enjoy classic entertainment and to watch the performances of great actors and actresses, many of whom have long since died. Over the years we saw several movies of one of the screen's greatest, Fred Astaire, who appeared in dozens of films over a span of four decades. We never seemed to tire of his movies, in spite of the predictable plots and mediocre acting. Astaire's dancing astonished us. He was a master on the dance floor—the quintessential example of grace, effortlessness, and sophistication. He looked at home in tails and a top hat.

After his death, Ginger Rogers, his most famous dancing partner, was interviewed on Nightline. She lauded his abilities. He was so good, she said, that he never seemed to be leading and she following. The film clips that were shown that night supported her claim. Astaire and Rogers were elegance in action. There was between them a fluidity, a seamlessness. They were so good that it was impossible, as she said, to tell who was leading and who was following. They were two people dancing as one.

Astaire and Rogers manifested in dance what God wants all of us to experience in life. He intends life to be whole; he wants relationships to be harmonious so that, regardless of the social status we have, the social role we play and the social order we live in, there will be little or no difference between leader and follower, powerful and powerless. Like Astaire and Rogers, our relationship will have a seamlessness.

Of course what God intends and how we live are very different. Astaire and Rogers only show how far we fall short of God's ideal. Their oneness exposes our disunity; their wholeness our brokenness. Their fluidity on the dance floor unmasks our competitiveness and hostility. In human society today—and that of course includes the church—we spend most of our time not dancing gracefully but tripping over each other's feet.[10]

When a group of Baptists, Mennonites, Messianic Jews, and Assemblies of God come together there is great potential for tripping over each other's feet. Not that we have to attend a dance class to learn how to function well as one, but there must be some serious practice sessions if ever we are to perform as one at the level of the heart, seamlessly woven together in the love of Jesus Christ. For the disciple in pursuit of spiritual health and vitality, there comes with this desire for oneness an earnestness to contribute to the fluidity of how the body of Christ loves, serves, worships, and lives together as one in him. Each of us has a part to play, and none of us are to stand on the sidelines and miss the opportunity to dance, nor are we to look out from the center of the dance floor and point fingers at others who aren't participating. Instead, we all join in and gracefully, seamlessly, lovingly advance the unity of the body of Christ. As Jesus has prayed, so we are to live.

Principle 9.1 Diversity of Connection

A starting place for many of us is to recount the variety of people with whom we find ourselves in relationship. Hopefully you will be surprised when you begin to realize the diversity of your existing connections. If you start to list indiscriminately the names of your neighbors, work associates, or even those within your closest circle of friends and extended family members, you'll be surprised to discover the diversity of that group. For example, our list would include our neighbors who are Irish Catholic, our friends down the street who are an interracial married couple (she's Korean and he's African-American), another couple on our street who is Hispanic, our neighbors around the corner who are Jewish, our tailor who is Armenian, and our daughter's friend and family who come from Brazil.

When you hone that list and keep it within the Christian community alone, we have friends who are Chinese Christians, Italian Pentecostals, African-American Baptists, Canadian Presbyterians, converted Jews, Episcopalians, and independent charismatics, just to name a few! When we start to put names and faces next to these people types, we are amazed at the diversity of our relationships within the Christian family and in all of these categories of worship and witness styles.

Unity in the body of Christ begins with our desire and willingness to extend beyond the normal contacts we have with those who are more like us and look for ways to network with others who differ from us. It is here that we begin to experience the beautiful tapestry of the body of Christ. Without having to go too far from home, we can enjoy the richness and flavor of the diversity of the body. We can indeed "taste and see" that the Lord is good, his faithfulness endures throughout generations, and his word is relevant to people of all nationalities, skin colors, and ethnic backgrounds.

Unity in the body of Christ begins with networking among the diverse Christian community that surrounds us. This is not ecumenism as it has become watered down to the least common denominator today. No, it's a new form of ecumenism that frankly claims the original purpose of ecumenism many decades ago—the coming together of God's people around the person of Christ, the Word of God, and the mission of the church worldwide. Here the coming together of God's people encompasses the Triune God, at work redeeming people around the globe from a variety of backgrounds and bringing them into the fellowship of the saints who claim the name of Christ as Lord.

We are a part of a diverse body of Christ. To experience the richness of that diversity requires that we make proactive steps forward in developing friendships with others who worship, witness, and relate outside the context of our typical weekly fellowship. How can you broaden your circle of friends to include greater diversity?

Principle 9.2 Holy Dissatisfaction

As we begin to acknowledge the importance of developing vital relationships with others in the body of Christ but outside our immediate fellowship and step out in faith to build those new relationships, we will begin to discover the richness of the church universal. Experiencing prayer, worship, or ministry with others who do so in a different way from our norm will begin to open up the eyes of our heart to the possibilities before us within our own fellowship. A very natural fruit that often emerges is a holy dissatisfaction with the status quo in our own churches.

When this happens, we need to be careful not to become judgmental or critical of what has been long established as the normal way of functioning within our home church. As often happens after people return from an exhilarating missions trip, Christian conference, or special retreat, they come back with zeal for change and an accompanying dissatisfaction with how things have always been. It's one thing when the youth group gets fired up on retreat or the missions team gets revved up with excitement for a particular people group in need. It's another thing altogether when either they come home and want to turn the church upside down with a new agenda or approach to ministry or they are greeted by yawns of inactivity or yells of displeasure by the adults minding the shop at home.

Having a holy dissatisfaction has both its positive, constructive elements as well as its potential negative, destructive results. Becoming dissatisfied with the status quo, the "same old same old," is generally good. It means that those who have experienced something more in their walk with Christ want to see that lived out in a transformed heart, life, and/or ministry. That's good, and it should be affirmed within the body of Christ. However, the flip side of that is there will inevitably be others within the fellowship who just aren't at the same place. Balancing the zeal of holy dissatisfaction with the status quo on one side with the innate patterns we've developed over many years on the other side takes wise leadership and spiritual discernment to determine the best response for the body of Christ.

It's exactly in this place that the variety of the church is in our favor. Directing or redirecting others into ministry settings that are most conducive to their personal, spiritual growth is key to their development in Christ. As we experience the diversity of the body of Christ, we may in fact discover there are a variety of places where our gifts, abilities, passions, and styles will fit better than others. It's okay to move on (physically, spiritually, and even theologically), as long as we remember, with gratitude and blessing, the place from whence we have come.

Are you dissatisfied in a holy way? Choose wisely the next step you are to take—either within your existing fellowship or in a new ministry setting—so as not to destroy the unity of the body. In your zeal for change, don't discard relationships, traditions, or experiences that have been effectively used of God in the lives of others. Keep the unity of the Spirit and the bond of peace foremost in your heart and mind.

Principle 9.3 Cross-Cultural Pollination

Choosing to participate in activities or service opportunities that take us into new cultural or ethnic environments broadens our understanding of the rich diversity of the body of Christ. Whenever I am with my African-American brothers, I remember afresh the place from which they have come and the struggles of previous generations that led to the vitality of their worship and witness today. As I join my Chinese friends in food, laughter, and vibrant conversation, I see the fruit of the Spirit of God emerge in their gentle, loving, kind, tenderhearted mannerisms. When I join hands in prayer with my Brazilian pastoral colleague and he prays over me in his native Portuguese tongue, I am touched with the Spirit of God and empowered to move ahead in the joy of the Lord.

In addition, having had the unique opportunity to participate in a handful of international missions experiences, I have seen firsthand how multiethnic and international the body of Christ truly has become. Through cross-cultural pollination among the people of God, we have gained so much in our perspective on world missions and international, multiethnic service.

When we participate in cross-cultural pollination among people groups locally, regionally, nationally, and internationally, we bring the worldwide church to the doorstep of our lives and our churches. Through the Internet, we see images of the international church. Through our personal experiences, we get to meet those from various cultural backgrounds. Through the stories of others, we listen in on their sharing and join in their excitement of God at work in the hearts and lives of people on every continent.

We have a choice to make. Either we closet ourselves within the enclaves of our monolithic Christian experience, or we broaden our interests, relationships, and experiences with others who share our faith in Jesus Christ and watch how God blesses and enlivens our spirit through the expanding diversity of our fellowship. The church is brilliant in colors, flavors, images, styles, experiences, ethnicities, cultures, and people groups. How much are you seeing the full spectrum of the mosaic that is ours to enjoy?

Principle 9.4 Multidenominational Investigation

According to Bill Hoyt, executive minister for the Baptist General Conference of the Southwest,

> Cultural borders are not always far away. They are not always obvious until you cross them. My native worship culture was New England, white, free church, low church, and restrained. It was marked by a Fundamentalist disdain for anything liturgical and a fondness for gospel hymns and choruses in the "saw dust trail" tradition. The "preliminaries," which preceded the only thing that really mattered, the sermon, were often planned on the spur of the moment.
>
> Then an uncle came to live with us. He was an Episcopalian. I began attending church with him and gained an appreciation for the majesty, mystery, and history of liturgical worship. I attended a Christian college that practiced a very Presbyterian form of worship. I experienced the enriching of order and planning. For four years I attended two African-American churches in Chicago. I discovered joy and spontaneity in worship. I learned the ease of celebrating Jesus through gospel music.
>
> About five years ago, I joined my son and about 500 other post-moderns at a conference in northern California. I learned that "ska" does not enhance my worship experience. I was, however, overwhelmed to see a new generation enthralled in the presence of God in a room reverberating with music that sounded to me like cats fighting. They didn't have to worship like I like to worship in order to praise God and enjoy Him. Crossing cultural boundaries in worship increased my tolerance and appreciation for a wide variety of worship experiences.[11]

For Bill and a large number of other believers, investigating other ways that believers worship God has enhanced their faith and renewed their commitment to the body of Christ. It doesn't mean that you have to leave the denomination of your choosing, but it gives you freedom to explore other ways that people of faith are expressing their love for God in worship, fellowship, and witness. When was the last time you captured a glimpse of this for yourself?

Principle 9.5 Prayerful Participation

Our network with the body of Christ is not only that which we see, hear, and touch. Our full network is eternal, worldwide, and encompassing all peoples everywhere. The enormity of the network is beyond comprehension, but the particular network God calls us to love and serve in his name is contained within our known experiences and relationships. God's provision for us is made clear as we live life to the full.

Therefore, our prayerful participation in networking with the body of Christ and joining prayerfully in the unity of the church of Jesus Christ, is found in our daily prayer closets, on the pages of our prayer journals, and in the daily experiences of our faith journey as members of the praying Christian family. As you reflect on this principle of discipleship health, you may wish to begin expanding your network simply through your prayers. By making this single choice, you open yourself up to the Spirit of God guiding you into places and relationships in which your network will more naturally expand. It won't happen overnight, but by paying attention to the need to participate more fully in the expanding network of the body of Christ worldwide, the enrichment of your life will occur over time. You will discover afresh how God has so creatively designed his body, the church, in the richness of her diversity and the strength of her unity around that which matters most.

When all is said and done, we return to the priority of Jesus in praying for oneness within the church. That oneness is expressed in our loving unity and commonality of service. *May we be one as he and the Father are one.* As we begin to pray this as our prayer, we will indeed reflect God's heart for disciples of all generations.

A DISCIPLE'S PRAYER

Lord Jesus, as I reflect upon your great prayer in John 17, I am reminded once again of the truth of your Word and the power of your love, grace, and mercy. You have extended that mercy to me through your life, death, and resurrection. You have promised to your disciples throughout every generation that you and the Father and the Spirit are One. You have pledged to us the provision for our unity within our diversity, as a visible reflection of your unity here in this world. Over and over again you have provided opportunities for the eyes of our hearts to be opened in order to see the beauty of the diversity of the body of Christ.

On this day, as my heart is joined with your heart in praying for unity in the church, I think of and pray for the following churches, denominations, ethnic groups, individuals, and ministries/missions that are extending your love to every corner of this city, state, nation, and world. [State particular names that are among your network of relationships.] I also ask that in the coming days you would lead your people into deeper relationships within the diversity of the body of Christ. Broaden our understanding of the expansive work of your kingdom, which is being fulfilled by those who faithfully live out your priorities. Knit the hearts of your people together as one as we join hands in unity in the days to come. This I pray with an earnest desire to see your prayers fulfilled in our generation. For your sake, Lord Jesus, and in your holy name I pray. Amen.

For Reflection and Renewal

The healthy disciple actively reaches out to others within the Christian community for relationships, worship, prayer, fellowship, and ministry.

1. List here the diversity of your existing relationships. Start with those you know in a general sense, and then write down those you know who are within the family of God. How can you foster new relationships with others in the Christian community who are more diverse and can enhance your understanding of the unity of the body of Christ?
2. When is the last time you participated in a worship service that was different from your norm? Jot down observations about the unique elements of that worship service. In what ways did the diversity of the body of Christ express itself in

that worship service? What about that service helped you engage at a deeper level with true, God-exalting worship?

3. As you review your personal prayer journal, how much diversity is expressed on the pages before you? In what ways can you expand the direction of your prayers on behalf of the larger body of Christ?

4. In the coming year, where can you go within the body of Christ to grow your connections with other ethnic communities or your experiences of multidenominational relationships? Who within your existing fellowship or small group can travel this new relationship journey with you and hold you accountable to taking this step forward?

5. What ministry opportunities can you take advantage of in the coming year that will take you into new arenas of service for the sake of sharing the gospel and expanding the kingdom of God? Explore and select one or more, and watch how God expands your horizons for service within the body of Christ!

10

Stewards a Life of Abundance

The healthy disciple recognizes that every resource comes from the hand of God and is to be used generously for kingdom priorities and purposes.

Unless a kernel of wheat falls to the ground and dies, it remains only a single seed. But if it dies, it produces many seeds.

John 12:24

Caleb Loring III is not only a friend and ministry colleague but also a former boss. He chaired the board of directors at Vision New England for the majority of my tenure as its president. He embodies this final principle of discipleship health more than anyone else I've met and has taught me more about stewardship from his life example than from the words he utters.

Caleb and his wife, Bonny, are known in our neck of the woods for their loving hearts and their generous service to the body of Christ. Most importantly, since becoming Christians in their thirties, they have grown to recognize that every resource entrusted to them comes directly from the hand of God and is to be used generously for kingdom priorities and purposes.

One doesn't have to sit with Caleb very long before discovering the genuine nature of his heart for God and for the work of his kingdom. Caleb is known for his stewardship and generosity not only among the evangelical Christian population but even among those in his hometown of Beverly, Massachusetts. The local chapter of B'nai Brith (an international Jewish organization) recently honored Caleb as Beverly's "Man of the Year." At that event, his wife and children surprised Caleb with a presentation of him as "Best Dressed Man of the Year," showing the audience the items that made up the bulk of his wardrobe—hats, t-shirts, jackets, and ties representing the organizations he supports. He's been active in the work of the YMCA, United Way, Salvation Army, Gordon Conwell Theological Seminary, and a host of other ministries and worthy causes (including a local music theater) in the New England region.

An active churchman in the Episcopal denomination, he's nudged the leadership of his local church, as well as the denominational hierarchy, to remain true to their Christ-centered roots and calling. An avid evangelist, Caleb has been actively involved with his wife in developing the Alpha course in Massachusetts through her North Shore Christian Network. He has hosted a weekly men's Bible study in his office's conference room for almost twenty years. He also serves on his church board and meets individually in a mentoring relationship with younger Christian men.

A devoted family man, Caleb and Bonny have raised two wonderful children, now married and raising their own families. He is faithful to serving the daily needs of his mother, who has been ill with Alzheimer's for the past few years, and he is on the tennis court for a weekly match with his beloved father (now in his eighties). In his unending desire to please his wife, Caleb can "cut a rug" like few others on the local dance floor. He is replete with stories of fun times with his family, and he models for the rest of us what it truly means to live life to its fullest.

Always a smile on his face, no matter the turmoil all around him, Caleb embodies what few others can offer to this world—a life of abundance that humbly benefits others. His life is abundant not because of his financial well-being but because of the health and vitality of his walk with Christ. His desire is to serve Christ in his harmonious relationships with others and through his vibrant life of service to the needs of the downtrodden, infirm, imprisoned, and endangered as well as to those who engage in leading such important work in numerous settings.

To know Caleb is to be inspired by his life and the testimony he has faithfully embodied all the days of his Christian walk. That he's a friend to many is an expression of his friendship with God. His daily pilgrimage with the Savior is obvious to all. He begins each day with readings from four or five daily devotionals and praying by name for every member of his huge extended family and all the Christian leaders and organizations he supports. He is a disciplined servant who keeps his priorities in order.

If only all of us were as generous in our stewardship of our lives of abundance—for if you are reading this book, you too are in that same category. Your life is an abundant life because you have faith in Christ. The question is, are you living life out of a spirit of abundance, or are you squandering life as if it's all yours to hold?

The Caleb Lorings of this world have come to realize that life—and all the resources it includes—is not to be held and guarded by us. Instead, the gifts that come directly from the hand of God are meant to be shared generously, openhandedly, in order for the purposes and priorities of God to be fulfilled. It is for the glory of Christ that we pour out our lives of abundance, and it is for the building of his kingdom that we reside on this great earth.

All that we have is God's, for it's from his hand that we receive all our many gifts. In releasing our resources for the purpose of stewarding generously a life of abundance, we let the kernels of our resources fall to the ground and be left there to die. Then, as we release them, they take root and multiply themselves through seedlings of new life, brought forth by our obedience to let them go. Then the harvest comes that only God through his grace can reap! This is how our life of abundance is multiplied in the hearts of others, founded after the example of Christ.

The Amazing Paradox

"The hour has come for the Son of Man to be glorified. I tell you the truth, *unless a kernel of wheat falls to the ground and dies, it remains only a single seed. But if it dies, it produces many seeds.* The man who loves his life will lose it, while the man who hates his life in this world will keep it for eternal life. Whoever serves me must follow me; and where I am, my servant also will be. My Father will honor the one who serves me" (John 12:23–26, italics added).

The hour had come for the Son of Man to be glorified! The Jews had waited since the time of Daniel for this to come to fruition. *The Son of Man* was the term used to describe the "undefeatable world conqueror"[1] who would be sent by God. So when Jesus uttered those words, his hearers held their breath, awaiting the trumpet call of eternity. The power of heaven was on the move, and the ultimate campaign toward victory would soon be ushered in.

Instead, when Jesus referred to being glorified, he meant crucified. "When the Son of Man was mentioned they thought of the conquest of the armies of God; he meant the conquest of the Cross."[2] The shock of this upside-down concept must have taken the first disciples by complete surprise. His words were of staggering and bewildering proportions. They anticipated conquest, but Jesus was talking about sacrifice and death. Their dream of victory was replaced by the vision of the cross, and this conquering, exalted, and glorified Savior was nothing like what they had anticipated for generations.

What was this amazing paradox that Jesus taught? He was saying three things, which are all variations of one central truth and all at the heart of the Christian faith and life.

1. *Jesus was saying that only by death comes life.* The grain of wheat was ineffective and unfruitful so long as it was preserved, as it were, in safety and security. It was when it was thrown into the cold ground and buried there as if in a tomb that it bore fruit. It was, for example, by the death of the martyrs that the church grew. It is always because men and women have been prepared to die that the great fruit

has come forth. Yet it becomes more personal than that. It is sometimes only when a person buries his or her personal aims and ambitions that one begins to be of real use to God. By death comes life. By the death of personal desire and personal ambition, a person becomes a true servant of God.

2. *Jesus was saying that only by spending life do we retain it.* The person who loves his or her life is moved by two aims—selfishness and the desire for security. Not once or twice but many times Jesus insisted that the person who hoarded life must in the end lose it, and the person who spent life must in the end gain it. Think what this world would have lost if there had not been men and women prepared to forget their personal safety, security, selfish gain, and selfish advancement. The world owes everything to people who recklessly spent their strength and gave themselves to God and to others. No doubt we will exist longer if we take things easily, if we avoid all strain, if we look after ourselves as a hypochondriac looks after his health. No doubt we will *exist* longer—but we will never *live*.

3. *Jesus was saying that only by service comes greatness.* The people whom the world remembers with love are the people who serve others. Once a school-age child was asked what parts of speech *my* and *mine* are. He answered—more truly than he knew—that they were *aggressive* pronouns. It is all too true that in the modern world the idea of service is in danger of getting lost. So many people are in business only for what they can get out of it. They may well become rich, but one thing is certain—they will never be loved, and love is the true wealth of life.

Jesus came to the Jews with a new view of life. They looked on glory as conquest, the acquisition of power, the right to rule. He looked on glory as a cross. He taught them that only by death comes life, only by spending life do we retain it, only by service comes greatness. The extraordinary thing is that when we come to think of it, Christ's paradox is nothing other than the truth of common sense.[3]

The paradox contained in this great passage in the Gospel of John is applicable to us today. *It is only as we give that we genuinely receive.* It is when we have sacrificed that we truly understand the fruitful blessing of the cross. It is when we die to ourselves, our own selfish ambitions, and our personal possessions, that we rediscover the true meaning of joy. Early on in my walk with Christ, joy was spelled out for me: J is for Jesus; O is for others; Y is for you. When our priorities are maintained in that simple order, we can truly experience the joy of the Christian life.

In the context of predicting his own death, Jesus reminded his followers that the time for judgment on this world is now. Therefore, while we still have the light among us, we are to walk in the light. He confronted the Jews once more (John 12:37–43), but their hearts remained cold even though he had performed so many miraculous signs in their presence. His call was one of obedience, and the blessing bestowed upon the faithful ones began with sacrifice but ended in glory. His appeal to the Pharisees, who loved praise from men more than praise from God, fell upon hardened hearts. As a result, they remained in darkness and never fully understood a life of abundance in Christ.

Jesus summarized his teachings and cried out:

> When a man believes in me, he does not believe in me only, but in the one who sent me. When he looks at me, he sees the one who sent me. I have come into the world as a light, so that no one who believes in me should stray in darkness.
>
> As for the person who hears my words but does not keep them, I do not judge him. For I did not come to judge the world, but to save it. There is a judge for the one who rejects me and does not accept my words; that very word which I spoke will condemn him at the last day. For I did not speak of my own accord, but the Father who sent me commanded me what to say and how to say it. I know that his command leads to eternal life. So whatever I say is just what the Father has told me to say.
>
> John 12:44–50

The entirety of John 12 provides for us illustrations of this principle of discipleship health and vitality. Preceding the main story of our chapter, in the first eleven verses, Mary of Bethany took a pint of pure nard, poured it out on Jesus' feet, and wiped his feet with her hair. As a result, the house was filled with the abundant fragrance of the extravagance of her love. In contrast, Judas Iscariot, the future betrayer of Jesus, was outraged by this action and objected to the wastefulness of this expression of love. Judas missed out completely and Mary knew fully—from the central core of her soul—what it means to steward a life of abundance.

Verses 12–19 show Jesus on a lowly donkey coming into Jerusalem as the King. Humility of heart had preceded his triumphal entry, not only into the city but into the hearts of his disciples. They shouted, "'Hosanna!' 'Blessed is he who comes in the name of the Lord!' 'Blessed is the King of Israel!'" (v. 13). Here was Jesus living an abundant life and attracting many others in search of that same expression of faith. They were exuberant on that great day of joy that spread throughout the city.

All the while, the Pharisees were more consumed with anger, saying, "See, this is getting us nowhere. Look, how the whole world has gone after him!" (v. 19). In a few short days, this same Jesus would hang on the cross, and many in the crowds would become disillusioned with the same King they ushered into the city with shouts of joy. Yet those who believed wholeheartedly would not only experience the fullness of the abundant life of faith here on earth but also would be ushered into glory to live in that same abundance forever.

Living in the abundance of eternal life is not only for the life hereafter but is to be lived in the here and now. Randy Alcorn, in his book *The Treasure Principle*, asks this poignant question: "Five minutes after I die, what will I wish I would have given away while I still had the chance?" He proceeds to challenge his readers to consider this question in light of six "treasure principles" that should be the guide of every Christ-follower who is interested in stewarding a life of abundance:

1. God owns everything. I'm his money manager.
2. My heart always goes where I put God's money.

3. Heaven, not earth, is my home.
4. I should live not for the dot [life on earth] but for the line [life in heaven].
5. Giving is the only antidote to materialism.
6. God prospers me not to raise my standard of living, but to raise my standard of giving.[4]

Stewarding our life of abundance includes how we handle our earthly treasures and grows outward into every aspect of our lives. Jesus calls us to place our treasures into the very areas that our heart resides. If our hearts are fixed on earthly priorities, then we will invest in worldly goods and the building of our reputations. If our hearts are focused on heavenly priorities, however, our investments will follow suit, and we will give to causes that advance the kingdom. It's a delicate issue for most believers who are honest about this issue and want to live abundantly and generously, all the while caring for the immediate needs of their family and loved ones.

Remember the paradox—unless the kernel of wheat drops into the earth and dies, we will not see new seeds bring forth new life! Which kernel(s) in your life needs to fall to the ground and die in order for your life of abundance to become fruitful for his kingdom? As the prayer of St. Francis reminds us, "It is in giving that we receive; it is in pardoning that we are pardoned; it is in dying that we are born to eternal life."

Attitude of Gratitude

Becoming a healthy disciple includes the fulfillment of God's call to abundant generosity in the stewardship of life. It means entrusting our time, talent, and treasures to God's purposes through us as his disciples. It begins with one's attitude toward life. Is our cup half empty or half full?

From our earliest days of childhood, we grow and mature in our ability to be grateful for what we have rather than always longing for things that are out of our reach. In our families, churches, and within ourselves, the heart of the matter is for us as believers to find strength, joy, and fulfillment in our contentment. The apostle Paul describes contentment for all circumstances in Philippians 4:11–13, "I have learned to be content whatever the circumstances. I know what it is to be in need, and I know what it is to have plenty. I have learned the secret of being content in any and every situation, whether well fed or hungry, whether living in plenty or in want. I can do everything through him who gives me strength."

Even from a prison cell, Paul found room in his heart to be joyful. The key to his gratitude was contentment. Learning to be content with what we have, rather than always longing for what we don't have, is the best place to begin to live a life of abundance. The glass is always at least half full, and an attitude of gratitude is reminder number one of that truth for the disciple in pursuit of spiritual health and vitality.

Our son, Nathan, has had to learn contentment the hard way. In the first seventeen years of his life he faced twelve surgeries to save, strengthen, and correct a weak, sickly tibia that he was born with in his right leg. It was only after the twelfth surgery that we began to see significant healing (in essence, he had lived the entirety of his life with a constant broken leg!). Teaching Nate to focus more on what he could do within his disability, as opposed to what he couldn't, required our constant monitoring and encouragement.

It has been amazing for us as parents to watch Nate develop an attitude of gratitude and contentment. He exudes the joy of the Lord in his relationships with others. He has chosen to be involved in athletics as a manager of a team every season for each of his four years of high school. He volunteers for backstage work at school plays, coaches middle school intramurals, helps park cars at various events, and generally makes himself available to serve others.

Nate never complained about the pain he was obviously experiencing, nor did he fight the doctors on the restrictions he had to follow whether on crutches, in a wheelchair, or in a hospital bed. He learned the hard way what it means to be content in every circumstance, yet he chose to live his life to the fullest rather than be brought low by the difficulties he encountered. We have all been blessed as we watch Nate deal with his disability with an attitude of contentment and joy. Suffering with integrity and honor has been a gift from God, and his attitude has been contagious.

What about you? Have you learned the secret of contentment that will transform your life forever? Begin today by counting your blessings, name them one by one, count your many blessings, see what God has already done. In your cup of abundance, begin to list the ingredients of blessing upon blessing that God has richly bestowed upon you. Noting the blessings of God is an expression of our reignited passion for God with all our heart, soul, mind, and strength. The attitude of gratitude will eventually become a habit of the heart that's worth cultivating for the rest of your life.

Abundant Life

Stewarding a life of abundance not only begins with an attitude of gratitude that grows out of a spirit of inner contentment, but it includes a life of joy, celebration, harmony, justice, continuity, effectiveness, faithfulness, obedience, resourcefulness, sacrifice, mercy, and love. The abundant life of the Christian is experienced when we prayerfully make God's priorities our daily priorities. North American Christians not only have the opportunity to live the abundant Christian life, but the majority of us also live an abundant life of earthly possessions. The latter abundance is what must be stewarded with a heart of generosity rather than multiplied for the sake of personal gain.

If we are not careful, the pursuit of a life of abundance will focus almost exclusively on the determination to acquire more and more things and experiences to benefit us personally. When we are in hot pursuit of such temporal values, we in essence are following after idols and losing sight of following fervently after the heart of God. By replacing God with our activities and acquisitions, we grow further and further away from developing a true understanding of Christ-honoring stewardship.

The ancients called them idols; today we call them addictions.

- Overabundance of food can lead to gluttony.
- Overabundance of passion can lead to lust.
- Overabundance of time can lead to boredom and sloth.
- Overabundance of resources can lead to selfishness.
- Overabundance of power can lead to manipulation.
- Overabundance of abilities can lead to pride.
- Overabundance of liberalities can lead to anarchy.
- Overabundance of chemical substances can lead to addiction.

To refer to the Christian life as the abundant life can be misconstrued and misunderstood to mean the abundance of things and experiences that satisfy our self-interests. No, the abundant Christian life is taking our abundance of heart, soul, mind, and strength and giving it all away for the sake of Christ and the needs of his kingdom. It includes a healthy satisfying of our family needs, all the while generously sharing our abundance with others. There is such joy in the abundant life of the Christian when we understand that everything we have comes to us from the generous heart of almighty God. He delights to see us steward all that we have with a heart of generosity for his almighty purposes here on earth.

Therefore, it is incumbent upon us as believers in search of spiritual health and vitality to be careful not to follow after those things that are an abomination to the Lord. Proverbs 6:16–19 articulates very clearly what the Lord loathes: "There are six things the LORD hates, seven that are detestable to him: haughty eyes, a lying tongue, hands that shed innocent blood, a heart that devises wicked schemes, feet that are quick to rush into evil, a false witness who pours out lies and a man who stirs up dissension among brothers."

This passage in Proverbs shows how we make a mockery of genuine life stewardship. That happens when we take even the basics of what we've been given by God—our eyes, tongue, hands, feet, mind, and relationships—and abuse them to the point that they lead to absolutely zero stewardship, no abundance, and certainly no life. Let's look at them one by one.

1. Haughty eyes—they are a reflection of a proud heart.
2. Lying tongue—exhibiting deceitfulness in one's speech.
3. Hands that shed innocent blood—accepting personal enrichment by theft or oppression of others; specifically, getting rich by exploiting others and/or via sexual immorality.
4. Heart that devises wicked schemes—acting out one's evil schemes against another.
5. Feet that are quick to rush into evil—destructive pathways of one's personal lifestyle choices.
6. False witness and verbal lies—speaking falsely and accusatorily against others.
7. One who stirs up dissension in relationships—through the slander of others, creating distrust that culminates in alienation and conflict.

As a disciple of Jesus Christ, I have not only been the recipient of some of the above from members of the body of Christ, but also I must admit that I have sinned against God and others in those very same ways. Allowing the things that are hated by God to enter the life of the disciple is not only a sin but a sign of our heart's true condition. This is why stewarding a life of abundance begins and ends with our hearts. When we replace God with activities, acquisitions, and attitudes unbecoming to him, then we begin to idolize what he abhors, and our passion for God's heart is replaced by the sin of our own.

What about your heart? Do you long for God more than the things of this world? Do you long for God more than what he can provide for you experientially or emotionally? Do you long for God more than his material blessings? If not, then you are being drawn more into idol worship than genuine, heartfelt, Christ-centered relationship with the living God. His life is an abundant life, and it's the life we are meant to live—to the fullest extent and always for his glory. Don't let the enemy steal your joy.

Principle 10.1 Serve Openhandedly

Henri Nouwen often wrote about the comparison between the life of openhandedness, which leads to joyful, prayerful service, and the contrasting life of the tightly closed, clenched fists of self-centeredness, which lead to inner tension and the desire to cling to those things that foster greed and create fear. He relates the story of an old woman brought to a psychiatric center: "She was wild, swinging at everything in sight, and scaring everyone so much that the doctors had to take everything away from her. But there was one small coin which she gripped in her fist and would not give up. In fact, it took two men to pry open that squeezed hand. It was as though she would lose her very self along with the coin. If they deprived her of that last possession, she would have nothing more, and be nothing more. That was her fear."[5]

Although more dramatic than we care to admit, this image also reflects many of our own lives. We are clinging to possessions, experiences, even people with such a strong-fisted grip that we fear ever releasing them, not knowing what will happen if we let them go. Nouwen reminds us that unless we open up our hands and release all that we are and all that we have, we will not experience the abundant life of Christ. Jesus gave all that he was and all that he had in order that we might be saved from the bondage of sin and self-absorption.

The antidote to a life of fearful clenched-fistedness is prayer. "To pray means to open your hands before God. It means slowly relaxing the tension which squeezes your hands together and accepting your existence with an increasing readiness, not as a possession to defend, but as a gift to receive. Above all, prayer is a way of life which allows you to find a stillness in the midst of the world where you open your hands to God's promises, and find hope for yourself, your fellowman, and the whole community in which you live. In prayer, you encounter God in the soft breeze, in the distress and joy of your neighbor and in the loneliness of your own heart."[6]

Stewarding a life of abundance begins with prayerfully releasing all that we are and have into the loving purposes of God. He is our source of life and the giver of all good gifts, so we must obediently open up our hands and generously discharge our life possessions so that others are subsequently served. Serving is not for self-gratification; it is for the glory of God and fulfillment of the needs of others. The only way we will be led into such an experience is if we become prayerfully attuned to God's priorities for us as his children. Serving openhandedly begins and ends with prayer.

Principle 10.2 Steward Prayerfully

As we are led into a life of prayerful openhandedness, the particulars of personal stewardship herald before us. In Matthew 25 Jesus recounts for his disciples the parable of the talents. In this parable, Jesus tells the story of "a man going on a journey, who called his servants and entrusted his property to them. To one he gave five talents of money, to another two talents, and to another one talent, each according to his ability. Then he went on a journey. . . ."

"After a long time the master of those servants returned and settled accounts with them. The man who had received five talents brought the other five. 'Master,' he said, 'you entrusted me with five talents. See, I have gained five more.' His master replied, 'Well done, good and faithful servant! You have been faithful with a few things; I will put you in charge of many things. Come and share your master's happiness.'" The same thing happened to the servant with two talents, who brought two more to the master.

The servant with one talent, however, thought he knew the heart of his master, and instead of multiplying his talent, he hid it in a hole in the ground. The master's response? "You wicked, lazy servant! So you knew that I harvest where I have not sown and gather where I have not scattered seed? Well then, you should have put my money on deposit with the bankers, so that when I returned I would have received it back with interest. Take the talent from him and give it to the one who has the ten talents. *For everyone who has will be given more, and he will have an abundance.* Whoever does not have, even what he has will be taken from him. And throw that worthless servant outside, into the darkness, where there will be weeping and gnashing of teeth" (Matt. 25:14–15, 19–30, italics added).

Here Jesus reminded his disciples that to steward a life of abundance (which as his servants comes directly from the hand of the Master), we are to prayerfully and intentionally seek to multiply all that has been given to us. To do anything less than multiplying our resources is to walk disobediently away from the Master's priority. Through this significant gospel story, the Lord is clearly articulating the need for every disciple, regardless of the number of talents given, to affirm the call to openhanded obedience.

All that we have is to be used for the glorifying purposes of God. Stewarding our life prayerfully brings us fully in touch with the following four very basic areas of consideration and evaluation:

Time—every hour of the day given over to him!
   Personal schedule reflective of God's priorities for you?
Talent—every gift and ability offered to honor him!
   Personal stewardship of your mission, roles, and goals?
Treasure—every dollar stewarded generously for him!
   Personal financial investments and checkbook generous to others?
Temple—every part of our bodies fit to glorify him!
   Physical body cared for, nourished, rested, and self-controlled?

Principle 10.3 Sacrifice Financially

"In God's eyes there's a vital link between our earthly possessions and our eternal soul," says Wesley Willmer, vice president for university advancement and professor at Biola University in La Mirada, California. "Giving is primarily a spiritual matter, an act of obedient worship to God. When we acknowledge that God owns everything, we realize God's priority is developing faithful disciples and seeing us mature spiritually through our generosity. How we handle our possessions on earth has far-reaching eternal consequences."[7]

As imitators of God, we are called to be generous just as he is generous. Giving generously requires sacrifice, but it's always a win-win situation for the giver, the recipient, and the glory of God! How then do we develop a generous heart? Since there is an irrefutable link between our earthly possessions and our eternal soul, how we give has eternal consequences worthy of serious consideration. Willmer outlines six values God holds about our possessions:

1. *God tracks how we use our possessions to determine what rewards we'll receive in heaven.* Rewards in eternity, Scripture teaches, are based on what we do on earth resulting in different levels of honor being granted in heaven. *Question to ask:* What have you done to earn crowns in heaven as "good and faithful servants" in the use of God's possessions? Consider Proverbs 24:11–12; Matthew 19:27–30; and Luke 14:12–14.

2. *Our use of possessions demonstrates how much responsibility we're worthy to assume in heaven.* If God can't trust you with small things on earth such as your house, belongings, or 401k plan, how can he trust you with true riches in heaven that will last forever? *Question to ask:* Can you cite examples of how you're using possessions entrusted to you on earth as evidence to God that you're capable of assuming truly important responsibilities in eternity? Consider Luke 16:10–12.

3. *Generous giving is an opportunity to reciprocate God's grace.* Since God is overwhelmingly generous with his grace, we should likewise be generous with the stuff (i.e., possessions) entrusted to us. Giving provides the opportunity to thank God for his kindness toward us. As imitators of God, we're called to be generous, just as he is. *Question to ask:* What evidence is there that you are a faithful dispenser of God's grace? Consider 1 Peter 4:10.

4. *God provides possessions as a tool to bring others to Christ.* Wise stewards will use all their possessions as tools on God's behalf. *Questions to ask:* Car, house, clothes, stocks, various collections: Are they being leveraged to glorify God? Who

will greet you in heaven saying, "We're here as the result of how you used your possessions as a tool to reach us for Christ"? Consider Luke 16:9.

5. *The stuff entrusted to us is a test of who is Master and Lord of our lives.* We cannot serve both God and money. God knows our attitudes and our actions better than we do. *Questions to ask:* Is God or money in charge of your life? Can you illustrate how you use God's stuff to demonstrate that God's eternal kingdom is your highest priority? Consider Luke 16:1–9.

6. *How we use possessions indicates our trademark.* One of the most visible signs of our values is our stuff. *Questions to ask:* As your neighbors, friends, or colleagues look at your life, what brand or trademark do they see? Is it clear from how you use your stuff that you value your home in heaven more than your stuff on earth? Try taking an inventory of all you have and ask, "Am I using this for God, or myself?" What specific evidence is there from how you use possessions that your trademark is that of a Christian? Consider Luke 16:13.[8]

Principle 10.4 Seed Generously

Whenever I address others about stewarding a life of abundance, I mention the two most telltale signs of how well we are doing in this area of our spiritual lives. Those two signs are our checkbooks and our calendars. As we look carefully at each, we see the truest condition of our stewardship of a life of abundance.

Those who seed generously are not afraid to show their checkbook to another believer. (I challenge you to try it!) Or they can at least discuss with others how their resources are being invested for kingdom-building priorities or what their goal is for the percentage of gross income they plan to give away in the coming year—not for bragging rights or comparisons, but for accountability and stewardship. How else will we make wise decisions about this all-important matter unless we have the freedom to talk openly about how we can grow in this area?

Frank grew in his company, and when he ultimately became president, he realized he didn't need all the money offered to him by his board. Instead of refusing the fabulous income, he and his wife made a deliberate choice not to spend it on themselves. Even though Frank was now holding a prestigious position in a thriving company, they didn't alter their living standards. Over time, they ended up giving 90 percent of their gross income away! The bundle he was making far surpassed their needs. As devoted Christians, they chose to proactively invest in kingdom priorities instead of adding to their personal portfolios or financial nest egg.

Who do you know who has made similar decisions? Unless you freely talk about issues of money from a Christian perspective with those in your fellowship, how will you ever know if you're making the best decisions for yourself? Knowing people like Frank has helped to shape our family priorities, and although we are nowhere close to the size of income Frank achieved in his career, we are seeking to grow the percentage we give away to others each year.

We don't need to continue acquiring more and more financial resources while the majority of our world is going to bed hungry. It may not be as readily apparent here in North America, but travel to almost any other continent and the abject poverty is a striking contrast to how we live in this land of abundance and wealth.

Not only are we to assess the stewardship of our financial resources on an ongoing basis, but the same kind of evaluation needs to be applied to our calendars. All too often we applaud each other for how full our days have become. We work, work, work, and don't find time to rest, refresh, and renew.

Instead of patting each other on the back for a full schedule of events each day, isn't it time to hold one another accountable for a more balanced lifestyle? If we are going to seed generously, we need to know how to seed appropriately. We don't just dump all the seed in one place or scatter it carelessly where it makes no difference whatsoever. No, the seeding of our gifts of time and service needs to be placed carefully and strategically so the greatest return on our investment can be achieved.

Take a careful look at your calendar for the coming week. What's on there of greatest priority? What could you eliminate or delegate to another? What needs to be changed in order that your primary relationship with God is advanced? And what about your closest human relationships? What's included that serves the needs of others? What kind of rest and refreshment is included? These are the kind of questions you need to ask yourself and invite others to speak to as well.

To seed generously is one of our greatest earthly joys for it's here that we ask God how *he* desires the fullness of our lives to be generously stewarded for his glory and purposes. There is no greater satisfaction than knowing at the end of the day, as we lay our heads down to sleep, that his words to us would be, "Well done, good and faithful servant! You have been faithful with a few things. . . . Come and share your master's happiness!" (Matt. 25:21). Having seeded generously throughout the day, we sleep well knowing he is pleased and honored in our stewardship of time, talent, treasure, and temple.

Principle 10.5 Smile Abundantly

One of my all-time favorite vision statements for a church is "to be a church that makes Jesus smile!" Just hearing those words brings a smile to my heart. Who wouldn't want to be a part of bringing that vision to life?

What about for us as individual believers? Imagine if every disciple in pursuit of health and vitality chose that same simple vision? If we were to make every decision, build every relationship, use every resource entrusted to our care with a desire to "make Jesus smile," how much brighter would be our hearts and how much more joy-filled would be our world.

Christians aren't known for their joy or their generosity. How unfortunate. Yet our generation can change that impression forever. We can choose the joy of the psalmist who prayed, "Satisfy us in the morning with your unfailing love, that we may sing for joy and be glad all our days" (Ps. 90:14). We can choose to steward our lives of abundance with generosity of heart, with the goal not only to make Jesus smile but also to bring the joy of the Lord into every situation of life and service.

Remember my friend Caleb? He chooses to make Jesus smile as he begins and ends each day. His life verse is Micah 6:8, "And what does the LORD require of you? To act justly and to love mercy and to walk humbly with your God." He has come to recognize that without the fullness and humility of Christ inhabiting the center core of his soul, what he gives to others is more of a frown than a smile.

What is the status of your heart today? What does God hear through his loving stethoscope as he listens carefully to the beat of your heart? Is your heart cold? Then let him warm it. Is it hard? Let him soften it. Is it wounded? Let him heal it. Is it divided? Let him unite it. Is it weary? Let him renew it. Give him your heart today—there is no place like home in the hand of almighty God. It is here that you begin to live the abundant life of Christ.

David's prayer of praise in 1 Chronicles 29:10–13 and 16–19 comes on the heels of the people giving freely and wholeheartedly to the Lord and is the basis of the following prayer.

A DISCIPLE'S PRAYER

Praise be to you, O LORD, God of our father Israel, from everlasting to everlasting. Yours, O LORD, is the greatness and the power and the glory and the majesty and the splendor, for everything in heaven and earth is yours. Yours, O LORD, is the kingdom; you are exalted as head over all. Wealth and honor come from you; you are the ruler of all things. In your hands are strength and power to exalt and give strength to all. Now, our God, we give you thanks, and praise your glorious name.

O LORD our God, as for all this abundance that we have provided for building you a temple for your Holy Name, it comes from your hand, and all of it belongs to you. I know, my God, that you test the heart and are pleased with integrity. All these things have I given willingly and with honest integrity. And now I have seen with joy how willingly your people here have given to you. O LORD, God of our fathers Abraham, Isaac, and Israel, keep this desire in the hearts of your people forever, and keep their hearts loyal to you. And give us . . . the wholehearted devotion to keep your commands now and forevermore. Amen.

For Reflection and Renewal

The healthy disciple recognizes that every resource comes from the hand of God and is to be used generously for kingdom priorities and purposes.

Stewarding a life of abundance means that we are willing to assess the true condition of our personal life stewardship in light of God's abundant gifts. For this final trait, the challenge for the disciple in pursuit of health and vitality is to begin looking carefully at the various stewardship issues raised in this chapter and move ahead in addressing each issue individually.

The following chart is designed to help you start working on each of these issues. As you edit and revise each category, share with others the direction you sense the Lord leading you in your desire to steward generously your life of abundance.

Take the time *now* to begin renewing a life of abundant stewardship. You will be so glad you did!

Stewarding a Life of Abundance
By God's Grace and Guidance . . .

God's Abundance	My Stewardship (when, where, how)
Personal life mission (WHY)	
Personal roles in life (WHO)	
Personal goals for life (WHAT)	
Priorities for my schedule (TIME)	
Proactive seeding, serving, sacrifice (TALENT)	
Physical body (TEMPLE)	
Personal finances (TREASURE)	
Prayerful joy! (TRUE HEART)	

Conclusion

But these are written that you may believe that Jesus is the Christ, the Son of God, and that by believing you may have life in his name.

John 20:31

We've been covering a lot of miles together, searching the Gospel of John, learning from Jesus' beloved disciples, and processing a plethora of important material along the way. The life and teachings of Jesus Christ provide the pinnacle of discovery for every disciple in search of spiritual health and vitality. There is so much more to learn about our Lord as we study the Gospel accounts of John's colleagues Matthew, Mark, and Luke and review the teachings of John's predecessors in the Old Testament and his many successors in the early church (from the Book of Acts to the Revelation). All of their teachings point us in one direction—toward Jesus.

As believers in Jesus, we read his Word so our faith can be deepened and by believing we may have life more fully in his name. That's the mission statement of the Gospel of John, and it should be our focus as well. "Did I not tell you," Jesus said, "that if you believed, you would see the glory of God?" (John 11:40).

The final few chapters of the Gospel of John put a wrap on the life and ministry of our Lord. Chapters 18 and 19 cover his arrest, crucifixion, death, and burial. Chapters 20 and 21 are all about his resurrection following the discovery of his empty tomb. Each of these accounts brings to light what he said to the disciples earlier: "In this world you will have trouble. But take heart! I have overcome the world" (John 16:33). His words of comfort and hope

239

reminded the disciples that their understanding of spiritual health and vitality in Christ will lead them to eternal life. Take heart—he has overcome the world.

We see this evidenced in the postresurrection "Jesus sightings" when he showed himself to his followers as the one who has conquered death and will live and reign forever and ever. "The risen Lord was not a vision, nor a figment of someone's excited imagination, nor the appearance of a spirit or a ghost; it was Jesus who had conquered death and come back."[1]

There are approximately a dozen such sightings recorded for us (e.g., Matt. 28:9, to the women; Matt. 28:17–20, giving the Great Commission; Luke 24:15–35, on the road to Emmaus; Luke 24:50–51, at his ascension; 1 Cor. 15:5, "to Peter and then to the Twelve"; 1 Cor. 15:6, "to more than five hundred of the brothers"; 1 Cor. 15:7, to James; 1 Cor. 15:8 and Acts 9:5, to Paul at his conversion). Yet, the four most remarkable postresurrection sightings in the Gospel of John are found in chapters 20 and 21.

Postresurrection Jesus Sighting #1

In John 20:10–18, Jesus appeared to Mary of Magdalene, the one out of whom he had previously driven seven demons. She was a scarlet sinner, one whom Jesus had reclaimed, forgiven, and purified, and she was the first on the scene at the empty tomb. Having sinned much, she loved much, and her love was all she had to bring.

Jesus said to her, "Woman, why are you crying?" (v. 15). The answer is obvious. Her Lord no longer resided in the place where he was laid only hours before. Her heart was filled with incredible pain, and the Conqueror of Death showed compassion and concern over her broken heart. As a result, he spoke into her pain and revealed himself to her out of amazing love. Love is the theme of the scene.

Postresurrection Jesus Sighting #2

In John 20:19–23 Jesus appeared to the ten disciples (not including Judas the betrayer nor Thomas). The disciples were behind a securely locked door, for fear they would be found out by the Jews. Jesus showed up and said to them, "Peace be with you!" (v. 19). After he showed them his hands and side, the disciples were overjoyed to see the Lord.

Jesus reminded the disciples of his previously spoken prophecy of himself, and their faith was strengthened and renewed. Then he breathed the Holy Spirit on the disciples, challenging them to proclaim forgiveness of sins in his name and under his divine authority. The room must have lit up with the light of the risen Christ, and the hearts of the downtrodden disciples were obviously lifted to greater heights having seen their risen Redeemer and Lord.

Postresurrection Jesus Sighting #3

When Thomas heard about Christ's appearance, he said, "Unless I see the nail marks in his hands and put my finger where the nails were, and put my hand into his side, I will not believe it" (John 20:25). A week later, Jesus appeared to the eleven disciples—this time with Thomas present and accounted for (John 20:26–31). Jesus' theme was still "Peace be with you" (v. 26), as if to repeat the previous theme so that doubting Thomas could be brought into the disciples' experience with the risen Christ.

Knowing Thomas's doubting heart, Jesus spoke directly into his concerns: "Put your finger here; see my hands. Reach out your hand and put it into my side. Stop doubting and believe" (v. 27). How much more direct could Jesus have been? He knew exactly where his disciples held doubt in their hearts and spoke peace into every corner of their troubled souls. Thankfully, he's still in that same business today.

Postresurrection Jesus Sighting #4

In John 21:1–14, Jesus appeared to the disciples as they were fishing and invited them to a shoreline breakfast like none other. In this miraculous story of catching fish, Jesus noticed they were not being very successful and encouraged them from the shore to "throw your net on the right side of the boat and you will find some" (John 21:6). When they did so, they were unable to haul the net in because of the large number of fish they had caught.

Realizing who it was speaking to them from shore, Peter impetuously jumped into the water in order to be with Jesus ahead of the rest of them. Jesus had a charcoal fire waiting for them, and they enjoyed a breakfast unlike any other they would have again. Jesus reinstated Peter (vv. 15–25) and poured courage on his heart as he commissioned Peter to feed the lambs, take care of the sheep—charging him to follow fervently after the priorities Jesus had established while they walked the Holy Land together. His calling and blessing was promised during one of their most intimate meals.

From these postresurrection Jesus sightings, we discover afresh how he ministers his grace upon his disciples.

- Jesus sighting #1: **From the depth of our *pain*** (which he recognizes and desires to heal).
- Jesus sighting #2: **He speaks *peace*** (through his promise of the Holy Spirit).
- Jesus sighting #3: **He leads us through a *process* of growth** (even when we doubt his presence and power).
- Jesus sighting #4: **He blesses our lives with *productivity*** (from the moment we are called, in his timing throughout our lives, and all by the gift of his unending grace).

What is it about the condition of your soul today that needs a touch of Jesus' healing grace? He longs to speak peace into your often troubled, depleted, and doubting soul. He promises his presence and power for every single moment of your day and will release Holy Spirit productivity through your faithfulness to his call. Trust in his tireless mercy, and turn yourself over to his constant and abiding care. There's no turning back for the disciple of Jesus Christ who is in search of his Spirit-filled vitality. Move forward, become a healthy disciple with vigor, and hold unswervingly to the hope he has planted within your heart—now and forever.

We Are People in Process

Congratulations! You've made it through the ten traits of a healthy disciple and considered prayerfully the five basic principles contained within each of the characteristics. Along the journey I have been encouraging you to think through all of this material within the context of your personal relationship with Christ and with fellow believers who are processing these same issues.

Now, if I may, I'd like to challenge you to review the notes you've made in the margins and the answers you've written out to the questions and urge you to move forward with one sweeping goal: *transformation!* What are the specific changes you need to make in order to embody more fully one or more of the traits or principles covered in this text?

The apostle Paul reminded us, "Therefore, I urge you, brothers, in view of God's mercy, to offer your bodies as living sacrifices, holy and pleasing to God—this is your spiritual act of worship. Do not conform any longer to the pattern of this world, but be transformed by the renewing of your mind. Then you will be able to test and approve what God's will is—his good, pleasing and perfect will" (Rom. 12:1–2).

Martin Luther put it this way: "This life is not righteousness, but growth in righteousness; not health, but healing; not being, but becoming; not rest, but exercise. We are not yet what we shall be, but we are growing toward it; the process is not finished, but is going on; this is not the end, but it is the road. All does not gleam in glory, but all is being purified."

Remember what the mystics of old said: "Action without reflection is meaningless action!" Therefore, if you want to make the best of your reading and processing of this material, it's important that you consider four very basic "-tions" that each of us should not "shun" at this stage of the process as we are becoming healthier disciples of Jesus Christ, being transformed more and more into his image and likeness.

1. *Reflection.* Press the pause button of your hectic life and consider ways in which the truths of God's Word are or are not being fulfilled through you. Don't walk away from opportunities for quiet reflection—that may be the greatest gift of all as you process the material contained in this book, the issues that were enlarged through answering the questions at the end of each chapter, and/or your discussion with others regarding each of the ten traits.

2. *Affirmation.* Be sure to listen carefully and confidently to the words of the Savior, "Well done, good and faithful servant," as well as the kind words of others as they confirm your gifts and abilities, your love and faithfulness.

3. *Evaluation.* Undoubtedly there will be places where you identify issues, relationships, and attitudes that will need to be not only assessed but addressed very specifically in the coming days. Don't be afraid to look honestly in the mirror and see the true you, knowing that where you are today isn't where you need to stay forever—praise the Lord.

4. *Application.* Once you've identified places within you that need some reconstruction, be sure to begin working on areas of heart, mind, and will that God directs you to change in order that his likeness can become more visible through you. Remember as well that all of this transformation is only accomplished by his grace, for his glory, and the fulfillment of his kingdom priorities through you.

Becoming a healthy disciple is a lifelong process, requiring patient steps taken one day at a time. It demands the very best of us, but the reality is that God is the one in full control of the process we encounter. George MacDonald said it well: "You must not imagine that the result depends on you. The question is, are you having a hand in the work God is doing? God will do his work in his time and in his way. Our responsibility is merely to stand ready and available to go where he sends and do what comes our way."[2]

Are you ready to take on this process throughout all the days of your life? If so, then "On your mark, get set, go!"

This is my prayer for you, my fellow disciple in pursuit of health and vitality. It is taken from Colossians 3:1–10, 12–17 and is spoken in love for you with the knowledge that our heavenly Father knows you intimately by name:

Since, then, you have been raised with Christ, set your hearts on things above, where Christ is seated at the right hand of God. Set your minds on things above, not on earthly things. For you died, and your life is now hidden with Christ in God. When Christ, who is your life, appears, then you also will appear with him in glory.

Put to death, therefore, whatever belongs to your earthly nature: sexual immorality, impurity, lust, evil desires and greed, which is idolatry. Because of these, the wrath of God is coming. You used to walk in these ways, in the life you once lived. But now you must rid yourselves of all such things as these: anger, rage, malice, slander, and filthy language from your lips. Do not lie to each other, since you have taken off your old self with its practices and have put on the new self, which is being renewed in knowledge in the image of its Creator. . . .

Therefore, as God's chosen people, holy and dearly loved, clothe yourselves with compassion, kindness, humility, gentleness and patience. Bear with each other and forgive whatever grievances you may have against one another. Forgive as the Lord forgave you. And over all these virtues put on love, which binds them all together in perfect unity.

Let the peace of Christ rule in your hearts, since as members of one body you were called to peace. And be thankful. Let the word of Christ dwell in you richly as you teach and admonish one another with all wisdom, and as you sing psalms, hymns and spiritual songs with gratitude in your hearts to God. And whatever you do, whether in word or deed, do it all in the name of the Lord Jesus, giving thanks to God the Father through him.

Soli Deo Gloria!

Overview

---

1. *Experiences God's Empowering Presence.* The healthy disciple understands the role of the Holy Spirit and lives daily with a fresh reality of his power and presence. "The Counselor, the Holy Spirit, . . . will teach you all things and will remind you of everything I have said to you" (John 14:26).

   1.1—Exemplify His Fruit
   1.2—Embody His Thumbprint
   1.3—Express His Gifts
   1.4—Envision His Call
   1.5—Experience His Presence

2. *Engages in God-Exalting Worship.* The healthy disciple engages wholeheartedly in meaningful, God-focused worship experiences on a weekly basis with the family of God. "The true worshipers will worship the Father in spirit and truth, for they are the kind of worshipers the Father seeks" (John 4:23).

   2.1—Preparation Begins on Monday
   2.2—Participation Begets Fulfillment
   2.3—Proclamation Styles Reflect Diversity
   2.4—Protection from Distraction
   2.5—Prescription for Enhancement

3. *Practices the Spiritual Disciplines.* The healthy disciple pursues the daily disciplines of prayer, Bible study, and

reflection in the quietness of one's personal prayer closet. "Remain in me, and I will remain in you" (John 15:4).

3.1—Prayer: ACTS and Relate
3.2—Scripture: Read and Discover
3.3—Reflection: Review and Preview
3.4—Proactivity: Rhythm and Rhyme
3.5—Accountability: Family and Friends

4. *Learns and Grows in Community.* The healthy disciple is involved in spiritual and relational growth in the context of a safe and affirming group of like-minded believers. "When they did [obey Jesus], they were unable to haul the net in because of the large number of fish" (John 21:6).

4.1—Safe Place to Share
4.2—Safe Place to Pray
4.3—Safe Place to Process
4.4—Safe Place to Care
4.5—Safe Place to Grow

5. *Commits to Loving and Caring Relationships.* The healthy disciple prioritizes the qualities of relational vitality that lead to genuine love for one another in the home, workplace, church, and community. "My command is this: Love each other as I have loved you. Greater love has no one than this, that he lay down his life for his friends" (John 15:12–13).

5.1—Agape Love
5.2—Absolute Joy
5.3—Affirming Communication
5.4—Resolving Conflict
5.5—Additional Time

6. *Exhibits Christlike Servanthood.* The healthy disciple practices God-honoring servanthood in every relational context of life and ministry. "I have set you an example that you should do as I have done for you" (John 13:15).

6.1—A Towel and Basin
6.2—A Servant's Heart
6.3—A Willingness to Give and Receive
6.4—A Listening Ear
6.5—A Life Well Lived

7. *Shares the Love of Christ Generously.* The healthy disciple maximizes every opportunity to share the love of Christ, in word and deed, with those outside the faith. "For God so loved the world that he gave his one and only Son, that whoever believes in him shall not perish but have eternal life" (John 3:16).

7.1—Evangelism

7.2—Social Concern

7.3—International Missions

7.4—Diversity of Friendships

7.5—Dispenser of Grace

8. *Manages Life Wisely and Accountably.* The healthy disciple develops personal life management skills and lives within a web of accountable relationships. "As long as it is day, we must do the work of him who sent me" (John 9:4).

8.1—Mission, Roles, and Goals

8.2—Balanced Lifestyle

8.3—Stress Reduction and Management

8.4—Accountable Relationships

8.5—Nine No's for Every One Yes

9. *Networks with the Body of Christ.* The healthy disciple actively reaches out to others within the Christian community for relationships, worship, prayer, fellowship, and ministry. "May they be brought to complete unity to let the world know that you sent me and have loved them even as you have loved me" (John 17:23).

9.1—Diversity of Connection

9.2—Holy Dissatisfaction

9.3—Cross-Cultural Pollination

9.4—Multidenominational Investigation

9.5—Prayerful Participation

10. *Stewards a Life of Abundance.* The healthy disciple recognizes that every resource comes from the hand of God and is to be used generously for kingdom priorities and purposes. "Unless a kernel of wheat falls to the ground and dies, it remains only a single seed. But if it dies, it produces many seeds" (John 12:24).

10.1—Serve Openhandedly
10.2—Steward Prayerfully
10.3—Sacrifice Financially
10.4—Seed Generously
10.5—Smile Abundantly

Afterword

When Jesus chose his first followers, there were twelve names on his list: Simon Peter, James the son of Zebedee, John the son of Zebedee, Andrew, Philip, Bartholomew, Matthew, Thomas, James the son of Alphaeus, Thaddaeus, Simon the Zealot, and Judas Iscariot.

None was theologically trained. None was a priest or religious teacher. Many had nicknames, most of which were given by Jesus: Simon was "Rocky"; James and John were "the sons of thunder"; Thomas was "the twin"; and the second Simon was "the Zealot." Thaddaeus also went by the name Judas the son of James. Two were brothers. Four were fishermen, one was a tax collector, one was a political extremist, and the rest never were known by their occupations. Three have books of the Bible named after them. A few became famous; some are unknown except for their names. They were ordinary men.

Eleven of the twelve did what disciples were supposed to do. They learned from Jesus and lived what they learned. They were empowered by the Holy Spirit and they empowered others. They became healthy disciples of Jesus Christ. For some, like John, it went easier than for others, like Simon Peter and Thomas, for whom it was difficult. They all made it but one: Judas. Although he had all the same information and opportunities, Judas flunked out.

Since the day Judas betrayed Jesus and left an opening on the team of twelve, there has been a debate about who replaced him. Some read Acts 1:23–26 and write in Matthias as Judas's replacement, although he never again is mentioned in the New Testament. Others point to Saul who became Paul and insist that he was not only the new number 12 but a vast improvement over the defective Judas.

Could it be that the Bible leaves the twelfth place intentionally vacant? Jesus is constantly looking for one more to add to his list of the top twelve disciples—ordinary women and men like you and me. Some of us come to discipleship more easily than others. Some of us are barely noticed while others rise to fame. The big deal is not name or fame. It is being on the list of faithful disciples of the Son of God.

Peter, James, John . . . Susan, Ralph, Meredith, Cooper, Kevin, Karen, Ahmed, Jose, Selina, Brian, Jessica, Rosie . . . and *you!* Hear the call of Jesus. Answer with a loud heartfelt "Yes!"

Become a healthy disciple.

Leith Anderson
Wooddale Church
Eden Prairie, Minnesota

Notes

Introduction

1. Stephen Macchia, *Becoming a Healthy Church* (Grand Rapids: Baker, 1999).
2. John Stott, *Basic Christianity*, as quoted in *Christianity Today*, 2 April 2001, 64.
3. William Barclay, *The Gospel of John*, vol. 2 (Philadelphia: Westminster John Knox, 1975), v.
4. Ibid., vol. 1, 24.
5. Margaret Campbell, *Renovaré Newsletter* 12, no. 1 (January 2002): 1.
6. George Barna, *Barna Research Newsletter*, September 2001.

Chapter 1: Experiences God's Empowering Presence

1. Barclay, *Gospel of John*, vol. 2, 154.
2. Ibid., 166.
3. Macchia, *Becoming a Healthy Church*, 32–35.
4. C. Peter Wagner, *Your Spiritual Gifts Can Help Your Church Grow* (Ventura, Calif.: Regal, 1994), 34.
5. Bruce Bugbee, Don Cousins, and Bill Hybels, *Network* curriculum (Grand Rapids: Zondervan, 1994).

Chapter 2: Engages in God-Exalting Worship

1. C. S. Lewis, *Reflections on the Psalms* (New York: Harcourt, 1986).
2. Barclay, *Gospel of John*, vol. 1, 159–61.
3. Ibid., 105.
4. Max Lucado, *Traveling Light* (Nashville: W Publishing Group/Thomas Nelson, 2001), 41–42.

Chapter 3: Practices the Spiritual Disciplines

1. Barclay, *Gospel of John*, vol. 2, 172.
2. Ibid., 173.
3. Ibid., 177–79.
4. Philip Yancey, "The Back Page," *Christianity Today*, 3 April 2000, 104.
5. Rueben P. Job, *A Guide to Retreat for all God's Shepherds* (Nashville: Abingdon, 1994), 136–37.
6. Dallas Willard, "Spiritual Formation for Real Life and Ministry in the Twenty-First Century" (speech, Pastors Convention, San Diego, February 2001).
7. Robert E. Coleman, introduction to *Resolutions of a Saintly Scholar*, by Jonathan Edwards, in *Billy Graham Center Collection of Classics* (Wheaton: World Wide Publications, 1992).
8. Christopher Lydon, "Remembering Sarah Small," *Boston Globe*, 28 December 2001.
9. Ibid.
10. Juan Carlos Ortiz, keynote address at Congress, Boston, 2002.
11. I highly recommend Richard J. Foster, *Prayer: Finding the Heart's True Home* (San Francisco: HarperSanFrancisco, 1992; Rueben P. Job and Norman Shawchuck, *A Guide to Prayer for All God's People* (Nashville: UpperRoom Books, 1990); Jonathan Edwards, *Religious Affections*, abridged and updated by Ellyn Sanna (Uhrichsville, Ohio: Barbour, 1999), Henri J. M. Nouwen, *With Open Hands* (New York: Ballantine, 1987); John Baillie, *A Diary of Private Prayer* (New York: Macmillan, 1949); Dallas Willard, *Renovation of the Heart* (Colorado Springs: NavPress, 2002).
12. Keith Anderson and Randy Reese, *Spiritual Mentoring* (Downers Grove, Ill.: InterVarsity Press, 1999), 97–99.

Chapter 4: Learns and Grows in Community

1. Diana Bennett, personal correspondence.
2. Barclay, *Gospel of John*, vol. 2, 281.
3. Ibid., 282.
4. Ibid.
5. Ibid., 283–84.
6. Henri J. M. Nouwen, *In The Name of Jesus* (New York: Crossroad Publishing, 1998), 62–63.
7. Bennett, conversation with the author.
8. Rueben Job and Norman Shawchuck, *A Guide to Prayer* (Nashville: UpperRoom Books, 1983).

Chapter 5: Commits to Loving and Caring Relationships

1. Barclay, *Gospel of John*, vol. 2, 109–10.
2. Ibid., 112.
3. Gary Chapman, *The Five Love Languages* (Chicago: Moody, 1992).
4. http://www.CNN.com/2003/world/europe/01/06/offbeat.happiness.equation/index.html.
5. Graham Kendrick, "Consider It Joy," *What Grace* (sound recording, Croydon, England, Make Way Music, 2001).

6. Stephen Macchia, *Becoming a Healthy Church Workbook* (Grand Rapids: Baker, 2001).

7. Lewis Smedes, *The Art of Forgiving: When You Need to Forgive and Don't Know How,* quoted in *Christianity Today,* 3 December 2001, 73.

Chapter 6: Exhibits Christlike Servanthood

1. Christina Wallace, "Sharing Faith and Strength," *Metro Boston,* 14–16 February 2003, Weekend Edition.

2. Ibid.

3. Barclay, *Gospel of John,* vol. 2, 137.

4. Ibid.

5. Ibid., 139.

6. Ibid., 143–44.

7. Richard Foster, *Celebration of Discipline* (New York: Harper & Row, 1978), 110–11.

8. Ibid., 112–13.

9. Ibid., 117–21.

Chapter 7: Shares the Love of Christ Generously

1. Barclay, *Gospel of John,* vol. 1, 124–27.

2. Ibid., 125.

3. Ibid., 134.

4. Ibid., 135.

5. Ibid., 137–38.

6. Ibid., 140.

7. Bob Jacks and Betty Jacks, *Your Home A Lighthouse* (Colorado Springs: NavPress, 1986); idem, *Divine Appointments* (Colorado Springs: NavPress, 2002).

8. Barclay, *Gospel of John,* vol. 1, 151.

Chapter 8: Manages Life Wisely and Accountably

1. Stephen Covey, *The Seven Habits of Highly Effective People* (New York: Simon and Schuster, 1989).

2. Barclay, *Gospel of John,* vol. 2, 40.

3. Covey, *Seven Habits*.

Chapter 9: Networks with the Body of Christ

1. Barclay, *Gospel of John,* vol. 2, 211–12.

2. Ibid., 212.

3. Ibid., 213–14.

4. Ibid., 215–16.

5. Ibid., 216.

6. Ibid., 217.

7. Ibid.

8. Ibid., 218.

9. Ibid., 219–20.

10. Gerald Sittser, *Loving Across Our Differences* (Downers Grove, Ill.: InterVarsity, 1994), 45–46.

11. Bill Hoyt, quoted in "Church Champions Email Update," ed. Dave Travis, Leadership Network, Dallas, 24 November 2000.

Chapter 10: Stewards a Life of Abundance

1. Barclay, *Gospel of John*, vol. 2, 122.

2. Ibid., 123.

3. Ibid., 123–25.

4. Randy Alcorn, *The Treasure Principle* (Portland: Multnomah, 2001), 23, 41, 45, 49, 56, 73.

5. Henri Nouwen, *With Open Hands* (Notre Dame, Ind.: Ave Maria, 1982), 12.

6. Ibid., 154.

7. Wesley Willmer, "Encouraging Generosity: Learning to Value What God Values," *Christian Management Report*, June 2002, 8.

8. Ibid.

Conclusion

1. Barclay, *Gospel of John*, vol. 2, 283.

2. George MacDonald, *Highlanders Last Song* (Minneapolis: Bethany, 1986), 169.

Stephen A. Macchia is founding president of Leadership Transformations, Inc. (LTI), a ministry focusing on the spiritual formation needs of leaders and the spiritual discernment processes of leadership teams in local church and parachurch ministry settings. In conjunction with his leadership of LTI, he also serves as the director of the Pierce Disciple-Building Center at Gordon-Conwell Theological Seminary. He is the author of *Becoming a Healthy Church* and *Becoming a Healthy Church Workbook*. Stephen and his wife, Ruth, are the proud parents of Nathan and Rebekah and reside in Lexington, Massachusetts.

For more information about Stephen Macchia or Leadership Transformations, Inc., visit:

www.LeadershipTransformations.org
www.healthydisciple.net